The Importance of Religion

T0374666

The Importance of Religion

Meaning and Action in Our Strange World

Gavin Flood

A John Wiley & Sons, Ltd., Publication

Library of Congress Cataloging-in-Publication Data

Flood, Gavin D., 1954-
  The importance of religion : meaning and action in our strange world / Gavin Flood.
    p. cm.
  Includes bibliographical references and index.
  ISBN 978-1-4051-8972-9 – ISBN 978-1-4051-8971-2 (pbk.)
  1. Religion–Philosophy. I. Title.
  BL51.F555 2012
  210–dc23   2011026338

A catalogue record for this book is available from the British Library.

This book is published in the following electronic formats: ePDFs 9781444399035; ePub 9781444399042; Mobi 9781444399059

Set in 10/12pt Sabon by Thomson Digital, Noida, India

1   2012

For Kwan

Hat man sein warum? des Lebens,
so verträgt man sich fast mit jedem wie?

He who has a why *to live for,*
can stand almost any how.

(Nietzsche, *Die Götzen Dämmerung* (1889),
Sprueche und Pfeile 12)

Contents

Preface

A prevailing idea from the Enlightenment, still with us today, is that the light of reason would dispel the darkness of religion and reveal the universe to us. While the desire for enlightenment and the attendant aspiration for a better human future are commendable, the identification of religion with darkness and ignorance is problematic. Religion has not gone away and is a topic of deep concern both because of its destructive capacity – most conflicts in the world have a religious component – and for its constructive capacity as a resource that gives people truth, beauty, and goodness. While secularization has developed in the West, this has not heralded the demise of religion. Christianity may be in decline in northern Europe but is expanding in Africa and the Americas. Islam is expanding in Europe and it is not inconceivable that it will be the majority religion in Europe in the course of time. With the demise of communism in Russia and Eastern Europe and the transformation of communism in China, religions are developing in those countries, both new religions and reinvigorated old religions, Orthodoxy in Russia, Buddhism and Taoism in China. In some western societies we also have the enhancement of privatized, individual spirituality linked with a quest for authentic experience and the true self.

This book is written in the context of these developments and in view of the persistence of religion in modern times. This is not a survey of religions or the contemporary religious field, of which there are plenty of fine volumes, nor is it a defense of religion as such, but is intended to develop new vocabularies and theoretical perspectives for the study of religion. It claims that the importance of religion is existential; religions provide significant meaning to life and guide people in their choices and practices.

Religions are not primarily propositions about the nature of reality, although they can be that, but ways of living and dying, ways of choosing a good life and guiding judgments about moral choice. Through actions the ways of life that we call religions mediate the human encounter with mystery. The world is a mysterious place, which scientific accounts do not exhaust but rather serve to add to its mystery. Religions show us ways of inhabiting our strange world that are transformative for individuals and for communities as a whole. Religious people in the modern world balance commitments to the secular public sphere – from voting in elections to educating children – with commitments to particular religious communities. This book attempts to describe the ways in which people are religious and to analyze the ways of being religious under the guiding thesis that religions are existentially important in providing people with meaning. While religions are, of course, important for macro-history, as large social and cultural forces moving through time, the argument here is that their primary importance lies in their significance for human persons in their communities.

The book is written broadly from within a phenomenological intellectual tradition, but a kind of phenomenology that is dialogical. It is also influenced by other intellectual traditions, particularly what might be called critical social science and what has come to be known as post-critical theology (theology chastened by postmodern critique). I tend to avoid the term "postmodern," which now has limited usefulness, although this book is written in the wake of that great intellectual flurry and energy even though some of its results were eccentric. But it seems to me that the ultimate questions that religions deal with (why is there something rather than nothing? who am I? what is the purpose of our life?) and their meaning in people's lives necessitates an approach that is both detached (and so attempts accurate description) and intellectually committed to truth (and so attempts accurate evaluation). The general orientation of this phenomenology is towards the world and this approach shows us that religions are fundamentally about how we are or should be in the world: they are about action, the repeated actions of the liturgical moment through history, the repeated actions of the ascetic life, and the unrepeatable moral actions of social being.

Because of the impossibly vast nature of the topic, I have dealt with some of these complex issues at a fairly theoretical level, bringing in concrete examples to illustrate points. Giving an account of religion in terms of subjective meaning takes us into a number of subject areas, including cultural anthropology, linguistic anthropology, philosophy, and theology. I hope that the reader will find application for the ideas and general argument presented here in their own contexts. Frits Staal speculates that the centre of civilization will return once more to China and India. This is probably an accurate prediction and while few predictions of the future prove to be correct, I think it safe to say that religions will continue to thrive, continue to endow lives with meaning, and will contribute to global, social, and climatic challenges facing the world. The new world citizen can also be a religious citizen.

After a substantial introduction outlining the general thesis I wish to present, that religion must be understood in terms of the human will to meaning and in terms of the desire for transcendence, the book is divided into three parts: action, speech, and world. We can understand religions as cultural forms that mediate the human encounter with mystery. Given this general thesis, in Part One, Action, I develop the idea that religion must be understood in terms of human meaning which finds expression in action: the encounter with mystery occurs through action which is of two kinds, ritual (within which I include spiritual practices) and moral. Chapter 1 examines the two processes of reification and rationalization in modernity and argues that these are not adequate accounts of religion; the latter needs to be understood in terms of the formation of subjective meaning. Chapter 2 develops this thesis arguing that religion calls people into the world through ritual and moral action. The chapter describes three examples of ritual action from the ethnographic literature. Chapter 3 links action to spirituality and describes the cultivating of an inner journey.

Part Two, Speech, shows how mystery is mediated through text which is received into the human world and internalized. It presents an account of religion and rationality and presents an account of the internalization of the sacred text as a form of encounter with mystery. Chapter 4 is about sacred text as characteristic or prototypical of religions, Chapter 5 on the problem of linguistic relativity, and Chapter 6 on rationality and religion. I present an account in these chapters of how religious language mediates the encounter with mystery and endows meaning to communities of reception. Finally, Part Three, World, shows how science, art, and politics are related to religions and how they move towards the world, which we might call the real, through action. Chapter 7 is about religion and science and offers a view of religions in the light of complexity and constraint. Chapter 8 is focused on art in relation to religion, the way art, like religion, mediates the encounter with mystery and its interface with religion. Finally, Chapter 9 examines religion and politics and the topical notion of how being a religious person is compatible with the idea of the citizen. We end with a summary of the general argument and an epilogue.

Gavin Flood
Oxford

Acknowledgments

I should like to acknowledge the people who have influenced this book in one way or another. Firstly I should like to thank my wife Emma Kwan, to whom the book is dedicated, for her constant encouragement, love, and support. She introduced me to a new world of contemporary art. My friend of many conversations, Luke Hopkins, years ago introduced me to Norman Brown's work, which has had an influence on my thinking about the present project. Another friend of many conversations, Oliver Davies, as always, has been an excellent interlocutor and I have been encouraged by his taking theology in the direction of a "new realism." My teacher John Bowker, whose work on religion and science is exemplary, has continued to stimulate my thoughts. Rebecca Harkin, the commissioning editor at Wiley-Blackwell, first suggested the project to me and I thank her for her thoughts, comments, and encouragement. I thank the anonymous readers for their very perceptive comments. One reader presented precise suggestions and corrected some factual errors and although I have not always followed specific recommendations, I have always taken these comments very seriously. Gavin D'Costa encouraged the project and made specific, insightful suggestions that I have generally adopted. I should also like to thank colleagues at the Oxford Centre for Hindu Studies, particularly Shaunaka Rishi Das, Jessica Frazier, and Rembert Lutjeharms, who have supported my work as have all the staff at the Oxford Centre for Hindu Studies. Among colleagues in the Theology Faculty I would like to mention Afifi Al Akiti, George Pattison, Guy Stroumsa, Joel Rasmussen, Johannes Zachuber, Mark Edwards, Pamela Anderson, Paul Joyce, Paul Fiddes, Peggy Morgan, Philip Kennedy, and Sondra Hausner for their support. I would also like to thank my family (especially Claire and Leela) for their love and good wishes. Last but not least, I should like to thank my students at Oxford on whom I tried out some of the material presented here, and who have provided such stimulating conversations over the past few years.

I am grateful to Faber and Faber for permission to use the Wallace Steven's quote on the title page of Part Three from his *Collected Poems*.

On occasion when I have used Sanskrit terms, and a few Arabic terms, I have Anglicized proper names and titles of books but retained conventional diacritical marks for technical terms that I cite in brackets beside their translation. Thus Shiva and Krishna rather than Śiva and Kṛṣṇa, Mahayana rather than Mahāyāna, and *Bhagavad Gita* rather than *Bhagavad Gītā*.

Introduction: Religion and the Human Condition

That religion is of fundamental public concern cannot be doubted as we move into the twenty-first century, central to global politics, cultural or identity politics, ethics, and the socio-economic processes of late modernity, as well as to the contested claims made in its name. Religions own vast tracts of land, have access to great resources which impact upon billions of the world's population, and 15 percent of the habitable surface of the earth is regarded as sacred.[1] Yet never has religion been so misunderstood. Never has there been a time when the understanding of religions has been more important and never has there been a greater need for such knowledge and critical inquiry to advise public debate which so often lacks informed perspectives. Some disparage religion as irrational, making claims about the world that simply cannot be substantiated in the light of modern scientific knowledge. On this view, religion is a series of propositions about the world akin to scientific theories, but erroneous propositions which have hampered, and still hamper, human progress and true knowledge and understanding. On this view, religions can be explained in terms of evolutionary psychology and are superstitions that we need to jettison. Apologists for religion react to the critique of the new atheism defending it on rational grounds, that its claims are indeed compatible with modern knowledge and scientific thinking. We only need to look around bookshops to see the proliferation of these kinds of works.

Yet both critique and apologetic have fundamentally misunderstood the nature and importance of religion in people's lives. This book is an attempt to understand religions and their attraction both in the adherent's view and in the context of the human sciences. Religions cannot be reduced to a series of claims about the nature of the world because they fulfill a much deeper,

The Importance of Religion: Meaning and Action in Our Strange World,
First Edition. Gavin Flood.
© 2012 Gavin Flood. Published 2012 by Blackwell Publishing Ltd.

existential function that drives human beings not only to answer or come to terms with the great, disruptive events of life such as birth and particularly death, but also compels us to go beyond ourselves and to transcend our limitations. Even the Buddha understood this when he declared that the test of religious teachings is whether or not they worked to relieve human dissatisfaction; a man with an arrow in his side should remove the arrow and not inquire about who shot it and to which family he belonged.[2] Religions are primarily ways of life rather than theories about the origin of the world (indeed, Buddhism and Hinduism think the world has no origin, a view even entertained by Aquinas[3]). Religions are not scientific propositions[4] but encounters with mystery and expressions of human needs that form ways of life, ways of acting, ways of responding to the strange world in which we find ourselves.

Religions are ways of being in the world which make strong claims and demands upon people and while they are concerned with socialization they primarily function to address questions of ultimate meaning at a bodily and temporal level in which human beings make sense of their experience. In other words, religions are responses to the human encounter with what is beyond us, to the encounter with mystery, paradox, and the overwhelming force and wonder of there being anything at all. Religions cannot be reduced simply to beliefs or propositions about the world but are visceral responses to the human condition and expressions of what might be called the will to meaning. Some of the claims of religion sound absurd to modern ears but religions continue to hold great power over billions of people who cannot simply be dismissed as irrational or deluded. Even if, as some claim, the churches in the United Kingdom and other European countries are emptying, it is far from clear that this signals the end of religion worldwide or a total disenchantment. (T.S. Eliot once observed that "(w)ithout religion the whole human race would die ... solely of boredom.")[5]

A strong secularization thesis developed in the sociology of religion[6] has proven not to be the case in the global context, with the rise of literalist understandings of religions ("fundamentalisms") and a new "recomposition of the religious field," to use Richard Roberts apposite phrase, in "spirituality" and religious pluralism.[7] Religions are expressions in action of human need and human striving to go beyond ourselves. This will to meaning and impulse towards transcendence we might call "the religious imperative" or "religious impulse," which rather more poetically Douglas Hedley describes as a "longing of the soul."[8] The phrase "will to meaning" was first coined by Viktor Frankl to denote the primary motivation in human life, an idea that he worked out in the desperate conditions of the concentration camp, that the will to meaning and its associated hope is the one thing that kept people alive.[9] While I take Charles Taylor's point that the concern with meaning itself is a modern one,[10] the deeply human concern for locating ourselves in relation to the world is not. It could be argued that human beings are fundamentally meaning-seeking creatures who try to make sense of the strange world not simply propositionally through philosophy (at least a modern view of philosophy) but through the body and action in religions; above all in ritual action, spiritual exercises, and in moral action.

In this book I therefore intend to show (a) that religions are forms of culture within which people live meaningful lives, (b) they fill the strange world with meaning though mediating the human encounter with mystery, and (c) there are political and social ramifications of these cultural forms. I intend to achieve these ends by developing the claim that religion accomplishes its mediating function primarily through kinds of action: ethical, ritual, and spiritual. I shall defer discussion of action until Chapter 1, but we need to foreshadow this key idea that religions endow meaning through action, through focusing on the world in collective, shared action, and in the personal responsibility of moral judgment followed by act.

Religion is linked to human meaning and need and above all to the encounter of something beyond us that cannot be contained within the usual human categories of knowledge. But even if this is the case, we have witnessed a gradual ebbing away of traditional religion, mostly in Europe, over the last two hundred years. In the nineteenth century Mathew Arnold wrote his famous poem about faith receding like the sea on Dover Beach, his only hope lying in human love. More dramatically, the German philosopher Nietzsche declared the death of God and so the end of religion through the voice of the madman in the market place declaring that God is dead and we have killed him.

These nineteenth-century voices articulated a skepticism about religion and supernatural agency that was to rise like a torrent in the twentieth century. The nineteenth century saw the development of the empirical sciences, particularly evolutionary science, faith in the power of reason and the value of individual self-assertion, which eroded traditional Christianity and the belief in God and Church. With the advance of secularism in the twentieth century and the growth (and, one might add, demise) of the secular ideologies of Fascism and Communism in Russia and Eastern Europe, religion, it seemed, was doomed to history. But while it is certainly true that church attendance in many countries in Europe, particularly the United Kingdom, is at an all time low, it is far from the case that religion has been assigned to a phase in humanity's past that we are now able to happily go beyond. Anyone who saw the terrible news coverage of planes crashing into the twin towers, or witnessed the event itself, can have little doubt about the negative force of religion in contemporary politics. A popular French magazine even declared that a "new clericalism" is threatening the world.[11]

For Nietzsche, that God is dead was not a regret but a liberating event that allowed humanity to go beyond irrational restriction and inhibition to explore new ways of being in the world (albeit a new kind of irrationalism) and a new kind of morality without transcendence. Freud was to echo the view that turning away from religion was inevitable as humanity grows out of its childhood, withdraws projection, and faces up to the reality of life.[12] Kristeva develops this idea that the symbolic realm, identified with the dominance of the Father in Theology, needs to be disrupted with the assertion of unconscious power of semiosis in order to achieve balance and health; we have to perform a kind of parricide or sacrifice,[13] although Kristeva herself recognizes the value of religion in upholding human freedom and creating meaning (although at the cost of repressing the other and the repression of sexuality).[14] The death of God was precisely supposed to free us from the kinds of violent irrationalism that had been perpetrated in the name of religion. Yet religions have not died out and have continued, as John Bowker has persistently highlighted, to be implicated and directly involved in many violent disputes, in Kosovo and the Balkans, Northern Ireland, China, Palestine, Kashmir, Tibet, Sudan, and Dafur to name but a few.[15]

For most religions, life is understood to be a journey to a better place for both individuals and communities; a journey guided (or constrained) by stories, prohibitions, and injunctions revealed in texts and expressed in religious laws. Sometimes this journey is conceptualized as a solitary, inner quest of the mystic, sometimes as a journey of an entire community or people. With the erosion of traditional Christianity in the West, other cultural expressions have taken over these needs for orientation – we have secular marriages and funerals for example – and meaning is constructed in other ways through art, environmental concerns, science, or politics. But religions generally claim that the meaning of human life must be understood in a much broader context and that the journey of this life leads towards an end-state that, at least for some if not for all, is a kind of completion or fulfillment. Such a completion is conceptualized in a number of ways in different religions, in collective terms as a vision of a utopian society, a heaven on earth as in some Christianity, a return to a spiritual home beyond the world as in some kinds of Hinduism, an awakening or realization in the here and now of a timeless truth, a transcendent or sublime power, the unnameable or reality limit, as in the idea of enlightenment in Buddhism. We shall encounter some of these concepts in the course of this study.

Religion is not only a force in cultural and global politics; it remains important in more subtle ways in contemporary culture. Often replaced by the more amorphous term "spirituality," religious ideas have not gone away from the secularized West; and the idea that human beings can change, improve, or access higher, non-material powers, to enhance their life is clearly still with us. This is because religion – and I shall turn to the vexed question of the usefulness of the category presently – addresses issues of fundamental human concern about being born, living, and dying, and religions are about the human encounter with the depth of the universe. Indeed, only religions address these concerns in a systematic way and only religions have provided structures for communities to negotiate the difficult transitions into and out of life and have provided forms of mediation or processes in which we can deal with, and attempt to understand, what we might call "mystery" or "transcendence" or "the invisible."

While religions are undoubtedly sources of grave concern for the future of humanity in many of their more literalist modes, they are also sources of great inspiration that death is not the end of hope, that humans can live in a better world, and that religions can provide models for peaceful cohabitation which recognize the human need for group identity while at the same time reaching out to others. Religions clearly have a function in terms of identity politics, the various tribes to which we all belong, but they must also be understood in terms of broader questions about shared human meaning and salvation or redemption from evil. While we must be cautious about generalization, as the religious field is so diverse and complex, we might say that religions provide a particular kind of orientation or route through the world and see human life in terms of a much bigger, cosmic picture. Religions provide fundamental resources for the formation of human lives in response to the strange world in which we find ourselves, claim to promote human flourishing, and emphasize the importance of finding wisdom, as David Ford has highlighted.[16]

But what prototypically differentiates religions from other kinds of meaning-seeking activity is a kind of narrative that incorporates theories of salvation or soteriology, that at the end of life or a series of lives, or at the end of time, all will be made complete, whole and healed, and that in life we encounter a limit to our understanding, a transcendence which can overpower us and which cannot be adequately articulated. Indeed, a soteriological dimension arguably marks out religions from other forms of culture that serve the same function of providing life with meaning, such as art or politics. There can, of course, be overlap between religions as soteriology and political ideologies that seek human perfection through history. It is also the case that many religions are concerned not so much with salvation as with worldly prosperity (magical protection of the family, predictions of death, the destruction of enemies, obtaining wealth, and so on). But nevertheless soteriology is an important, theologically articulated, ideal in religions that seek completion to human life.

The nature of this completion has been highly contested and a source of passion and violence from the Inquisition to forced conversions in Islam and Christianity, alongside the more sober reflections of theologians and philosophers. Often within religions we find great conflict and tension over these issues – whether a sense of the sublime or mysticism should take precedence over law, for example, or whether connection between human beings and a higher power needs to be mediated through hierarchical, social institutions such as the church. The basic point that I wish to make is that religions are somatic responses to human need in real space and time, responses to our strange world, and sources for the construction of human meaning that we might call expressions of the will to meaning.

These meanings are formed in ways of life, spiritual practices, and in the stories we tell each other. While for the majority world, religion is less of a choice and more of a way of being brought up, in the West there is generally voluntary election to a particular religion. Religions are ways in which the human encounter with mystery, transcendence, or what we might call the invisible, are mediated. The mediation of this encounter is also an orientation within subjectivity towards a power beyond us that marks a limit to our comprehension: mystery, the invisible, the transcendent, the sublime, the unnameable, or even the impossible. But we are racing ahead of ourselves here and the terms we choose and those we exclude will have different resonances and implications.

Mediating Our Strange World

There is a constellation of ideas at the heart of this study, namely the strange world, mediation, and action that will become clearer as the argument unfolds. But first we need to say something more about "our strange world." There is an intuitive sense that most of us share that the world is strange, a place where we are not at home. Let us probe this idea a little further before proceeding. Many thinkers have highlighted this: the philosopher Heidegger spoke of our being "thrown" into the world and philosophy's task to understand this thrownness, and Freud spoke of the uncanny.

In his perspicacious essay "The Uncanny" ("Zur Psychologie des Un-heimlichen") Freud observes a phenomenon of how the familiar or "homely" (*heimlich*) can become unfamiliar or "uncanny" (*unheimlich*), as if the familiar were strange as "when one is lost in a forest in high altitudes."[17] A range of experiences falls within the remit of the uncanny in both real life and in literature; the familiar can become strange and what we are accustomed to suddenly take on a new, unfamiliar appearance. Freud gives us an account from personal experience how in a town in Italy he wandered from the piazza and found himself in the red light district. He tried to leave this particular street but found himself returned to it on three occasions before he finally, and thankfully, made his way out. Streets that would normally prove no difficulty became strange to him and tinged with anxiety.[18] One of the features of Freud's experience was repetition; involuntary repetition "which surrounds with an uncanny atmosphere which would otherwise be innocent enough, and forces upon us the idea of something fateful and unescapable where otherwise we should have spoken of change only."[19] The unconscious provides a repetition-compulsion that is perceived to be uncanny.

Freud links these experiences to the childhood condition in which the child does not differentiate between his or her thoughts and reality; Freud called this the "omnipotence of thought," which he associates with an animistic conception of the universe as being populated by spirits and "by the narcissistic overestimation of subjective mental processes."[20] This overestimation of subjective thinking – that thought can affect reality – is furthermore linked to the development of the human species as a whole: "It would seem," writes Freud, "as though each one of us has been through a phase of individual development corresponding to that animistic stage in primitive men, that none of us has traversed . . . without preserving certain traces of it which can be re-activated."[21] The uncanny is a reactivation of this animistic mental activity: a resurgence of an earlier phase of our development.

I would not wish to argue for the problematic association of individual with species development, but I do believe that Freud is on to something when he identifies a subjective dimension to our sense of the uncanny that corresponds to an external situation. The uncanny – that might embrace such experiences as *déjà vu*, meaningful coincidence, a significance to existence almost, but never quite, grasped – is a dimension of human life that contains subjectivity but always an externality. The strangeness of the world is linked to the idea of the uncanny but while we might accept Freud's description, we do not need to take on board his explanation. Indeed, the strange world resists explanation (as we will see in Chapter 8) but is saturated with meaning and can be experienced as the eruption of transcendence, to use Schutz's phrase, into everyday life.[22]

I have used Freud here not to agree with his etiology of the uncanny, but to highlight something about the strangeness of the world. The uncanny is a way of articulating the mystery of the world. Otto senses something of this in his conception of the holy (*das Heilige*) but for our purposes, Otto's is an insufficiently social concept to convey the full sense of strangeness and he wishes to restrict the sense of the holy to "the sphere of religion."[23] Freud's uncanny points to something more everyday and mundane that I would wish to emphasize in the strangeness of the world. The strange world is not different from the world, from the "lifeworld," of our social and cultural interactions that is perceived from a different angle as unfamiliar, mysterious, or uncanny. The sense of our strange world is thus linked in modernity to a sense of alienation although in a pre-modern context, the obverse of this is a sense of wonder and enchantment.

This strange world is always culturally mediated. We experience the world through cultures and systems of signs and symbols that link us to each other, to the past, and to the future. By mediation, then, we mean the symbolic systems that necessarily form our encounter with the world (in other words, culture); this is a process, the means whereby human beings encounter the world, which translates that encounter into meaning and allows us to make sense of experience. Others have made a not dissimilar observation; Csordas, for example, speaks of religion as developing from a primordial sense of otherness or alterity as "the phenomenological kernel of religion."[24] While a detailed and nuanced understanding of cultural process will be dealt with more extensively in later chapters (particularly in Chapters 1, 2, and 4), we need to say something about this at the outset. Cultural process can be understood in terms of "translation," in phenomenological jargon the translation of intentional objects or *noema*, that is, the objects of knowledge, into the process of intentionality, the *noesis*, that is, the processes of knowing. It can also be understood in terms of signification and representation: the sign system that forms a culture translates the human encounter with mystery into socially sanctioned, acceptable, and understandable forms (such as a university course or a church service or even a sporting event). But above all, mediation must be understood in terms of action: religions process the human encounter with mystery through ritual and ethical action. It is through action, particularly religious action, that people encounter and come to terms with mystery, the uncanny, the strange.

The strangeness of the world especially takes focus in the extreme situations of life, notably death and bereavement but also love, where religions come into their own as resources for mediating these encounters and allowing us to deal with life in suitably expressive ways. Mediation is thus linked to the idea of symbol as a cultural form that points to a reality beyond itself while at the same time participating in that reality, which is a uniquely religious understanding.[25] For example, the Eucharist in Catholic and Orthodox Christianity is a symbol in this sense of participating in the reality to which it points (that is, the body and blood of Christ). Similarly, in Hinduism a mantra is understood as the sound-body of the god: a symbol that both points to something beyond it and participates in that reality to which it points. We can, of course, have failed process when the symbol system does not adequately deal with the strangeness of the world, as we find in late modernity. This alienation is well articulated in the opening of Camus's *L'étranger*, when Meursault's mother has died and he is alienated from her death and from the process of her funeral; cultural process has here failed. It is not that mediation makes the strange world familiar, but rather that the unfamiliar is given meaning through cultural process.

Theories of Religion

There are many theories of religion linked to definitions. Recent debate can perhaps be encapsulated in three statements within which different theories can be located, namely religion is politics by other means, religion is nothing but the genes, and religion is a cultural response to life. These tend to be mutually exclusive but not necessarily so. The first two claims are forms of reductionism: a cultural reductionism, on the one hand, that says that the analysis of religion shows that it is really only about power in human relationships, and an eliminative or materialist reductionism, on the other, that says that religion is really part of a cultural mechanism to ensure the successful transmission of the genes through the generations.[26] Both of these positions generally take the view that the claims of religions are false. A third view, that religion is an encounter with and response to life, or we might say the strangeness of the world, claims that religions cannot be fully understood in terms of the two reductionisms.

This last view includes a number of theoretical orientations within phenomenology and anthropology. It is a claim that religion is a realm of human theory and practice distinct from other fundamental human activities such as politics and art but is intimately related to them. There is also a group of theorists whose work crosses boundaries between social science and religious studies or between cognition and theology. One such example is a stimulating book by Thomas Tweed, who locates religions in terms of crossings over and dwelling on the borders. Theories of religion are provisional, always from a perspective: "they are positioned representations of a changing terrain by an itinerant cartographer."[27] We glimpse religion from a particular viewpoint as we pass through. Tweed's emphasis on space (and his spatial metaphors of sighting) and the physical location of religion is important and a welcome balance to an overemphasis on history. Another example in the same spirit as Tweed is Kim Knott's work on the location of religion and the need to develop a spatial analysis of the everyday practices of religious people that draws on philosophers of space such as Lefebvre.[28] These works, like my own project, place emphasis on the body as our location in the world and the basis of spatial awareness.

Thirty or forty years ago there was a sense that religion was in decline and would inevitably die out with the rise of secularism, the development of science, and a general incredulity towards the claims of religions that were seen as eccentric irrationalities. While there has been a rapid decline in church attendance in some countries in Western Europe, particularly the United Kingdom, elsewhere in the world we have, on the contrary, an increase in religious activity and commitment of a kind that directly challenges secular modernity. The rise of a highly political Islam, Hinduism, and Christianity bear witness to this. But neither has religion disappeared from those most secularized nations, and the impulse to religion can be seen in a multiplicity of groups and ideas that affect mainstream forms of life, economics, and politics, from business employing "new age" management techniques to public debates about euthanasia, the environment, animal experimentation, and genetic research.

Nor is it simply a question of choice between secular modernity and religious fundamentalism. Probably the vast majority of people wish to live materially comfortable lives in a technologically developed, global world while at the same time adhering to their religious traditions. Modernity and tradition are not necessarily at odds. As Tariq Ramadan has observed, traditions such as Islam contain within them the resources for their own transformation and adaptation to the conditions of modernity. While some within the Moslem world will see Ramadan as too westernized, his is an important voice and a view to be taken very seriously as demarcating a mode of religious being in the world which is not regressive or nostalgic.[29] As David Ford persistently points out, we live in a secular *and* religious society.[30] While religions cannot be separated from cultures, they nevertheless lay claim to life and present fundamental orientations to the world and responses to its strangeness.

Intellectuals in secular modernity, its contemporary "cultured despisers," have perhaps been surprised at the persistence of religion and now recognize its importance, particularly in the wake of religiously inspired terrorism and the presence of religion in cultural and international politics. Whereas thirty years ago secular modernity might have thought religion to be nonsense, it is now considered by many to be *dangerous* nonsense. Religion is a political force in the modern world and some analysts would see it purely in these terms. On this view, the discourse of religion covers a discourse about power in a community and nation. The secularist critique of religion, which sees itself as an emancipatory critique that strives for social justice and human rights, is that once the conditions that give rise to religion are unveiled by criticism, then religion dissolves.

Behind this critique is the Marxist dictum that religion is ideology or false consciousness, the opiate of the people that keeps us deluded and imprisoned. Religion is ideology and therefore not true but useful in the interests of political power and control. To realize our freedom we need to give up this opium, to accept responsibility, and to stop being in thrall to some higher power expressed through hierarchical institutions. Some of the greatest human minds have thought this, particularly Marx and Freud. The secular modernist might think that religion is against the human good and once religion is dissolved through uncovering the conditions of its production, then we can move forward through reason to more realistic, and achievable, human goods. The counter position from the religious perspective is that, on the contrary, secular modernity leads to social breakdown, moral chaos, abjection, a fragmented sense of self, and human suffering.[31] A religious worldview, by contrast, leads to human flourishing and the collective good of a people. I believe there is truth in both these claims and, as I will develop later in the book, I would wish to argue for a religious humanism that recognizes the shortfalls of both tradition and modernity.

A second kind of reductionism has said that religion can be exclusively accounted for in terms of evolutionary biology, that genetics can explain why we are religious and that religious positions are simply errors and, often dangerous, errors. But the scientists are not united and while some are avowed atheists intent on debunking the "superstition" of religion, others are committed to a religious perspective. Indeed, a religious counter-argument might accept, for example, evolutionary biology but would reject this as an explanatory account of religion. Evolutionary biology might explain how living beings are in the world as they are or specify a particular range of constraints, but it does not explain why beings are in the world, the meaning of being in the world, or the mystery of life itself. Another aspect of this kind of explanation is brain science or cognition theory, which locates particular kinds of activity in particular areas of the brain and develops neurological accounts of certain kinds of human behavior. There is a burgeoning development of this kind of work in relation to religion, with many excellent scholars working in this field; the names Harvey Whitehouse, Lewis-Williams, and Pascal Boyer on cognition, Guthrie on projectionist theory, and Scott Atran on cognitive theory in anthropology come to mind.[32] Yet it would be highly surprising if certain areas of the brain were not related to the development of the religious impulse and the development of religion as a set of skills. Inevitably there are cultural assumptions in cognitive work that some scholars regard as unjustified, such as Carrette's well-formed critique that the cognitive science of religion is "embedded within a wider cultural environment of the knowledge economy."[33]

While the idea of religions as resources for the formation of human lives goes against the grain of some recent scholarship, it nevertheless seems to me that the data of religions require that we understand them in broadly existential terms. But such an existential understanding of religion does not mean that religion is set aside from specific cultures and societies. Indeed, there is no religion outside of culture and religions are inseparably connected to culture and particular languages. It is through language and culture that our somatic responses to the mystery and strangeness of the world take place; these somatic responses we call religions. As de Certeau observes, in emphasizing cultural, economic, and social factors, historians of religion have often overlooked religious and spiritual dimensions, hardly referring to religious literature as such, while theologians, conversely, hardly refer to cultural, economic, and social dimensions of religion.[34] This book therefore seeks to account for the importance of religion in terms of the human will to meaning and in terms of responses to our world, thereby locating religions within existential human concerns. Religions are best understood as ways of living, forms of culture, and kinds of skilful action that address the limits of human life and express wonder along with a desire for meaning, wisdom, and transcendence. Theories of religion are always provisional, perspectival, and inevitably limited. It is not clear what kind of theory could explain the Hindu holy man Sadhu Ludhkan Baba (the "rolling" Baba), who rolled from Madhya Pradesh in the centre of India to Lahore in Pakistan in 2004. He wanted to convince the President of Pakistan to reach a permanent peace with India.[35]

Religion and Religions

The reader will have noticed that sometimes I refer to "religion" and sometimes to "religions," thereby apparently gliding over an issue about the very category "religion" and how it is defined. Are the many "religions," species of the single genus "religion?" Can we speak about an essence of religion? Or is talk about "religions" simply a way of speaking about the diversity of human cultures? Must we restrict the category "religion," which some argue arose between the Renaissance and the Enlightenment, to a particular historical development in the history of the West linked to the development of the private realm in contrast to secular governance? Is religion a social construct or a natural category? Are there any more difficulties in defining or isolating "religion" from other spheres of human activity such as "art," "music," "politics," or "economics?"[36] All of our European categories or abstractions are the product of secularization and what Derrida refers to as our "theologico-political heritage."[37] Can we speak of religion in the singular or must we speak of religions? Indeed, can we only speak of religion in the singular because religion is only the product of western thinking? The general thrust of much scholarship has been in this direction although we would do well to remember, as Stroumsa shows, that religions in the plural was used as early as 1508 by Catholics to refer to systems of belief and behavior.[38] Wilfred Cantwell-Smith many years ago argued that the idea of religion was a European construction that emerged in the seventeenth and eighteenth centuries as "a concept of polemics and apologetics,"[39] an abstraction or reification of piety and faith. Others have followed this trend, skeptical of the category and its universal application.[40]

There is a rich literature on these questions, and weighty volumes dedicated to the question of "religion" or "religions,"[41] but it does seem to me that Douglas Hedley makes a valid point when he says that simply because there was no term for something does not mean that what it refers to did not exist; this is the "no name no thing" fallacy. In the medieval period, he notes, there was no term for architecture and the Enlightenment had no terms for linguistics or sociology.[42] We might add that Panini "discovered" linguistics and Vico, in a sense, "discovered" culture although they had no name for these sciences or areas of life in earlier periods, and that while the history of category formation is culture specific, this does not necessarily mean that categories are simply constructed rather than discovered or revealed through a discourse. It seems to me that it is no less difficult to differentiate "the political" or "the cultural" as categories of knowledge than "the religious."[43]

While politics, culture, and religion are categories that we vaguely understand, the precise definition of these terms is fraught with difficulty as each entails the others. While I do believe we can speak of "religion" in the singular, this does not mean that we can speak of it independently of these other categories. There is no uncontaminated essence of "religion," and I do not intend to reify it. As Derrida observes, religion "is inseparable from the social nexus, from the political, the familial, ethnic, communitarian nexus, from the nation and from the people; from autochthony, from blood and soil, and from the ever more problematic relation to citizenship and the state."[44]

The category religion is an etic category developed within western intellectual tradition. The term "etic" is from "phonetic" and denotes an "outsider" discourse in the sense that phonetics is the science of the sound of words which is available to all, in contrast to "emic," from "phonemic," designating the semantic properties of words availably only to those who speak the language. "The etic viewpoint," writes the linguist Pike, who coined the distinction, "studies behaviour as from outside of a particular system, and as an essential initial approach to an alien system. The emic viewpoint results from studying behaviours as from inside the system."[45] The etic description is constructed by the analyst, whereas "the emic structure of a particular system must ... be discovered."[46] Religion might be seen as a western emic category that has become an etic category with the development of scientific discourse. Thus an etic account and an emic account could have a surface similarity although the former examines data "in tacit reference to all parts of the earth" in contrast to the emic perspective which is orientated "to the particular function of those particular events in that particular culture ...".[47]

The actual word "religion" is from the Latin *religio* which has been derived from two Latin verbs, from *relegere*, "to re-read" (according to Cicero), and from *religare*, "to bind fast" (according to Lactantius), that is, binding the people to the state.[48] Thus in its very beginnings, religion was implicated with politics. At first, Christianity distanced itself from the category, St Paul associating religion with false paganism,[49] but in time it became an indigenous Christian self-description. After years of religious war in Europe, Locke advocated the relegation of religion to the private realm as distinct from governance restricted to the public realm, thereby instigating a separation of religion from politics, of the sacred from the secular, which is now regarded as quite normal in mainstream political discourse at least in Europe.

Peter Harrison has argued that "religion" originated with the Deists and developed during the Enlightenment from the Lutheran tradition.[50] Hegel in particular is important in the development of religion as a general category that incorporates within it other "religions" as an expression of the unfolding of the Spirit.[51]

Yet the history of the term does not demonstrate that it can only be restricted to a history of the West.[52] Our use of the term beyond these boundaries will, of course, depend upon what we mean by it and how we define it. If we define religion as developing only by reference to the secular or only in terms of a *theos*, then this will exclude many other cultures and histories. If, however, we define religion more inclusively, then I do believe that the term highlights an important aspect of culture and of being human that might otherwise elude attention. While I take Frits Staal's point (and Weber's) that definitions come at the end of inquiry, I would like to articulate some general characteristics of the central term of this book, taking on board the fact that definitions are always preliminary.

There are other related terms, such as "sacred" and "holy," which have direct analogues in other languages and which are, indeed, implicated in the history of "religion." Emile Beneveniste has studied terms for the "sacred" in Indo-European languages, observing that while there are no terms to designate religion itself, there are terms that are applied to gods and supernatural power such as Latin *sacer*, Greek *hieros*, Gothic *hails*, and so on. These terms, or rather sets of terms, point to the prehistoric period where a notion of the sacred has a double aspect: positive – "what is charged with divine presence" – and negative – "what is forbidden for me to contact."[53] But both divine presence and prohibition are incorporated within the term "religion" and are also related to the idea of sacrifice. The "sacred man" (*homo sacer*) in Roman law, Beneveniste tells us, was stained with a pollution that put him outside of society and contact with him was to be shunned,[54] a theme which formed the basis of Agamben's thesis about sovereign power over the "bare life" of the individual.[55] This ambivalence of the sacred, the double aspect of sacredness as something set aside but also negatively powerful, is a dimension of religions that points to their processing of something transcendent to human communities.

Defining Religion

Religion is a vague term and this is to be welcomed, as vague terms in language have broader applicability. The criticism that religion has no applicability outside of the West (and the consequent absurd claim that, for example, there is no religion in South Asia) reflects a fundamental misunderstanding about category formation, naming, and the nature of vagueness in language.[56] For example, the term "celt" and the adjective "celtic," used to refer to old Welsh, Manx, Scottish, Cornish, and Brittanic cultures and languages, is an etic category not used by those cultures themselves, but which nevertheless denotes a range of historical development and related peoples in northern, particularly north-western Europe. "Celtic" is a term of analytic identity and is not an emic or insider category,[57] but is used to bring to light or discover emic understandings and categories. The category religion as an etic term functions in a similar way.

There are many definitions of religion which introductory texts list, some adequate, some prolix, some humorous. Some of these, particularly those of Marx, that religion is the opiate of the people, of Freud, that religion is an illusion and sublimation of our instinctual desires (like Marx, he called it a "narcotic"), and of Durkheim, that religion is a social glue that unites people who adhere to certain beliefs and practices into a single moral community, express theories of religion that are part of the broader projects of those thinkers (political, psychoanalytical, and sociological, respectively). Within the sociology of religion there has been a tradition of theorists (to be encountered in later chapters), who have emphasized how religions provide meaning in the face of a meaningless world.

But while religions only exist within cultures – within particular social systems, kinship structures, ways of speaking, ways of acting, cultural memories, kinds of art, and so on – it is also arguable that religions show us something about or point to a world outside of culture. There is a reality that human beings encounter which shows itself to us through religion. We need therefore to understand religions as cultural forms that mediate the human encounter with mystery. We could substitute "mystery" with a number of terms such as "the invisible," "transcendence," "the para-doxical," or even "the impossible," and the choice of terms is important as each entails a certain set of concepts. But we cannot substitute "mystery" with "God," however empty that category might be understood, because God is a theological term specific to traditions, particularly what have been referred to as the "Abrahamic religions," although this category itself might be disputed. Buddhism, for example, would not fall within this definition nor would the Chinese traditions of Confucius and Lao Tzu, yet these traditions arguably do mediate human encounters with mystery.[58]

In brief, I wish to stress that from the practitioner's standpoint, religions are not primarily abstract systems but lived realities experienced within subjectivity, within the body, within community, and in the messy cut and thrust of history and human life. Religions give us a sense of identity, a path to walk, and a place in the world from where to act. Religions are ways of life, ways of living in the body, which encounter and respond to the raw fact of being, to the human condition, concerned with the formation of transcendent or sublime meanings that offer explanations of, and sometimes solutions to, suffering and death. They do this through ritual in which people act out the commands or injunctions of their sacred texts, they do this through narratives with which people identify the particularity of their lives, and they do this through inner practices of prayer, meditation, asceticism, and silence. All of these involve the development of skill, both behavioral skill and the skill of wisdom. We could argue that transcendence or the sublime accessed through inner practices is a structure fundamental to the workings of religions, and that if religions were not concerned with subjectivity and the truth of people's lives, they would cease to exist. It is hard to imagine a purely exterior or external religion concerned only with its own perpetuation through time and with adherence to law. Religions respond to human existential suffering, and bring death, that apparently meaningless event, into the realm of meaning. While this might be nothing new – even Marx and Freud thought that religion offered a satisfaction, albeit a false one, of human need – the explanation of religion in terms of science or political power often fails to grasp this fundamental point.

The cultural encounter with something beyond culture is mediated by the structures of tradition, primarily through text and ritual, and when religions fail to be relevant they die out. By "tradition" I mean kinds of knowledge handed down through the generations along with the practices that embody that knowledge; "transmission of practices," to use Salvatore's phrase.[59] In the secular context of late modernity, the situation is made more complex by the proliferation of spiritual technologies divorced from tradition and linked to a consumerist *Zeitgeist*, on the one hand, and an increasing environmental awareness on the other. While it remains to be seen just how important to contemporary culture and historically significant this amorphous spirituality is, it would seem to be an important transformation of practices and ideas whose origins lie in the old religions. In what remains of the introduction we need to look at religions as responses to the human condition, at the related problem of the primacy of lived bodily experience in contrast to being born into a semiotic system or culture, and to the problem of what "mystery" denotes.

Can we, then, speak of religion? And in speaking of religion are we speaking *about* religion or *for* religion? Generally in speaking of religion I am speaking *about* religion, but when speaking about religion there is a boundary beyond which we cannot go and that boundary is not so much between the insider and outsider but between science and theology or even philosophy as the history of being. That is, if religion is restricted to an object of science – as implied by the "science of religion" – then a deeper understanding of it in terms of mystery and invisibility is out of reach. I do not wish to foreclose this possibility and Chapter 9 ventures into speaking about the ontological referent (the ontology of process) that supplies such meaning.

The Argument

In the broad context of the positions I have just outlined, the aim of this book is to present a general account of religion as mediating the human encounter with mystery or the invisible, as a human quest for meaning, and as an impulse towards transcendence. Another way of expressing this in more phenomenological language is that religions speak from the world, from the real, or that the world shows itself through religions. That is, religions while clearly within culture, give voice to or express a reality outside of or larger than culture; we might designate this by the necessarily vague terms "the world," or "the real," or "mystery," or "the invisible" that point to a pre-cognitive ontology necessitated by phenomenological description. Religions mediate the encounter with mystery particularly by developing practices rooted in the body and through language. This encounter takes the forms of action (or doing) and speech (or meaning), and shows us the world.

1 Action is of two kinds, religious practices or the *habitus* comprising ritual performance (collective and personal) and moral action (political and personal).
2 This encounter takes the form of speech, which comprises speech acts (illocutionary acts such as promising) and locutionary statements (such as narratives, doctrines, and cultural knowledge).
3 Lastly this encounter shows us the world, which is the real (the material world and the socio-political world or culture) and the invisible (which comprises metaphysics).

Body and language are intimately connected in encountering the world in religiously important ways. These different categories are part of a single process. They can be represented diagrammatically (see Figure 1).

Alienation and the Human Condition

The phrase "human condition" has been in existence from at least the nineteenth century, although the phrase "la condition humaine" seems to have been popularized in post-war France by Sartre[60] and, especially, by Malraux's *La condition humaine* (1946). If by this we mean the brute facts[61] of human life – that we are born, that we die, that we are subject to disease, that we seek to make our lives meaningful in the face of the apparent indifference of an impersonal universe – then this human truth has been found throughout history in all continents from Homer's *Odyssey*, to the great, rambling, tragic epic of the *Mahabharata*. The sense of human suffering is attested in all literatures and the recognition of human limitation

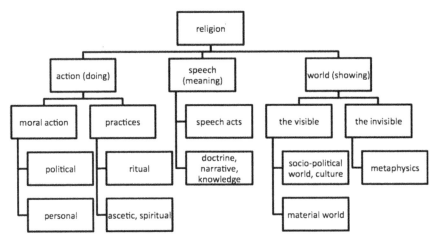

Figure 1   Religion as concerned with action, speech, and world

and suffering has been recognized across cultures and histories. But it is with modernity that there has developed a strong sense not simply of human suffering but that this suffering is linked to alienation or a sense of the strangeness of the world.

With the rise of modernism in the arts over the last hundred and fifty years, the parameters of the human condition have been keenly outlined by painters, sculptors, poets, and novelists, especially in the context of the terrible historical events of the twentieth century. Indeed, it could be argued that a sense of the strangeness of the world is a characteristic of modernity and that alienation or estrangement, the sense that humans are separated from the world, has its origins in Hegel and develops through Feuerbach and Marx, on the one hand, and through Kierkegaard and Nietzsche, on the other, into the existentialism of the twentieth century. While alienation means different things to these thinkers – for Hegel it is the self-alienation of Spirit from itself, for Feuerbach and Marx it is human nature as self-alienation, for the existentialists a sense of the absurdity of human life – we can identify here a trajectory of reflection characteristic of modernity. As Kierkegaard remarks in *Repetition*:

> One sticks one's finger into the ground to tell what country one is in; I stick my finger into the world – it has no smell. Where am I? What does it mean to say: the world? What is the meaning of that word? Who tricked me into this whole thing and leaves me standing here? Who am I? How did I get into the world? Why was I not asked about it, why was I not informed of these rules and regulations but just thrust into the ranks as if I had been bought from a peddling shanghaier of human being? How did I get involved in this big enterprise called

actuality? Why should I be involved? Isn't it a matter of choice? And if I am compelled to be involved, where is the manager – I have something to say about this. Is there no manager? To whom shall I make my complaint?[62]

There is a certain despair for Kierkegaard at the heart of the human condition that no act of will on our part can rescue us from the failure of our life to access the infinite.

While Kierkegaard's response to these issues is a Christian one that we need a "leap of faith" to rescue us from "sin," there are others who have responded to such questions nihilistically; that there is no meaning in the world. Indeed, there is a late modern view that philosophy itself is an atheism, in Simon Critchley's terms "a mood of unease" from which philosophy "begins its anxious and aporetic dialectics, its tail-biting paradoxes ...".[63]

While the languages are specific and the related concepts distinct, there is a sense in this historical trajectory that the human condition is characterized by alienation from the world and from ourselves, a sense borne witness to in literature from Kafka, to Beckett, to Camus. With the death of God values become non-universal and culture-specific, and historicism wins out over universalism. There is a profound sense in which human beings in modernity and late modernity are not at home, are not at ease, and for whom the world is strange. Not only philosophy but literature might be seen as responses to human alienation from the world and from ourselves. Beckett, that supreme modernist master of the humorous absurd, captured the spirit of what appears to be a futile life and utter pointlessness in a meaningless universe and the tragic pathos of the human struggle – "can there be misery loftier than mine?"[64] asks Ham rhetorically in *Endgame*. Thus Beckett can say that "at the end of my work there is nothing but dust ...".

Some might argue that late modernity is not even characterized by Ham's lofty ennui, but rather by a cultural indifference to questions of meaning and truth in favor of a vapid conformism in which consumerism and a kind of hedonism is the highest ideal. But while there may be some truth in this, western cultural productions clearly demonstrate that humans in late modernity are fundamentally concerned with questions of meaning and purpose; tendencies towards social fragmentation in the West combined with ecological concern serve to highlight these questions rather than occlude them and serve to demonstrate human alienation and helplessness in the face of immense global climate and environmental changes.

But is this sense of alienation and of the strangeness of the world unique to a particular history in the West? Partly "yes" and partly "no." "Yes," in the sense that never before have societies been in the grip of ideologies in which meaning is understood to be wholly a human construction; "no," in the sense that the human condition – which is actually shared by all creatures – of being born, suffering, and dying is universal. There is a sense of human suffering, of discontent, and of philosophical unease due to our ignorance articulated in all philosophical speculation. The Buddha clearly understood the sense of unease and the human predicament expressed in the first truth of the noble one[65] that "all is suffering" or "discontent" (*dukkha*), an idea at the beginning of other systems of Indian philosophy. Homer clearly understands human restlessness and the desire to find "home" in the wanderings of Odysseus. Indeed, the very existence of religions is response to the existential human condition of being born, living, and dying. This is not only a romantic conception of religions but born witness to throughout history.

In speaking about the human condition are we thereby committed to some idea of a common or essential human nature? This is a widely debated topic and the idea of a common human nature, derivative largely from Christianity, has come under attack, especially in postmodernity and the "death of man," but even much earlier. Sartre criticizes the idea on the grounds that since there is no God to conceive it, there is no essence to "man," no human nature, and "man" makes himself from nothing and is what he does ("il sera tel qu'il se sera fait").[66] We are condemned to be free: free to choose ourselves and to create ourselves in a world without absolute values. No longer seduced by the "perpetual end called God," as de Certeau says, we are nevertheless caught in a movement of "perpetual departure."[67] As there is no common or universal essence found in all human beings, Sartre claims, the universality of the human condition lies in its being a *condition*; a historical situation that sets the limits to our existence and which varies in different societies and temporal locations.

While we may disagree with Sartre's rejection of an essential human nature, his emphasis on historical situation along with our locatability in particular times and places is apposite and important. Fictional and historical stories of human suffering along with the realization of human dignity and redemption are found throughout history and in all religions. In Judaism we have an acute sense of human vulnerability from the early books of the Hebrew Bible – one immediately thinks of *Job* – to post-holocaust theology. In Christianity we think of the pathos of the fall and the hope of healing the broken human condition through Christ. In many Hindu traditions, as with Buddhism, we begin with a sense of suffering and dissatisfaction, and in Islam we think of Muhammad's wrestling with the burden of the revelation placed upon him and of a wayward human nature that needs to be controlled through law. While often being the cause of suffering, religions also offer resources for dealing with suffering and the oppressive power of one group of people over another. Religions can be sources of both personal and political liberation. We witness this in the selfless compassion of Etty Hilesum in Westerbork camp before her murder in Auschwitz, drawing courage from her Judaism[68] or, in the same war, the courage of the theologian Bonhoeffer facing the violence of his death with a Christian composure.

But we need not be too jeremiad in our assessment of the function of religions. In some ways it is a truism that religions are responses to the human condition, but it is pertinent that we share being born and dying, that we share grief and sorrow, and that we share hope for ourselves and for our families in this or in some other life. All religions respond to our need to make sense of our lives, suggest ways of living them, and offer ways of transcending our worldly life where that is seen to be a supreme good.

Taking from Sartre the emphasis on the historical location and temporality of life, we might say that in mediating the encounter with mystery, religions create moral communities and values – and we might add, virtues – that guide people's lives. Religions offer responses to the human condition and, while these responses vary a great deal, they share strong narrative bases that form communities. Such narratives – the story of the Exodus, the story of Jesus, the story of Krishna – give shape to religious communities and provide moral resources that allow human beings to function creatively.

But not only religions, secular ideologies can do this too and we think of Mao's long march or Lenin's return to St Petersburg. Such stories are accompanied by significantly divergent doctrines and practices. What Moosa has called the "grammars of religion," the "network of ideas and meanings,"[69] differ widely from Buddhism to Judaism and there can be contesting grammars (often many) within a single religion. Even the so-called "Abrahamic religions," Judaism, Christianity, and Islam are quite distinct. As Rémi Brague has shown, Judaism as it emerged in the common era was not connected with a sovereign state whereas Islam and Christianity were; Christianity separated itself from the political from its inception in contrast to Islam which inseparably bound itself to the political; and the idea of God distinct from the Trinity emerged in Islam only towards the end of the seventh century.[70] But the grammars of religion are set within a narrative context and the stories a community tells about itself along with its injunctive doctrines provide moral frameworks that guide or dictate people's lives from their sexual and dietary behavior to their philosophical attitudes. In providing stories to live by religions help form moral persons, and people are formed through community in conformity to the structures of tradition. At their best religions offer freedom from "the destructive bondage that the worship of the creature brings,"[71] to use Nicholas Lash's phrase, and at their worst they nurture that bondage and limitation. Indeed, we are all too familiar with the ways in which religions can be dysfunctional and restrictive of human flourishing, from priest child abuse to stoning women for adultery.

In being responses to human need and to the human condition, religions are thereby fundamentally concerned with subjectivity. I shall develop this idea in due course but for now we can say that subjectivity is formed in tradition-specific ways; through religious practices and the development of virtue, subjectivity conforms to tradition and is thereby transformed. By subjectivity I do not mean a western individuality but a kind of inwardness that is formed within community and set within a web of relationships. Such subjectivity is *will* expressed as narrative unity, constrained by the larger narrative of tradition. If by common human nature we mean a unity of the self provided by narrative, a recognition that we are temporally bound beings limited by birth and death, then this is basic not only to a description of human beings but to religions as responses to our needs.

Religious subjectivity is not the Cartesian subjectivity of the isolated individual, but rather is formed in community, in intersubjectivity. Sartre makes this point well in contrasting the dualism of Cartesian subjectivity with existential subjectivity, which is the discovery of others as a condition of my own existence.[72] If we qualify this by characterizing subjectivity as the narrative unity of the self then we have the basis for a religious subjectivity in which the person, through action, internalizes tradition and constructs him or herself as a religious person. This is generally done through mimesis, through copying the master, and has been the main structure for conveying religions through the generations. The language of construction implies the freedom to act, but we must remember that for many religious persons, the freedom or even desire to act otherwise is limited through the historical conditions in which we find ourselves. In earlier centuries people's choices were far more limited than our own.

Given the existential character of religious subjectivity, we see that the body is so important in understanding religions, a point recognized by John Bowker, who characterizes religion as "somatic exploration."[73] Through the body, which of course includes the brain, religions provide pathways to understanding the world. "(R)eligions," Bowker writes, "should be conceived as route finding activities, mapping the general paths along which human beings can trace their way from birth to death and through death …".[74] The aporias, the serious perplexities about the world which offer no way out – an *a-poria* means "no pathway" – are offered resolution by religions.

If religions address fundamental human needs and express the will to meaning, they are rooted in the body and bodily experience rather than being simply ideologies. Yet the meaning of the body is found in relation to a whole set of signs or semiotic system which forms culture. We are born into a semiotic system and yet there is also the experience of the body that resists assimilation into systems of language and signs. This is a difficult issue but one that has implications for our understanding of religion. If there is an experience of the body prior to language and sign – the primacy of perception, in Merleau-Ponty's terms – in which there is a somatic encounter with transcendence or the sublime, then religion might be understood not as a construction but as a natural category.

If, on the other hand, the body is understood as being primarily part of a semiotic system formed through culture, then religion can be seen as a cultural construction, a human rather than a natural category.

This issue relates to methodology and the question of how we best understand religions, in terms of phenomenology or in terms of semiotics? But we do not need to choose between the lived body as the basis of experience and semiotic system, as it is both the case that we inherit a system of signs and that our encounter with the world is primarily somatic.

The Primacy of Perception and the System of Signs

In his *Phenomenology of Perception*, Merleau-Ponty rejects the idea of a detached self or transcendental ego, distinct from the world and the Augustinian subjectivity proposed by the German philosopher Edmund Husserl, who even quotes Augustine at the end of *Cartesian Meditations* that "truth dwells in the inner man" (*in interiore homine habitat veritas*).[75] Merelau-Ponty writes:

> Truth does not 'dwell' only in 'the inner man', or rather, there is no inner man: man is within the world; it is in the world that he knows himself ... I find not a home of intrinsic truth, but a subject dedicated (*voué*) to the world.[76]

In place of Husserl's consciousness, Merleau-Ponty attempts to unveil a pre-theoretical layer of human experience upon which other theoretical formulations, particularly scientific ones, are based. Phenomenology is a reflection on this pre-theoretical experience and an attempt to see the world anew and to recognize and expound the importance of perception. The body is central to this enterprise, being the vantage point of perception and perceived world, and giving us access to a world. "The world is not what I think," writes Merleau-Ponty, "it is not in words, but what I live through, I am open to a world, I communicate indubitably with it ...". We are presented with the world's "facticity," with the "worldliness of the world," its *Weltlichkeit*.[77] To encounter this worldliness in our bodies, through our perception, is simultaneously to encounter meaning. We are therefore "condemned to meaning" by virtue of being here at all.[78] This account of meaning is something that is prior to sociality and language; it is a sense of presence and completion inherent in our experience of the world itself.

We are born into a given, human world: the world we inhabit and expand into is meaningful prior to our personal experience of it. This meaningful world has generally been called "culture" in anthropology or the "lifeworld" in phenomenology.[79] And yet while culture gives us language, the body, symbolic action, morality, and all ways of dealing with each other and with the world, the world itself, the horizon of time, and the very amazement of being here at all, are never exhausted by cultural accounts and always resists closure. It is in this sense that we are condemned to meaning; meaning is part of the very structure of the world.

The great questions of life are not and cannot be answered by science (such as the classic Leibnizian/Heideggerian question why is there something rather than nothing?), and we must understand religions primarily in terms of responses to these fundamental, existential questions that have confronted human beings throughout history and are arguably integral to the kind of beings we are. We can put this even more strongly by saying that religions are not merely responses to questions but responses to the *encounter* with the problems posed through the human experience of being here. Merleau-Ponty speaks about wonder in the introductory sections of his text. There is a wonder at the heart of the world, at its inexplicability, and at the very fact of wonder itself.[80] And I think this is surely what Merleau-Ponty is getting at when he refers to a pre-linguistic layer of experience. This is fundamental to religions. Religions are concerned with the body as the locus of encounter with mystery, the invisible, or transcendence, through well-winnowed practices of prayer, fasting, breathing, meditation, and silence, and to understand religions we need to understand the ways in which they inhabit human subjectivity through bodily and community modes of being in the world.

There is therefore not necessarily a contradiction between human experience of the primacy of the body and the experience of world as a system of signs or, one could say, a culture, although culture is a further elaboration or objectification built upon the lived-body. Religions can certainly be understood in terms of systems of signs but the existential ground of religions lies in the bodily encounter with the world, with the invisible that pervades the world, and in the complex relationship between bodily being (that embodiment prior to language) and the elaborate systems that are religious traditions at the interface of the visible with the invisible. The meaning of religion is intimately connected to the meaning of the body and the meaning of being in the world.

The Invisible and the Transcendent

If an account of religions as expressions of meaning is a first-level phenomenology, then a second-level phenomenology[81] raises ontological questions and presents an exploration which is not an account of various theologies, nor is it an attempt at synthesizing various religious standpoints; it is rather a claim that religions share an orientation to the world that recognizes mystery, transcendence, the sublime, or the invisible and its impact upon the visible.

This impact or constraint, the way transcendence is found in the folds of the world, is imaged – and can only be imaged – through human imagination. Religions are structures or forms of culture that allow human beings through the imagination and through action, to enter into the invisible and to bring the invisible into conceptualization, often in conflicting ways. In this sense, returning to my original definition, religions are cultural forms that mediate the encounter with mystery.

The invisible is resistant to objectification and explanation or complete understanding. Yet while it resists explanation, we also see in religions the pliability or adaptability of the invisible to the structures of the visible, to the world. It is this pliability or adaptability that allows the kinds of exploration of reality that constitute religions. This exploration is always in the body and through the body, through the flesh acting within the religious imagination. Religions arguably conform to the structures of reality and mediate the interface of the visible with the invisible. This exploration of the real and access to the invisible is through ritual action and through ethically informed action. Arguably ritual is effective on people's lives because, over time, it has discovered the fault lines or modes of pliability of the visible in which the invisible is given expression. Thus the Orthodox divine liturgy has effects on people who perform it as does the practice of meditation. By "effect," I mean an influence on the flesh through the flesh in the form of action; through action religions impact on history.

The body sees and touches and simultaneously has the propensity to be seen and touched; it is "a being of two leaves, from one side a thing among things and otherwise what sees them and touches them,"[82] says Merleau-Ponty. The body is both objective and phenomenal, part of the visible and yet constituting the visible within it, enfolded within the visible and enfolding the visible. This is the flesh of the visible in Merleau-Ponty's terms, which is the precondition of experience, the "wild being" or uncultivated being of the sensible. This visible that constitutes the world is the body in the world and the seer in the body. In Merleau-Ponty's words:

> What we call a visible is ... a quality pregnant with a texture, the surface of a depth, a cross-section upon a massive being, a grain or corpuscle born by a wave of Being. Since the total visible is always behind, or after, or between the aspects we see of it, there is access to it only through an experience which, like it, is wholly outside of itself.[83]

Pervading or assumed by the visible is that which makes the visible possible, namely the invisible. This is closely related to the idea of transcendence which we can take in the Kantian sense of the condition of possibility of the world as well as in the sense of something that goes beyond the world (and so is recognized or imaged only in the imagination). Behind the "pellicle of the visible" is a depth beneath the surface of things that they are dependent upon. But this invisible is not:

> a *de facto* invisible, like an object hidden behind another, and not an absolute invisible which would have nothing to do with the visible. Rather it is the invisible *of* this world, that which inhabits this world, sustains it, and renders it visible, its own interior possibility, the Being of its being.[84]

The invisible is therefore inexhaustible and endlessly explorable through traditional religions and in new cultural forms in the future.

The Truths of Religion

There used to be a desire in the study of religions to remain at a descriptive level and not to venture into questions of truth. While this book does not wish to shy away from a phenomenological ontology as the presupposition of inquiry into the importance of religions, one of the problems that it cannot develop in a sustained way is that religions make often passionate claims to truth which are incompatible: for example, that the soul is repeatedly reincarnated in a physical body versus the claim that the soul goes to heaven or hell for all eternity, versus the claim that the person becomes one with the elements. While the book does examine the relation between religion and rationality, I do not intend to comment directly on the issue of the truth of particular religious claims, taking seriously the "first-level" phenomenological move of bracketing the question of being or truth behind appearances and leaving this question to the philosophy of religion.

But while I do not directly address the question, "what of conflicting truth claims?", I would nevertheless wish to uphold a realist position for religions in general, by which I mean that religions are ways of life that inform us how to inhabit and act in the world, how to lead a good life, and teach us how to die well. Having made this comment about the suspension of examining truth claims, there is a case for a deeper phenomenological engagement, a phenomenological ontology (that, following Bowker, we might call a second-level phenomenology). Such a phenomenology seeks to raise ontological questions in relation to religions and their claims. Indeed "the real," "the mystery," or "the strange" is arguably what, in the end, is the ontological referent that supplies the meanings of religions.

This is a complex and potentially controversial claim that concerns the relationship between a phenomenological ontology and a theological reality.[85] Theological claims are specific to traditions and often, perhaps inevitably, in conflict: issues that are generally dealt with in the philosophy of religion. I do not argue for any theological position regarding the real. But I do posit the notion of the real as a necessary constraint on a descriptive phenomenology. Religions bestow meaning for human communities not as illusions – although they do that too – but because they access the ontological referent that gives rise to those meanings. This is not to defend absurd empirical claims that religions have sometimes made in their histories, or to defend a particular theological language, but it is to claim a primacy to somatic experience and material causation that religions access. It is on the grounds of material causation that the real can be differentiated from the unreal, although this idea must inevitably remain vague: the real cannot be described with any fullness except through particular theological languages although it must be posited as being without content in terms of a phenomenological account. I develop this somewhat in Chapter 7, where I argue for an ontology of process which examines the ways religions appear in human history and consciousness. Through this we see the importance of religion in articulating the relationship between the invisible and the visible expressed through speech acts, through ritual acts, and through ethical acts.

Conclusion

By way of summary then we can reiterate the claim that religions are cultural forms that respond to the encounter with mystery that I have characterized as the invisible. We might also claim that religions offer transcendent solutions to the human experience of life. Because of the centrality of subjectivity and body in living within a religious tradition, the explanation of religion purely as a cultural construction is inadequate. There is an encounter with the world prior to culture and language that we can describe as somatic and which has importance for the way we understand religions.

So, if religions are non-propositional ways of responding to and articulating the human condition of being born, living, and dying, then we need to develop an account of religious action and to show how such action can be read in terms of shared human responses to mystery, the invisible, and the strangeness of the world in which we find ourselves. This response has often been dysfunctional in the history of religions – there are long histories of religious dysfunction from the Inquisition to Jains being impaled on stakes by a Shaiva king – and in late modernity we know these stories well. There is no need to retell the dysfunctional history of religions here. I hope to make our understanding more complex. In concentrating on the more positive side of religions as ways of choosing a good life, as forms of community, as meaning-giving systems, I do not wish to present an apology but rather an analysis. In the coming chapters we will see how religions are central to our understanding of the human experiment and how, while they all disagree over metaphysics, they need to be understood as kinds of action rooted in the body, as kinds of narrative, kinds of injunction, and unique kinds of inwardness. Religions speak to us of human reality.

Notes

1. To quote the Alliance of Religion and Conservation (ARC) website: "The 11 faiths in ARC own seven percent of the habitable surface of the planet, and if they invested together, would be the world's third largest identifiable block of holders of stocks and shares" (http://www.arcworld.org/about.asp?pageID=2; accessed June 7, 2010). In a conversation, Martin Palmer told me that the figure at the time of writing is now closer to 8%. Also see Joanne O'Brian and Martin Palmer (eds), *Atlas of Religion* (Berkeley: University of California Press, 2007).

2. Gombrich, Richard, "Religious Experience in Early Buddhism" (1997) BASR Occasional Papers.

3. Eagleton, Terry, *Reason, Faith and Revolution: Reflections on the God Debate* (New Haven and London: Yale University Press, 2009), p. 6.

4. A point also made by Leszek Kolakowski, *Religion* (Glasgow: Fontana, 1982), p. 165, by John Cottingham, *The Spiritual Dimension: Religion, Philosophy and Human Value* (Cambridge: Cambridge University Press, 2005), pp. 1–2, and by Terry Eagleton, *Reason, Faith and Revolution: Reflections on the God Debate* (2009). Eagleton, responding to the idea that because of science religion ceases to be an explanation, writes with reference to Christianity: "But Christianity was never meant to be an explanation of anything in the first place. It is rather like saying that thanks to the electric toaster we can forget about Chekov" (p. 7).

5. Eliot, T.S., "Thoughts After Lambeth," p. 360 in *Selected Essays* (London: Faber and Faber, 1932), pp. 353–77.

6. As Heelas and Woodhead point out, secularization theory contains within it a variety of positions. On the one hand there is the disappearance thesis that religions will simply fade away in the West, the differentiation thesis that pushes religion even further into a purely private realm, a de-intensification thesis that religion will remain in a weak form, and the coexistence theory that in some contexts religions grow and thrive. Heelas, Paul and Linda Woodhead, *Religion in Modern Times: An Interpretative Anthology* (Oxford: Blackwell, 2000), pp. 307–8. On a strong version of secularization, see Steve Bruce, *God is Dead: Secularisation in the West* (Oxford: Blackwell, 2002). For a nuanced discussion, see Charles Taylor, *A Secular Age* (Cambridge, Mass., and London: Belknap Press, 2007), pp. 223–45; David Martin, *On Secularisation: Towards a Revised General Theory* (Aldershot: Ashgate, 2005).

7. Roberts, Richard, *Theology and Social Science* (Cambridge: Cambridge University Press, 2001), p. 288. See also his *Religion and Social Theory* (Oxford: Wiley-Blackwell, forthcoming). On the contemporary religious field, see Paul Heelas and Linda Woodhead. *The Spiritual Revolution: Why Religion is Giving Way to Spirituality* (Oxford: Blackwell, 2005). But compare Steve Bruce. *God is Dead: Secularization in the West* (Oxford: Blackwell, 2002), who defends a

strong secularization thesis and claims New Age spirituality to have little impact on the wider social body.

8. e.g. Hedley, Douglas, "'The 'Future' of Religion," in Julius Lipner (ed.), *Truth, Religious Dialogue and Dynamic Orthodoxy: Reflections on the Work of Brian Hebblethwaite* (UK: SCM Press, 2005), pp. 96–111.

9. Frankl, Viktor, *Man's Search for Meaning* (London: Random House, 2004 (1959)), pp. 105–6.

10. Taylor, *A Secular Age*, p. 308.

11. *Marianne 2* (3/26/2010), "Les Nouvelles Guerres des Religions: comment les clericalismes menacent la planète."

12. Freud, S., *The Future of an Illusion*, in *Civilization, Society and Religion, Group Psychology, Civilization and Its Discontents and Other Works*, trans. W.D. Robson-Scott (London: Penguin, 1985 (1928)), p. 227.

13. Kristeva, Julia, *Revolution in Poetic Language*, trans. Margaret Waller (New York: Columbia University Press, 1984), pp. 78–9.

14. Kristeva, Julia, *Hatred and Forgiveness*, trans. Jeanine Herman (New York: Columbia University Press, 2010), p. 211

15. Bowker, John (ed.), *Conflict and Reconciliation: The Contribution of Religions* (London: Key Publishing House, 2008), "Introduction," pp. 9–10.

16. On the theme of wisdom, see Ford, David, *Christian Wisdom: Desiring God and Learning in Love* (Cambridge: Cambridge University Press, 2007).

17. Freud, S., "The Uncanny," p. 390, in *Collected Papers* vol. IV, trans. Joan Riviere (London: Hogarth Press, 1925), pp. 368–407.

18. Freud, "The Uncanny," pp. 389–90.

19. Freud, "The Uncanny," p. 390.

20. Freud, "The Uncanny," p. 393.

21. Freud, "The Uncanny," p. 394.

22. Schutz, Alfred, *On Phenomenology and Social Life* (Chicago: University of Chicago Press, 1970), p. 248.

23. Otto, R., *The Idea of the Holy: An Inquiry into the Non-Rational Factor in the Idea of the Divine and its Relation to the Rational*, trans. John W. Harvey (Oxford: Oxford University Press, 1923), p. 5.

24. Csordas, Thomas J., "Asymptote of the Ineffable: Embodiment, Alterity, and the Theory of Religion," p. 164. *Current Anthropology*, vol. 45 (2), 2004, pp. 163–85. Thanks to Hrvoje Cargonja for this reference.

25. On this view of symbol see Robert Cummings Neville, *The Truth of Broken Symbols* (Albany: SUNY Press, 1996), p. x.

26. For a defense of reductionism see the work of Robert Segal, particularly *Explaining and Interpreting Religion, Essays on the Issue* (New York: Peter Lang, 1992).

27. Tweed, Thomas A., *Crossing and Dwelling: A Theory of Religion* (Cambridge, Mass.: Harvard University Press, 2006), p. 15.

28. Knott, Kim, *The Location of Religion: a Spatial Analysis* (London and Oakville: Equinox, 2005).

29. Ramadan, Tariq, *Radical Reform: Islamic Ethics and Liberation* (Oxford: Oxford University Press, 2009).

30. Ford, David, *Shaping Theology: Engagements in a Religious and Secular World* (Oxford: Wiley-Blackwell, 2007), p. 129.
31. Williams, Rowan, *Lost Icons* (Edinburgh: T&T Clark, 2003).
32. Whitehouse, Harvey, *Cognitive Theory of Religious Transmission* (Walnut Creek: Alta Missa, 2004); Lewis-Williams, David, *Conceiving God: The Cognitive Origin and Evolution of Religion* (London: Thames and Hudson, 2010); Boyer, Pascal, *Religion Explained: The Evolutionary Origins of Religious Thought* (London: Basic Books, 2001); Guthrie, S., *Faces in the Clouds: A New Theory of Religion* (Oxford: Oxford University Press, 2011). There is no room for a critical review of this work here, but for some of the general issues, see my *Beyond Phenomenology: Rethinking the Study of Religion* (London: Cassell, 1999), pp. 57–63.
33. Carrette, J., *Religions and Critical Psychology* (London and New York: Routledge, 2007), p. 165.
34. de Certeau, Michel, *The Writing of History*, trans. Tom Conley (New York: Columbia University Press, 1988), pp. 32–3.
35. Cited by Tweed, *Crossing and Dwelling*, pp. 127–8.
36. See the comments by Tweed, *Crossing and Dwelling*, p. 30.
37. Derrida is citing Carl Schmitt, the German political philosopher who recognizes the secular origin of categories in his critique of the attempt to neutralize politics in his time. Derrida, J., "Faith and Knowledge," p. 26, in J. Derrida and G. Vattimo (eds), *Religion* (Stanford, CA: Stanford University Press, 1998), pp. 1–78.
38. Stroumsa, Guy G., *A New Science: The Discovery of Religion in the Age of Reason* (Cambridge, Mass.: Harvard University Press, 2010), p. 27.
39. Cantwell-Smith, Wilfred, *The Meaning and End of Religion* (Minneapolis: Fortress Press, 1991), p. 43.
40. I cannot review or critique this literature here but would draw the reader's attention to two engaging if polemical books by Fitzgerald who presents an argument for the construction of the concept of religion. Fitzgerald, T., *The Ideology of Religious Studies* (Oxford: Oxford University Press, 2000) and *Discourse on Civility and Barbarity: A Critical History of Religion and Related Categories* (Oxford: Oxford University Press, 2007). Also see Tomoko Masuzawa, *The Invention of World Religions Or, How European Universalism was Preserved in the Language of Pluralism* (Chicago: Chicago University Press, 2005). This offers a good survey of the history of scholarship, but, as the author admits, offers no "particular programmatic scheme or a change of course in the way the study of religions is to be done" (p. 10). Other significant scholars share this skepticism particularly Talal Asad, *Genealogies of Religion* (Baltimore: The Johns Hopkins University Press, 1993) who disclaims the universality of religion because "its constituent elements and relationships are historically specific" and because "definition is itself the historical product of discursive processes" (p. 29). Also see Richard King, *Orientalism and Religion: Postcolonial Theory, India and "The Mystic East"* (New York: Routledge, 1999); Daniel Dubuisson, *L'Occident et la Religion: Mythes, science et idéologie* (Bruxelles: Éditions Complexe, 1998); Frits Staal, *Rules Without Meaning* (New York: Frits Lang,

1989), pp.387–406; and from a completely different perspective Nicholas Lash, *The Beginning and End of "Religion"* (Cambridge: Cambridge University Press, 1996). For a sober historical account, see Peter Harrison, *"Religion" and the Religions in the English Enlightenment* (Cambridge: Cambridge University Press, 1990). Guy Stroumsa presents a detailed historical survey of The category religion and the science of religion in his *A New Science: The Discovery of Religion in the Age of Reason* (Cambridge, Mass.: Harvard University Press, 2010). For a discussion of the category "religion" see Flood, *Beyond Phenomenology: Rethinking the Study of Religion* (London: Cassell, 1999), pp. 42–64. For a fuller bibliography, see Bianchi, Ugo (ed.), *The Notion of "Religion" in Comparative Research* (Rome: Bretschneider, 1994). For an engaging collection of essays reflecting on the concept of religion, see Vries, Hent de (ed.), *Religion: Beyond a Concept* (New York: Fordham University Press, 2008).

41. e.g. Bianchi, Ugo (ed.), *The Notion of "Religion" in Comparative Research: Selected Proceedings of the XVI AHR Congress* (Rome: Bretshneider, 1994). On the issues of defining religion, see Peter Clarke and Peter Byrne *Religion Defined and Explained* (London: Macmillan, 1993). For a lucid overview, see Keith Ward, *The Case for Religion* (Oxford: Oneworld, 2004), pp. 9–25.

42. Hedley, Douglas, "'The 'Future' of Religion," p. 97, in Julius Lipner (ed.), *Truth, Religious Dialogue and Dynamic Orthodoxy Reflections on the works of Brian Hebblethwaite* (UK: SCM Press, 2005), 96–111.

43. Tweed makes a similar point see *Crossing and Dwelling*, p. 30–1.

44. Derrida, "Faith and Knowledge," p. 4.

45. Pike, Kenneth Lee, *Language in Relation to a Unified Theory of Structure of Human Behavior* (The Hague and Paris: Mouton, 1967), p. 37.

46. Pike, *Language*, p. 38.

47. Pike, *Language*, p. 41.

48. Flood, *Beyond Phenomenology*, p. 44.

49. Betz, Rudolf, "Christianity as Religion: Paul's Attempt at Definition in Romans," in Bianchi, *The Notion of "Religion"*, pp. 3–9.

50. Harrison, P., *Religion and the Religions in the English Enlightenment* (Cambridge: Cambridge University Press, 1990).

51. For an engaging account of this, see Arvind-Pal D. Mandair, *Religion and the Specter of the West: Sikhism, Indian, Postcoloniality, and the Politics of Translation* (New York: Columbia University Press, 2009), pp. 127–61.

52. I do think the term "religion" can be used in a comparative context. For a rigorous and entertaining defense of comparativism, see Wendy Doniger, *The Implied Spider: Politics and Theology in Myth* (New York: Columbia University Press, 1998), pp. 64–77.

53. Beneveniste, Emile, *Indo-European Language and Society* (London: Faber and Faber, 1973 (1969)), p. 445.

54. Benveniste, *Indo-European Language and Society*, p. 453.

55. Agamben, Giorgio, *Homo Sacer: Sovereign Power and Bare Life*, trans. Daniel Heller-Roazen (Stanford, CA: Stanford University Press, 1998), pp. 8, 81–6. For Agamben, the sacred man who can be killed but not sacrificed has its analogues in modern politics. Here "bare life," the realm of the original sacred man, is

controlled by politics. This, for Agamben, displays a paradox at the heart of democracy, namely that it seeks happiness and freedom yet wants to control bare life.

56. For example, Masuzawa seems to be critical of the vagueness of the term "world religions" but arguably this is where its strength lies. Masuzawa, Tomoko, *The Invention of World Religions Or, How European Universalism was Preserved in the Language of Theism* (Chicago: University of Chicago Press, 2005), p. 1.

57. I am indebted to Oliver Davies for pointing out this parallel. See his "Celtic Christianity," pp. 26–7, in Mark Atherton (ed.), *Celts and Christians: New Approaches to the Religious Traditions of Britain and Ireland* (Cardiff: University of Wales Press, 2002), pp. 23–38.

58. As Philip Kennedy has observed, the idea of God is relatively recent in the history of the human species: "Naming the Divine: A History of the Concept of God" (Oxford, February 2011); see also his *God's Career: The Evolution of a Deity* (forthcoming). See also Mark Smith, *The Origins of Biblical Monotheism: Israel's Polytheistic Background and the Ugaritic Texts* (New York/Oxford: Oxford University Press, 2000).

59. Salvatore, A., *The Public Sphere: Liberal Modernity, Catholicism, Islam* (New York: Palgrave Macmillan, 2007), p. 80.

60. Sartre, Jean-Paul, *L'Existentialisme est un humanisme* (Paris: Gallimard, 1996), pp. 59–60.

61. I take "brute fact" to be something which resists complete explanation. See G.E.M. Anscombe, "On Brute Facts," *Analysis*, vol. 18, 1958, pp. 69–72.

62. Kierkegaard, Søren, *Fear and Trembling/ Repetition*, edited and translated with introduction and notes by Howard V. Hong and Edna H. Hong (Princeton: Princeton University Press, 1983), p. 200.

63. Critchley, Simon, *Very Little, Almost Nothing; Death, Philosophy, Literature* (London and New York: Routledge, 1997), p. 3.

64. Beckett, S., *Endgame* (London: Faber and Faber, 1976), p. 1.

65. I am indebted to Alexis Sanderson for his observation that *āryasatyāni* (noble truths) is a *tatpurusa* compound and so "the truth of the noble one" is a more accurate translation than "noble truth."

66. Sartre, *L'Existentialsme est un humanisme*, p. 29.

67. de Certeau, Michel, *The Mystic Fable*, vol. 1: *The Sixteenth and Seventeenth Centuries*, trans. Michael B. Smith (Chicago: University of Chicago Press, 1992), p. 299.

68. Hilesum, Etty, *Etty Hillesum: An Interrupted Life the Diaries, 1941–1943 and Letters from Westerbork* (New York: Henry Holt and Co, 1996 (1981)), trans. Arnold J. Pomerans.

69. Moosa, Ebrahim, *Ghazali and the Poetics of Imagination* (Oxford: Oxford University Press, 2008), p. 139.

70. Brague, Rémi, *The Law of God: the Philosophical History of an Idea*, trans. Lydia G. Cochrane (Chicago: Chicago University Press, 2007), pp. 36–7.

71. Lash, Nicholas, *The Beginning and End of "Religion"* (Cambridge: Cambridge University Press, 1996), pp. 21–2.

72. Sartre, *L'Existentialisme est un humanisme*, pp. 58–9.

73. Bowker, J., "Introduction," *Oxford Dictionary of World Religions* (Oxford: Oxford University Press, 1997), pp. xvii–xviii.
74. Bowker, John, *The Sense of God*, p. 82.
75. Husserl, E., *Cartesian Meditations*, trans. Dorion Cairns (Dordrecht, Boston, London: Kluwer, 1950), p. 157.
76. Merleau-Ponty, Maurice, *Phénoménologie de la perception* (Paris: Gallimard, 1945), p. 11. My translation, guided by *The Phenomenology of Perception*, trans. Colin Smith (London: Routledge, 1962), p. xii.
77. Merleau-Ponty, *Phénoménologie de la perception*, p. 17; *Phenomenology of Perception*, p. xix.
78. Merleau-Ponty, *Phénoménologie de la perception*, p. 20; *Phenomenology of Perception*, p. xxiv.
79. On the links between phenomenology and anthropology, see Michael Jackson (ed.), *Things As They Are. New Directions in Phenomenological Anthropology* (Blooomington: Indiana University Press, 1996).
80. Merleau-Ponty, *Phénoménologie de la perception*, p. 22. This is also akin to Csordas' "surprise." For an interesting discussion of this and a good account of Merleau-Ponty's understanding of embodiment as alterity or *écart*, "gap," "interval," "distance," see Csordas, "Embodiment, Alterity, and the Theory of Religion," p. 171. See also the responses to Csordas' argument, particularly by Fiona Bowie (pp. 176–7), who argues that more stress needs to be placed on "the world" itself rather than the world as "a cipher for language and culture" (p. 177).
81. On this distinction, see John Bowker, *The Meanings of Death* (Cambridge: Cambridge University Press, 1991), pp. 28–9. I discuss levels of phenomenology on pages 164–5.
82. Merleau-Ponty, Maurice, *The Visible and the Invisible* trans. Alphonso Lingis (Evanston: Northwestern University Press, 1968), p. 137.
83. Merleau-Ponty, *The Visible and the Invisible*, p. 136.
84. Merleau-Ponty, *The Visible and the Invisible*, p. 151.
85. I would like to thank one of the Wiley-Blackwell readers for highlighting the issue in this way.

Part One

Action

karmaṇaiva hi saṃsiddhim āsthitā janakādayaḥ/
lokasaṃgrahamevāpi sampaśyan kartum arhasi//

It was by action Janaka
and the others reached perfection.
Looking only to grasp the world,
your obligation is to act.

Bhagavad Gita 3.20

1

Clearing the Ground

As human beings we enter history through our actions which are unrepeatable and the consequences of which we can never completely predict. We can make amends but we can never take back what we do; we can never keep a broken promise and never retrieve good or bad done to others. This fundamental human truth exists at different levels and at different degrees of intensity; thus an act of marriage to a particular person at a particular time is unrepeatable, with significant consequences for those involved, although usually without large historical consequence. A government that goes to war, on the other hand, an action as the result of a number of decisions by a number of people, has considerable historical consequence that could affect thousands of people. The relation of action to history is complex and highly pertinent to the importance of religion in that religions mediate the human encounter with mystery through action and so can affect history. On the one hand we have macro-historical forces operating over large stretches of time – characterized as the *long durée* by the French annales school – in which human persons seem to be of little consequence,[1] while on the other we have subjective human action that impacts upon the world.

The human subject is both the consequence of history, the product of a certain time and space, language and culture, economic and social forces, yet also acts upon history and in some sense stands outside of it. We are both the products of history and its agents. In sociology this is formulated as the problem of which has priority, structure or agency? We are social actors as products of the social system and yet we act upon the social system to change it. My claim that religions express a human will to meaning needs to be located in the broader context of this complex problem. We need to present

The Importance of Religion: Meaning and Action in Our Strange World,
First Edition. Gavin Flood.
© 2012 Gavin Flood. Published 2012 by Blackwell Publishing Ltd.

an account of the theorizing about religion in macro-historical terms and to locate religious practice in relation to this debate. While I would wish to make claims about religion that holds up across traditions, we first need to be historically sensitive to the conditions of late modernity within which religions continue to flourish. Although we will develop these themes in later chapters, we need to place religion not only in the context of the will to meaning, but in the context of the historical processes that have created our modern condition.

This understanding of religion as a cultural form that mediates the encounter with mystery needs to be located within the history of social theory. It is a claim of social realism in so far as the encounter with mystery is expressed as action and is a claim of religious ontology in so far as it reveals a truth about the nature of our strange world. In its purest or simplest articulation, the will to meaning is the human act itself framed by the imagination; we do things for a reason, which is conceptualized or repre-sented in our minds, and which in turn is based on a pre-cognitive sense of bodily being. Religious actions are framed by a religious imaginaire and the purpose of such acts, the meaning of such acts, is directed towards a transcendent goal even when simultaneously directed towards the world. That is, the ultimate goal of many religions is a salvation or liberation that both transcends the world and is achieved only through and within it. The human encounter with mystery is mediated by action (and so the body) informed by a religious imagination. The Buddhist meditating in the morning along with the Moslem call to prayer are intentional actions driven by distinct imaginaries or ways of conceptualizing the nature of reality and the human place within it. People's actions have been driven by the religions they inhabit which, traditionally, have formed systems of total meaning. Historically, the majority of human beings have made sense of their lives through religions; religions have formed their daily behavior as well as their political actions, and in modernity religious people need to negotiate multiple identities which hold together the religious imagination along with advanced economic, technological, and scientific knowledge. People make meaning, as Hughes reminds us, from the meanings which are available to them.[2]

The importance of religion lies in the way religious action is a kind of mediation; the form in which people encounter mystery. People interact or dwell within the world through action and so action is also the point of intersection with history. This is not to conflate history with mystery, but clearly they are linked in temporality and the conundrum of time (Augustine's point that we experience time but cannot explain it). We live our lives through time within societies and within religions, and it is this complex relationship between history, society, and religion and the rela-tionship of that complex to the particular subject, to subjective meaning, that will allow us insight into the nature of religion as mediation.

The complex relationship between history, society, and religion has been analyzed in critical sociology since its inception with Compte in the nineteenth century. In the classical sociological terms of Durkheim, religion can be distinguished from society and yet explained by it: religion is social effervescence that functions to bond a community, the glue of the social group. But two other sociological traditions, those of Marx and Weber, have been especially significant in their explanation of and impact on religion. In particular two processes need to be discussed as they impact upon religious action, namely reification and rationalization. Reification is emphasized in a theoretical trajectory beginning with Marx and developing into the Frankfurt School while rationalization is emphasized by Max Weber and Weberian sociology. Traditionally the way these processes have been theorized have been at odds: on the one hand the Marxist trajectory sees religion as the consequence of the social economy and the reification of social and political relationships, on the other hand the Weberian tradition sees religion as directly affecting the social economy through the process of rationalization. The contemporary, global condition of modernity and global capitalism can be seen as the result of these processes. We need therefore to understand the claim that religions mediate the encounter with mystery, firstly in the context of historical process and secondly in the context of subjective meaning.

When understanding religions in terms of historical process there has been a general skepticism towards religion: religion is no mediation of mystery but rather an illusion that keeps us bound and trapped in an unjust world. On this view, religion does not develop from within the real but is rather an ideology imposed upon the real that takes us away from it. Ideology in Karl Marx's sense is "false consciousness" that keeps people entrapped within their social conditions. The counter-argument to religion therefore proceeds from a consideration of reification as a feature of the contemporary human condition, to a consideration of how processes of rationalization have contributed to this reification. The counter, counter-argument is that religions offer alternative conceptualizations or antidotes to reification and provide subjective meanings that cannot be reduced to ideology. This is not simply a normative claim about religion but also a methodological claim about how we understand religions, how any "science of religion" needs to proceed.

In clearing the ground for what follows we need then to discuss firstly the idea of reification, that one of our problems is that we turn ideas into things, and secondly rationalization, that reality can be explained in terms of our reasoning about it. Modern sociology has attempted to explain religion in terms of these processes but in so doing it has missed an important point that religions provide subjective meaning through action. Through action religions mediate the human encounter with the mystery and strangeness of the world.

Reification: The Marxist Legacy

Developing from Hegel, Marx identified alienation as the key experience of the individual in relation to the socio-economic processes in which s/he was born and religion as ideology being instrumental in this alienation. For Hegel, alienation was the Spirit departing from itself (from the condition of "being in itself" to the condition of "being for itself"), moving through the historical process, through the stages of art, religion, and philosophy, to its final self-realization as the "in and for itself" at the end of history. Religion in this view is part of the manifestation of the Spirit. Marx famously reversed this idea claiming that religion was not a manifestation of Spirit, an idealist position, but rather a product of matter. Religion, along with ethics and traditional German metaphysics, was a representation of material reality, but a false representation that was mistakenly taken to be real. To overcome alienation we must give up religion as people's illusory happiness in order to establish the conditions for real happiness, which is to abandon the condition which needs illusions. Some of Marx's best "sound bites" concern religion: it is "the sigh of the oppressed creature" and "the opium of the people."[3] Religion does not speak from the real but on the contrary is an illusion or ideology that he defined as false consciousness. Indeed, religion is the opiate of the people that gives us succor but in the end keeps us deluded, in slavish thrall to the capitalist industrial machine. This is a familiar story which develops into the twentieth century Marxism of Lukács, Gramsci, Mannheim, and the Frankfurt School.[4]

The Hungarian Marxist Georg Lukács developed the thesis that there is a disjunction between experience and social reality that needed to be resolved. In an early work, *The Theory of the Novel*, the self is alienated or estranged from the world and experiences life as fragmented; in its reflecting on the world, the "I" creates an image of itself and sees the world not objectively, but purely as a broken reflection. This "elevation of interiority" fragments the subject and creates a disjunction between self and world.[5] Lukács identifies the human need for meaning but because he accepts the Marxist critique of religion, this meaning cannot be located in any transcendence and nor can it be found in the current, modern conditions of the subject whose relationship to the world is dissociated.

The retreat into metaphysics cannot give us real meaning because the retreat from the material world is illusory. Drawing not only from Hegel but embedded within a neo-Kantian tradition that has privileged the subject of knowledge, the central problem Lukács deals with is the relation of subjectivity to history or of the human subject to the totality of the social system. The distorted perception and experience we have of the world he called "reification," the turning something into a thing, which is a form of alienation and characteristic of the modern social and political life of his time (and arguably still is). Reification, which creates the relationship between subject and object as a primary reality, appears normal to us and has become second nature.[6] The factory worker who devotes ten or more hours a day selling her labor for a mere pittance, believing this to be her duty and is a regular church goer where she learns respect for the social system of which she is a part and the unchangeable nature of her social relationships, is in thrall to ideology; her human relationships and relationship with the commodity she helps produce are reified. In this view, the modern, industrialized subject lives an inauthentic and tragic life, tragic in so far as she is unable to give meaning to the "fatalistic" laws of nature and unable to overcome the distance between self and world; we live isolated and alienated due to reification.

Lukács wants to humanize the subject and give meaning to human life, but the historical conditions in which we find ourselves militate against this.[7] In *History and Class Consciousness* (1923) he developed the idea of reification in terms of the analysis of commodities which he saw as "the central, structural problem of capitalist society."[8] The relationships between people, economic and political, take on the characterization of a thing. In turning social relationships into things they become "fetishized" to use Marx's term. Society as a whole is a totality, an idea that is derived through Marx from Hegel, and the subject tries to grasp or understand this totality but cannot. Instead our tragedy is that we experience estrangement from the social world. The true subject and object of history for Lukács is the proletariat or working class, a realization that dissolves the alienating distinction between subject and object. This collective subject can realize its potential, realize that it itself is both subject and object of historical process and in this realization, enacted in revolutionary acts, finds fulfillment with the dissolution of reification. The classless society will be achieved once the working class is, in a sense, eradicated, which will also be the eradication of reification.

Lukács launches his attack against reification not only in terms of religion but more particularly in terms of philosophy. In "The Antinomies of Bourgeois Thought," the second chapter of *History and Class Consciousness*, Lukács begins with the astute observation that problems of modern philosophy spring from their being grounded in the reified structure of consciousness which has occurred within a specific time and location, namely the history of the West; thus it is futile to find Kant in Plato. The fundamental problem of modern philosophy is that (as Kant had claimed) "it refuses to accept the world as something that has arisen (or e.g. has been created by God) independently of the knowing subject."[9] This confidence in and justification of human reason displays itself before Kant in, on the one hand, a skepticism that knowledge can be universally valid (Berkeley, Hume) and on the other in an "unlimited confidence" in the ability of philosophy to apprehend "the true essence of things"[10] (Leibniz, Spinoza). This tendency to abstract or pull reality back to the mind is erroneous for Lukács because it misses the fundamental priority of the material. Linked to the tendency to abstract we have the alienation of the human subject and the reification of social relationships inscribed within a material reality, and Lukács offers an insightful account of the conditions of modernity. Reification therefore affects individuals and groups of individuals who comprise any particular society in both their perception of the world and in their actions: the systemic distortion of reification is perceptual and practical.[11]

But there are three problems with Lukács' insightful work. Firstly, his desire to critique the subject–object relationship as a consequence of reification. For Lukács the goal of history is to realize that the real, authentic subject is in fact the working class. But a collectivity cannot be the subject of history. While it is possible to speak about a group will, this is a metaphorical extension of the meaningful sense of will being located within a person; there is no true collective will or collectivity as a centre of consciousness (at least as thematized in mainstream history of the West; there are esoteric traditions that make such a claim).

The proletariat cannot be the subject of history for it cannot contain a singular will; only human persons can act through will governed by the ability to imagine a particular outcome. In this sense persons are free and independent of social structure. Secondly, reification assumes that we can separate religion from society and culture. However, such a separation is a modern phenomenon that has developed in the history of the West with, for example, Locke's relegation of religion to the private realm in contrast to the operation of governance in the public realm. While many cultures do distinguish between the religious realm and the secular realm (Tibetan Buddhism, for example, has a distinction between the monastic community and laity), many do not; the religious is inseparably combined with the social. Milbank, echoing Troeltsch, makes the point that in some locations it might not be possible to abstract religion from society; in Islam, for example, society has been "inside" the religion and so the social "dissolved into nothingness,"[12] which some might argue is a bad thing. Lastly, for Lukács inwardness is a sign of alienation. Indeed so long as we do not realize the true, collective subject of history we are under the influence of this estrangement. But it could be argued, conversely, that inwardness can be decoupled from alienation and that religious identity is the intensification of inwardness which is simultaneously an intensification of meaning. This is not individuality – we are not back with the Cartesian self – rather it is a kind of subjectivity that is formed through tradition. This kind of religious inwardness is identity through time along with narrative identity that makes a life coherent and explicates the way a life conforms, or otherwise, to tradition. This kind of inwardness, religious traditions claim, brings us into the mystery of the world and only exists within the world as a mode of the world, again, always expressed in action.

In Honneth's lucid study, reification is not merely an epistemic category mistake nor a morally objectionable act, but a distorted form of praxis.[13] "Reification," he writes, "signifies a habit of thought, a habitually ossified perspective, which, when taken up by the subject, leads not only to the loss of its capacity for empathetic engagement but also to the world's loss of its qualitatively disclosed character."[14] This form of distorted praxis involves us in perceiving both objects and persons as "things" that we can make profitable: both people and things on this view are reduced to a perception of their usefulness and become mere instruments in the activity of profit.

Honneth re-examines Lukács' thesis and its contemporary relevance, arguing that there are striking affinities between this concept and ideas of John Dewey and Martin Heidegger. For Heidegger, objectivity envisaged as the privileging of a neutral, epistemic subject[15] is called into question. The world is given to us prior to conceptualization and our practical relation to the world he characterized as "care": "humans in fact exist in a modus of existential engagement of 'caring', through which they disclose a meaningful world."[16] Honneth gives empirical support for this idea from developmental psychology and presents an argument for "recognition"; prior to conceptualization, prior to "cognition" and the objective or neutral understanding of reality, we have a direct, empathetic engagement with the world and with others, but this engagement is distorted through reification. Honneth's extension of reification to a pathology of intersubjectivity takes it beyond economic determination and places the idea more centrally in the structure of human being, of social ontology; reification is part of the structure of who we are and yet can be counteracted by positive forces within the social order.

These forces, existential care, praxis, and the pre-conceptual engagement before subject and object reification, are fundamental to human being in the world entailed in taking over the perspective of another person.[17] In terms of ontogenetic development, this ability to empathize so fundamental to being human has its genesis in imitation or mimesis of the parent by the child. Recognition, according to Honneth, is therefore prior to cognition, an idea that is shared by Lukács, Dewey, and Heidegger.[18] On this view, forgetfulness of recognition is reification and so recollection is the overcoming of reification, overcoming the neutralization of "empathetic engagement"[19] that has occurred through the socialization processes of modernity.

A different version of fundamentally the same problem is found in Habermas' theory of communicative action, which seeks to overcome distorted communication (which we might read as reification). The natural human condition of empathy is distorted by reification that occurs due to the unjust political-social system in which we are reared. On this view, religion is an expression of reification and bolsters up injustice. Although religion gives us comfort – like an opiate – it is an illusion, albeit a powerful illusion that contributes to inequality and injustice. Religion is part of the structure of reification. The solidification of social relationships – such that conditions of oppression seem natural – is reinforced through religion, through the ideological superstructure of society. Religion on this account is an ideology that serves to reinforce the illusion of the subject in relation to the world. Through reification our unequal social relationships are solidified, taken to be real, and religion supports this fragmented view of reality.

For Lukács and other Marxists from Karl Mannheim through to Althusser, to repair the modern condition we need to understand how "the inauthentic subject ... becomes the reified subject of capitalism."[20] We do not need to follow Lukács' adherence to the Marxist revolutionary dictum which has affected extremely destructive political regimes in the name of achieving utopian harmony, but we can take from him the analysis of reification as a feature of the modern, capitalist economy. But the criticism of religion, or rather of Christianity, as reinforcing reification, while containing some truth in that religion has clearly historically reinforced unequal social conditions, ignores the liberating and transformative dimensions of religion. It is not enough to identify the conditions of reification and through that to anticipate the dissolution of religion; rather, we need to recognize the importance of religious meaning in subjectivity and the importance of transcendent goals that motivate and drive human reality. To understand the process of reification further we need to understand the parallel process of rationalization or instrumental rationality that in fact produces reification.

Rationalization: The Weberian Legacy

A second sociological trajectory distinct from the Marxist is that of Weber. Lukács' thought was influenced by Max Weber and the idea of reification and can be reconciled with the Weberian analysis of rationalization.[21] The more the rationalization of life in modernity, the greater the intensity of reification and so the more alienated we become. Without religion there is a process of disenchantment accompanied by nostalgia for a time of religious enchantment when human beings' place in the cosmos was assured. Rationalization is central to Weber's philosophy of history which points to the process whereby magical explanations of the world are replaced in favor of scientifically reliable ones. There is an inevitable progress as human beings move from a magical worldview, through religion, to a world governed by reason. For Weber rationalization is a process that occurs in different realms of civilization, in the economic realm, in law, in the military, and in religion, and is integral to the development of civilizations.

Weber's understanding of religion might be summarily abbreviated as follows. Religion is a key force in the history of civilizations that cannot be reduced merely to social or economic factors but which influences the socio-economic level. The earliest tribal cultures had simple forms of religion characterized by magical practices that sought to manipulate supernatural powers for human benefit. Magical practices came to be replaced by religion characterized as worship, rather than manipulation, of those supernatural powers, the gods. As societies become more complex, with religion we have the formation of ethical rationalization, which develops codes of conduct and laws by which a people might live. Such ethical development is accompanied by the rise of specialists who deal with issues of morals and law, that is, a priesthood. Thus religious "virtuosi" – the monks, priests, renouncers – are concerned with salvation, liberation, or eternal life, while the ordinary population is still concerned with magical manipulation for protection against disease, warding off premature death, abundance of crops, and so on.

Along with the development of ethical social structures we have the development of a bureaucracy and administration linked to the state. We see this most clearly, according to Weber, with Confucianism. Yet we also have individuals from different social groups, particularly outside the mainstream, who criticize and reform the social structure. These are charismatic leaders and prophets who have arisen in all religions. Charisma is a property possessed (or endowed to) certain individuals who have undergone some extreme religious experience brought about, for example, by asceticism. The charismatic prophet both founds a religion and can challenge an established religion when often religious revival or sectarian break-off occurs as a result. In highly centralized, bureaucratized cultures such as China, prophesy is highly controlled, whereas in non-centralized cultures such as biblical culture, prophesy becomes rife. Through history, the doctrine and practices of the charismatic leader undergo a process of rationalization – the routinization of charisma – and in turn become traditional, established institutions. There is then a dialectic between charisma (a property possessed by important individual social actors) and routinization (the process of instrumental reason wherein lies the stability and progress of a society). Perhaps one of the most influential contributions Weber has made to the sociology of religion is his thesis of how the protestant spirit influenced the development of economic practices that became capitalism. With Protestantism, the other-worldly asceticism of the monasteries became a this-worldly asceticism as part of everyday life. Hard work along with an abstemious lifestyle became part of a religious ethos which allowed a surplus of wealth to develop and hence the development of capitalism.

Weber is important to us on a number of accounts. Firstly, in contrast to Lukács who saw the subject of history as the self-conscious proletariat which must be galvanized into action through uncovering the mechanisms of its own oppression, Weber understood the subject of history to be the individual social actor who has causal priority. While we certainly work in shared communities, these communities are of human persons with intentionality and direction into the world. Rather than the group, it is the individual person that is the agent of action, and meaning must be located primarily in the social actor. Indeed, a long sociological tradition develops from Weber that lays emphasis on the way social meaning is formed for the particular social actor and how religion as a motivating factor within culture is integral to this process.

Talcot Parsons, following in Weber's wake, both privileged individual action as having causal efficacy and held that meaning is public. The sociological tradition stemming from him, which includes Geertz, Berger, Bellah, and Luckmann, along with the French sociologist Hervieu-Léger, shares this view that religion primarily belongs to the individual realm. Secondly, Weber is important in showing the interactions between economies and cultural and religious systems, and in offering comparison in terms of ideal types. This is a brave sociology that flies in the face of both extreme relativism and any crude economic reductionism,[22] but a sociology that nevertheless relegates religion to the margins. What is important is the broad unfolding of rationalization that on this view drives history. Religion is certainly important in this formation, but is nevertheless marginalized. This marginalization is typical of sociology which, Milbank argues, "polices" the social order, restricting the scope and importance of religion.[23] In this sense sociology is a thoroughly secularist and, as Richard Roberts observes, modernist enterprise.[24]

Knowledge and Action

Our discussion so far has established that we can understand western modernity and the effects on the subject of action through the dual processes of reification and rationalization. While instrumental rationality is positive in so far as it facilitates action and social cohesiveness, it is negative in so far as it also produces alienation and reification when persons regard relationships as things. This dual process that underpins the development of modernity has resulted in the sweeping acceleration of modern humanity in the last fifty to a hundred years with the development of technology that enables globalization. While I agree with Oliver Davies' claim that religions offer models of solidarity and cross-cultural cooperation through liberating potentials of technology for the human good,[25] we need here to understand the narrower claim that religions mediate the encounter with mystery through constraining human action usually in ways that are considered to be for the betterment of the group or in ways that are conducive to salvation. To return for a moment to our starting point with the idea of reification: It is far from clear that religion is ideology that operates to reinforce the status quo through the mechanism of reification.

The main problem is that Marxist thinkers such as Lukács identify religion with ideology as the epiphenomenon of the socio-economic base and a commodification of the means and relations of production. While we might agree with Lukács that one of the problems with the western history of philosophy has been its tendency to abstraction and the confusion of what is real with what is thought, along with the tendency to make the object of knowledge conform to the subject, we must part from Lukács in claiming that religion too is reification on the grounds that religions consistently claim to bring us into the world and to speak from within the world. Even in strongly idealist modes, for example Hindu forms of idealism such as Abhinavagupta's monistic Śaivism, religions draw their practitioners into the experienced world, into the bodily habitus as the location of redemption and transformation.

To question whether religion can be exhausted by the idea of reification is not simply to replace a hermeneutics of suspicion with a hermeneutics of faith, it is not a claim about content, but is rather to identify a process whereby religions mediate the encounter with mystery. The revelations of religions, the *Qur'an*, the Hebrew Bible, Buddhist and Hindu scriptures, claim an authority by those who adhere to them that persists through the generations. The claims of these traditions, their content, vary greatly but a pattern can be identified, what we might call a phenomenological structure of tradition, which is constant. I have given a name to the structure, the mediation of mystery, and need here to highlight three processes namely (i) the identification of knowledge and action, (ii) temporal mediation, and (iii) subjective meaning. I shall deal with these in fairly brisk terms here, as the concrete instances will be developed in the following chapters.

(i) *The Identification of Knowledge and Action.* In religions we have a union or fusion of knowledge and action. Religious actions as moral acts, ritual, and asceticism are forms of cultural knowledge through which practitioners become aware of a world. These knowledge systems are passed through the generations by the imitation of action. Clearly the origin of knowledge-acts is in human intention and the will. In modernity such religious actions interact with technology to produce globalized religions of today. In religion we have dualities of will and action, along with knowledge and action, being overcome or fused without being eradicated. Religions offer a kind of "sublation" or *Aufhebung*, to use Hegel's term, a synthesis of action without the abolition of the parts: will and knowledge combine in movement; the movement of the moral speech act in the promise, for example, or the movement of the hand in a ritual gesture (see next chapter). Action itself is meaning.

(ii) *Temporal Mediation.* The self meets the world in intentional act and act is always movement in time. Through religious action practitioners encounter mystery, which is always a temporal encounter; even an ecstatic or extraordinary experience is within time (as William James observed with regard to mystical experience). Temporal mediation refers to a fundamental mode of encountering the world within a religious framework. That is, there is a constellation of events witnessed by a practitioner that is translated into memory including cultural memory and thence through inscription into history. We will examine this constellation with regard to revealed text more closely in Chapter 3, but for now we need simply to note this structure which operates at the micro- and macro-levels of religious encounter. An event, at least a human event, is an action. In the case of religions this is a kind of action that mediates the encounter with mystery, such as taking Holy Communion or a Jain monk practicing asceticism. The act of communion lives in cultural memory and is brought into the present moment through repeated acts of remembrance. These acts of remembrance can enter history both as a point in temporal sequence and as the object of a historiography.

In the religious act, the practitioner simultaneously remembers tradition and recalls the meaning of the act, perhaps as future goal. This understanding is always mediated through signs, symbols, and texts, as Ricoeur has emphasized with regard to self-understanding.[26] The religious act embodies a shared memory into which generally one is born and itself bears witness to common or shared knowledge by a community.

(iii) *Subjective Meaning.* Lastly, the phenomenological structure of mediation involves action as the performance of subjective meaning. An action embodies a mode of thinking (which some call "praxis") and always involves understanding. Denys Turner puts this well with reference to Merleau-Ponty's contention that "a praxis is a meaning." He writes: "Far from it being the case that to engage in a praxis is a performance by rote, repetition without understanding; it is only an understanding of the 'meaning' which a praxis incarnates which makes any repetition possible."[27]

The particular religious actor, guided by the cosmology of tradition, acts in a particular way – such as taking Communion or meditating – and in so doing expresses the meaning of that act for that time. Action results from intention and is meaningful because not random or arbitrary. The act is religiously meaningful because it mediates the encounter with mystery – each act of

Communion, each call to prayer, each *puja*, repeats in action the memory of tradition. In privileging an existential subjectivity we are emphasizing agency over structure, yet acknowledging that structure informs agency (as structuration theory would have it). Agency is sociological discourse for the problem of freedom in philosophy found either in the moral sense (for Kant) or within thought (for Hegel). Arguably religious subjective meaning entails an idea of freedom which is located neither in autonomy nor within dialectical reason, but in a performed subjectivity, whose intention is to replace its own will with a higher power that transforms it. In the coming pages we will substantially develop this idea of subjective meaning as being formed by tradition and through self-narrations that interface with broader historical processes: tradition is internalized within subjectivity through religious action.

Methodology

Finally we need to examine the methodological point about reification. Some have argued that scholars of religion are themselves complicit in the reification of religion and thereby in the "ideological processes" of domination.[28] Such critique itself implicitly, if not explicitly, comes out of a neo-Marxist position that sees religion as an epiphenomenon of other social and historical forces. The general argument is that "religion" as an object of scholarship has been taken to be a real object (i.e. reified) and is an essence that can be studied as something in itself, outside of social and political institutions.

But, the argument goes, this is not the case. Religion has been constructed through a phenomenology of religion that is blind to its own presuppositions without reference to socio-political and geopolitical implications. Scholarship has constructed a mythical essence of religion abstracted from historical location.[29] In contrast, the argument goes, as scholars we need to be aware of our presuppositions and rather than trying to identify an essence of religion, examine the socio-political conditions under which certain kinds of discourse (and practice) arise. This has been the argument of genealogical scholarship, particularly by Foucault. On this view the object of the science of religion would dissolve into culture and the politics of representation.

I have some sympathy with this position, but only some. Religions arise only within human history at particular times, in particular societies, and are associated with particular social and political institutions; but the argument is problematic. Firstly it assumes that religion is an epiphenomenon of social and political forces, even to the extreme that the category religion functions to legitimate American political hegemony.[30] However, this is to dismiss religion on a priori grounds which have no greater basis than theological claims themselves. On the contrary, we can posit a realist understanding of religion that sees religions as forms of culture that penetrate the world of life or perhaps more accurately, should not be relegated to the irreal, as sociology has done, but taken seriously as cultural forms that bring us into the strange, but real world. Religion is a different kind of cultural object to other abstractions such as politics or society, although a cultural object necessarily devoid of content. A first-level phenomenology, in which religion shows itself in the ways I have suggested here, gives way to a second-level phenomenological claim about religious action, from mystery or the invisible and that we might call a "religious ontology" (see p. 165). Such a religious ontology is a philosophical rather than a sociological claim and is necessitated by the data of religions. A second-level phenomenology is open to the probability that religions speak from the real.

Conclusion

By way of conclusion the material presented here has been necessarily condensed. Within what we can call the sociological tradition of western thought there are at least three important trajectories: the functionalism of the Durkheim tradition, the Weberian tradition, and the Marxist tradition. Of particular importance is the Marxist thesis about religion as false consciousness or ideology expressed in the process of reification, along with the Weberian thesis about the process of rationalization and the way religion influences the socio-economic base.

We have pointed to some of the limitations of this work and suggested that understanding religion in terms of cultural forms that mediate mystery through action and thereby articulate a religious subjective meaning is a more adequate description. The *how* of mediation is in the action as an expression of the will to meaning, whereas the *place* of mediation is the here and now, wherever that is, and in places of semantic density, the temples, churches, mosques, and synagogues of the religions. Having cleared some of the theoretical ground here, we now need to develop the thesis about the mediation of the encounter with mystery, specifically how this plays out in religious action characterized by the moral act and the ritual act. To do this we will need to consider more sociology in the process.

Notes

1. On a recent history of the annales school, see Burguière, André, *The Annales School: An Intellectual History*, trans. Jane Marie Todd (New York: Cornell University Press, 2009).
2. Hughes, Graham, *Worship as Meaning: A Liturgical Theology for Late Modernity* (Cambridge: Cambridge University Press, 2003).

3. Marx, Karl, *Contribution to the Critique of Hegel's Philosophy of Right*, in Saul K. Padover trans. and ed., *The Essential Karl Marx* (Ontario: Mentor, 1978), pp. 286–88.

4. Siebert, R.J., *Critical Theory of Religion: The Frankfurt School – From Universal Pragmatic to Political Theology* (Berlin, New York: Walter Gruyter, 1985); *The Critical Theory of Religion: From Religious Orthodoxy through Mysticism to Secular Enlightenment and Beyond: The Totally Other and the Rescue of the Hopeless* (Leiden: Brill, 2006).

5. Lukács, Georg, *Theory of the Novel*, p. 114, trans. A. Bostock (London: Merlin Press, 1971). I am indebted to the excellent discussion which guided my thinking by Caroline Williams, *Contemporary French Philosophy: Modernity and the Persistence of the Subject* (London: Athlone Press, 2001), pp. 40–54.

6. Lukács, Georg, *History and Class Consciousness*, trans. Rodney Livingstone (Cambridge: MIT Press, 1971), p. 89.

7. For a good discussion of this issue, see Caroline Williams, *Contemporary French Philosophy*, pp. 40–54.

8. Lukács, *History and Class Consciousness*, p. 83.

9. Lukács, *History and Class Consciousness*, p. 111.

10. Lukács, *History and Class Consciousness*, p. 112.

11. Honneth, Axel, *Reification: A Recognition-Theoretical View: The Tanner Lectures of Human Value* p. 95 (www.tannerlectures.utah.edu/lectures/documents/Honneth_2006.pdf; accessed August 11, 2010).

12. Milbank, John, *Theology and Social Theory: Beyond Secular Reason* (Oxford: Blackwell, 1990), p. 89; see also p. 109.

13. Honneth, *Reification: A Recognition-Theoretical View*, p. 96.

14. Honneth, *Reification: A Recognition-Theoretical View*, p. 109.

15. Honneth, *Reification: A Recognition-Theoretical View*, p. 104.

16. Honneth, *Reification: A Recognition-Theoretical View*, p. 106.

17. Honneth, *Reification: A Recognition-Theoretical View*, p. 113.

18. See the discussion by Raymond Geuss, "Philosophical Anthropology and Social Criticism," in Axel Honneth, Judith Butler, Raymond Geuss, and Martin Jay, *Reification: A New Look at an Old Idea* (Oxford: Oxford University Press, 2008), pp. 120–30.

19. Honneth, *Reification: A Recognition-Theoretical View*, p. 126.

20. Williams, *Contemporary French Philosophy*, p. 45.

21. Honneth, *Reification: A Recognition-Theoretical View*, p. 97.

22. For the importance of Weber in contemporary considerations of the relationship between economy and religion, see Richard H. Roberts (ed.), *Religion and the Transformations of Capitalism* (London and New York: Routledge, 1995).

23. Milbank, *Theology and Social Theory*, p. 110.

24. Richard Roberts, *Theology and the Human Sciences* (Cambridge: Cambridge University Press, 2002), p. 208; Giddens, A., *Consequences of Modernity* (Cambridge: Polity, 1990), p. 43.

25. Davies, private communication, July 13, 2010.

26. Ricoeur, Paul, *Hermeneutics and the Human Sciences*, trans. John B. Thompson (Cambridge: Cambridge University Press, 1981), pp. 142–4.

27.   Turner, Denys, *Marxism and Christianity* (Oxford: Blackwell, 1983), pp. 21–2. This stress on praxis in regard to religion has also been emphasized by John Cottingham; see his *The Spiritual Dimension: Religion, Philosophy and Human Value* (Cambridge: Cambridge University Press, 2005), pp. 5–8.

28.   e.g. McCutcheon, R.T., *Manufacturing Religion: The Discourse on Sui Generis Religion and the Politics of Nostalgia* (Oxford: Oxford University Press, 1997), p. 24; Fitzgerald, T., *The Ideology of Religious Studies* (Oxford: Oxford University Press, 2000).

29.   See Flood, Gavin, *Beyond Phenomenology: Rethinking the Study of Religion* (London: Cassell, 1999), pp. 131–2.

30.   Fitzgerald, Tim, *Discourse on Civility and Barbarity: A Critical History of Religion and Related Categories* (Oxford: Oxford University Press, 2007), p. 41.

2

The Meaning of Religious Action

We live in a secular age where belief in a transcendent reality, or rather the experience of a transcendent reality as a fact in our lives, has been replaced by skepticism towards transcendence as the default position for many if not most of us in the late modern West. As Charles Taylor observes, not to believe in God was almost impossible in 1500 in the West whereas in 2000 unbelief is easy or even inescapable.[1] Meaning is found in other ways, through love, family, work, sport, science, art, literature, and other forms of culture. While in previous ages whether to be religious or not was not an option for the vast majority of people – they were simply born into a tradition and community – in the late modern West we have a variety of options open to us with religions as one of them. Religions have undergone transformation in the secular age and attenuated or watered down versions of ancient traditions are represented for contemporary consumption. But although secularity is the dominant paradigm in Europe, religions have not died out as secular sociology predicted and (as they have always done) re-invent themselves in contemporary contexts.

Whether or not we are religious, questions about meaning, about the kinds of beings we are, and about the very nature of the world that religions address are common in the history of human beings and at some point touch every human life. Neanderthal burials at the mouth of Shanidar cave in Iraq, 85,000 years ago, one of which may have been filled with flowers, are viscerally recognizable actions by all of us, a symbolic act that expresses hope and love.[2] Laying aside truth claims, to understand religions, both in their power to positively influence our lives and as terrible destructive forces, we need to understand them as responses to fundamental or existential questions

The Importance of Religion: Meaning and Action in Our Strange World,
First Edition. Gavin Flood.
© 2012 Gavin Flood. Published 2012 by Blackwell Publishing Ltd.

about who we are and where we are; the strange place in which we find ourselves.

While religions have always been integral to the cut and thrust of history, to power politics, and to justifications for one group oppressing another, as Karl Marx so astutely observed, at a deeper level they function to articulate the mystery and strangeness at the heart of the world and respond to questions of meaning in existence and to human experiences at the boundaries of reason. Religions are responses to the strangeness of the world that claim to show us something about the world and our place in it, and which offer us ways to explore that world and the invisibility behind it, in our bodies, in our communities, in our cultural productions, and in our subjectivities. In other words, religions are expressions of what we might call the quest for human meaning and more specifically, transcendent meaning that locates us within a broader, cosmic perspective. As Levinas claims, prior to philosophy, religion is the pre-philosophical stuff from which philosophy arises.[3]

The importance of religion lies in this impulse towards transcendence, in the power of human imagination that gives us the ability to conceptualize and frame our lives in terms of something outside of ourselves. Rather than being explained purely through science or politics, religions are kinds of action which express a quest for understanding life and a desire to go beyond our limits. While such actions are forms of culture, they are cultural forms that seek to penetrate, order, and make sense of the world of life beyond culture; they attempt to express and explore our strange world, to express the invisible and, indeed, the unsayable. Limited by the kind of beings we are, humans nevertheless strive to understand the world and the shared experiences of birth, death, joy, despair, and transcendence, not only in propositional terms (or philosophy) but more importantly in terms of meaningful action and speech, located and experienced in the body.

If my claim is that religions express the will to meaning, the concern to understand life, then we need to raise questions about the nature of this meaning, how it differs from other kinds of meaningful activity and where religions point beyond the boundaries of human meaning. What is "religious meaning" in contrast to any other kind of meaning? What meaning is in general and what religious meaning is in particular are notoriously difficult questions and there is a wide philosophical and theological literature to draw on. There are different kinds of meaning. The most obvious is linguistic meaning, especially in social contexts or "linguistic practices within wider cultural practices."[4] But we can also speak of the meaning of action, aesthetic meaning which includes the meaning of the plastic arts and music, political meaning, and scientific meaning that includes mathematical meaning. These kinds of meaning involve a relationship between ideology and action (praxis).

But does it make sense to speak about religions in terms of meaning when religions themselves are so diverse and the very category questionable? Arguably it does because religions are meaningful in so far as they address questions of ultimate human concern and attempt to locate human beings within an ordered cosmos. It is difficult to imagine a world without religion or its analogues. This point has been a theme in both theology and sociology. In theology, Paul Tillich famously identified religions as responses to ultimate concern,[5] although this is arguably at the cost of historical specificity. In sociology, by contrast, there is a tradition of explaining religion in terms of meaning and in terms of social function. To bring our sense of meaning into sharper focus we need to consider some of this work.

The Sociology of Religious Meaning

Weber understood religion in terms of systems of meaning and Thomas Luckmann, developing the phenomenological sociology of Alfred Schutz, sees religion in terms of meaning which has shifted from "great otherworldly" transcendence to the intermediate or political, to the minimal transcendence "whose main themes ('self-realization,' personal autonomy, and self-expression) tend to bestow a sacred status upon the individual."[6] A stream of sociologists have, like Luckmann, understood religion in terms of meaning systems, including Talcott Parsons, Peter Berger, Robert Bellah, Milton Yinger, and, in France, Hervieu-Léger. Berger, for example, discusses religion as offering a "sacred canopy" within which to live a meaningful life, keeping away the difficulties of living in a meaningless state, a life constructed in terms sacred power which is maintained by the social order and which individuals appropriate in their own life. Society is legitimated in terms of an "all-embracing order of the universe"[7] and locating life within this order gives people meaning. Religion maintains this socially defined reality. With secularization people are threatened with meaninglessness once the sacred canopy is dismantled. The general tendency of sociology has been to see religion in evolutionary terms, as developing, and progressing, from a primitive state to a more refined state and, although generally not explicitly stated, to the view that religion will eventually fade away as technology and science develop and people experience a general disenchantment with the world.

An example of an evolutionary sociology of religion is NiklasLuhmann, who develops a systems theory approach. Luhmann has developed a sophisticated model of the function of religion particularly in modern societies throughout his career.[8] From a condition where ritual dominates in archaic societies, religion moves to the predominance of doctrine and in modern society has become a subsystem of the total social system. The modern subject is a result of a "semantics of transition" from feudal society to modernity. Modern society is characterized by a functional differentiation and can no longer be integrated into a total, ethical or religious worldview. Indeed, complex functional differentiation is a better designation than secularization, thus we have various subsystems operating concerned with the satisfaction of needs (i.e. economics), the making of decisions (politics), secondary socialization (education), and truth production (science).

Within this complexity, religion is one of these differentiated subsystems that has shifted from its central place where it provided an all-encompassing worldview to a situation in which there is no longer room for a "sacred canopy." But religions are still important in modern society for Luhmann, as they deal with the unity of a distinction between the observable and the unobservable which maps onto a distinction between immanence (indefinite) and transcendence (definite). Religions function to transform the indefinite into the definite through "chiffres" such as "the sacred" and "God." Religious meaning is created when events in the world are viewed from the perspective of transcendence and thereby integrated into a system of communication. Thus what is important is the system of communication rather than subjective actors or persons. Part of this communication is the resolution of the paradox that an ultimate reality is unspeakable and yet must be designated, and religions do this through paradoxical language as we find in Zen Buddhism and in mysticism. All of this serves to distinguish between immanence and transcendence.

There is much in Luhmann's approach to commend it. Religion as communication is very important, as the communicative act is integral to religions as collective bodies that relate subjectivity to a broader, more complex entity beyond the agent. But there are problematic areas which we might condense into the problem of whether religions evolve and the problem of subjective meaning.

The evolutionary model of society, according to which we move from primitive to less primitive forms has been with us for a long time. Evolutionary models influenced by Darwin emerged towards the end of the nineteenth century with the idea that ontogeny, the development of the individual, reflects phylogeny, the development of the species. In Luhmann's model, under the conditions of modernity religion shifts from the center to periphery and becomes one among other subsystems with society as the more fundamental category; religion on this view moves from an archaic condition in which ritual is inseparable and undifferentiated from other areas of social life, to a condition in which religion is the central, world ordering system, to the complex fragmentation of modernity. Luhmann remains a critical sociologist and does not comment on the value of this shift (in contrast to John Milbank's critique on the grounds that the religion–society dichotomy could always easily be inverted and the skepticism towards religion inherent in sociology questioned).[9]

This is a complex issue. On the one hand there is the argument that rationality is shared by all human beings in equal degree and has been so since the arrival of *Homo sapiens*: Cro-Magnon man was no less intelligent than a Californian computer expert. On the other hand we can see a sense in which societies progress with modernity – science offers better explanations of natural phenomena (see Chapter 8) and religions seem to shift from ecstatic and magical practices to an emphasis on doctrine. Thus in Shaivism, popular possession (*āveśa*) by ferocious goddesses became transformed in the later tradition to the metaphysical doctrine of immersion (*samāveśa*) in the light of consciousness. We might see this as a shift from a model of the self in which the self is subject to influences by external forces (what Heelas and Lock, following Lienhardt, have called a *passiones* model of the self[10]) to a model in which the self is in control. This is a shift from what Martin Hollis once called "plastic man," a passive conception of the self who is subject to external forces, and "Autonomous" man who has some substantiality and independence[11], and is reflected in Taylor's distinction between the porous and buffered self. But whether there is progress in understandings of the self and the way these are present in religions is contentious; there are clearly *passiones* type models operating in contemporary society, and social ecstasy has been present in youth cultures for many decades.

We have then to be hesitant about the idea of evolution or progress in religion. Accepting that the social matrix in the West has changed and religion in northern Europe has become another subsystem in the complex, global web, does not mean that there is evolution in the history of religion and that things are improving. Indeed, Milbank questions the reduction of religion to the social partly on the grounds that there is no "social" as such, and that while we think of the religious as problematic, the social is not:[12] the social is an abstraction as much as the religious.

But the main problem with Luhmann's thesis is the distinction between meaning and communication, where meaning is a property of "psychic systems" (i.e. persons) and communication a function of social systems. It is not that Luhmann denies the validity of psychic systems as "a unified self-referential nexus of conscious states,"[13] his thesis is too sophisticated for that, but it is rather a matter of emphasis. Meaning is a closed circle in that every meaning is given reality only by reference to some other meaning, and so meaning is fundamentally unstable.[14] Meaning is thus the actualization of potential or the horizon of possibility. He writes:

> But because meaning can be meaning only as the difference between what is actual at any moment and a horizon of possibilities every actualisation always

also leads to a virtualisation of the potentialities that could be connected up with it.[15]

This restriction of meaning to "psychic systems" is a criticism of the tradition of humanist scholarship (indeed Luhmann sees his work as post-humanist) which thereby neglects the importance of social system and the reliance of persons upon the broader structure that gives rise to them.

In many ways we can see that this is a valid criticism of the location of meaning in the private realm in modernity. However, it is arguably to miss a fundamental point about religious subjectivity that, as we will see, religions' concern with meaning is not private although it is subjective. The private realm of the individual is the invention of modernity – as Luhmann shows – but religious meaning within subjectivity is not. Indeed, religion is meaningful precisely because it is not private but is the intensification of subjectivity in tradition specific ways. Moreover, this intensification occurs only through action: the religious actions of ritual, meditation, reading, asceticism, and so on, which brings people into the world. Thus rather than being self-referential within "psychic systems," we have meaning arising by contact with the world through action. As I hope to show, religions bring us into the world through action, which is also an intensification of subjectivity (and not the individuality of modernity). Thus on the one hand we have the private individual of modernity, on the other the subjectivity of tradition and the making the world real through action.

Meaning and Action

It is primarily through action that religions respond to human need, both constructive and destructive; through human action religions impact on individual lives, on politics, and on history. We need therefore an account of religions as meaningful action which must be an account of how they are orientated towards materiality and the world of action. It must also be an account of how religions point to the invisible within the visible and how this interface is explored in the body, in the flesh. At first this might seem contradictory, as most religions point beyond the world to their ultimate point of reference. But religions function in history and impact on history only through action, and so operate through material causation.[16]

Religious meaning must be understood in terms of action that expresses imagination rather than as propositions about the world. Such action is akin to developing a skill; a ritual skill, such as rites of passage, exorcism, sacrifice, enacting sacred texts, and interior practices of prayer, meditation, and asceticism, along with a moral skill of acting correctly in particular situations. This in turn entails an account of how persons or subjectivity are located within a cosmos through such practices. Finally we can say that religion is not exhausted by human meaning and points to the transcendence of human limitation which might be said to go beyond meaning; there is always an excess, an abundance in the religious imagination that cannot be accounted for except in terms of wonder, where that which can be articulated fades into the inarticulate.

Through symbolic action religions offer access to the mystery of life and reveal the mystery of life through symbolic actions. It is not enough simply to agree or rationally explain the world, it must be understood in our bodies in a complex way that involves speech and action and yet is not restricted to or by speech and action. T.S. Eliot understood this point when he wrote:

> ... You are not here to verify,
> Instruct yourself, or inform curiosity
> Or carry report. You are here to kneel
> Where prayer has been valid ...[17]

Here Eliot understands something very important about the nature of religion; it is above all action that seeks both to bring us into the world of life, action that seeks to penetrate the strangeness of the world, and transcendence, to go beyond cultural restriction through cultural restriction. Religious action is a way in which human meaning can be understood and the meaning of a life performed. Indeed, the performance of such meaning is the expression of a basic human drive; it is the expression of Frankl's "will to meaning."[18]

There can be, of course, no religious action which is not simultaneously a cultural action; there is no religion outside of culture, as Geertz so masterfully wrote,[19] so what is the force of the adjective "religious" that distinguishes some kinds of cultural action from others? A common sense response to this might be along the lines of protypicality, that there are some actions that clearly fall within the category "religion" – such as going to church, burying the dead according to a particular set of rites – while others fall outside of that category – cooking a meal or riding a bike. There are many actions that fall between these – when we prepare a meal with a devotional attitude or lay a wreath at the cenotaph in London. But what is it about religious actions that distinguish them from non-religious actions? This is complex question and there are number of ways of categorizing ritual. Richard Scheckner usefully divides ritualization into different categories with human ritualization subdivided into social ritual, aesthetic ritual, and religious ritual (which includes observances, celebrations, and rites of passage).[20] We could argue that what marks religious ritual off from other kinds of human ritual behavior is text or specifically the text set aside as sacred, as we will see in Chapter 4.

My general argument is that religious meaning is given primarily through the act, which is the causal impact of subjectivity on the world, or the impact of the "I-body" on the visible. There are two forms of religious action, one is ritual, which is habitual although intentional, and the other is ethical, which is unrepeated and unrepeatable and impacts upon history. Both are intimately related in that ritual, especially in the sense of the performance of a sacred text, can become action and the repetition of ritual has effect on ethical action. We need therefore to pursue two lines of inquiry at this stage, one into ritual and the other into moral action as determining features of religious meaning.

Moral Acts

Human action is meaningful in so far as it is intentional although the actor's intention does not exhaust its meaning and the meaning of an action will always be beyond the control or predictability of the agent. As Paul Ricoeur has argued on analogy with language, human action is meaningful in so far as it displays *sense*, coherence internal to itself in relation to other actions, and *reference*, the projection of a possible world, and in this way is akin to language.[21] We act as agents in order to secure a particular kind of world which involves decisions about what to do and when, although such decisions might not be fully rational and involve judgments driven more by instinct. The meaning of a life – the meaning of my life – entails judgment followed by action. If we take action to be what is done intentionally by an agent through the body, as opposed to simply what happens, then such doing entails judgment or mental decision alongside its bodily enactment. In Kantian terms, judgment is what happens when the rules that determine understanding (such as the categories of space, time, and the moral imperative) are applied to intuitions (what is given to us in perceptual experience), particularly judgments about causal relationships between objects or substances[22] which occur within the imagination but which have real consequences when translated into action.

An act, in Bakhtin's phrase, is unrepeatable and answerable. We are responsible for each act which is the enactment of a decision and this actualization of a decision is not theoretical or in an abstract realm but is actual, historical, and real.[23] Through action which is answerable or responsible we enter history and it is such action that religions call us to make. While ritual is habitual and routine, although still intentionally enacted, ethical action is the result of judgment and so is answerable and responsible, the consequences of which we do not and cannot fully know.

Such ethical action may be informed by ritual habit, but ethical action in itself is unique and particular to historical situation. Religions call us to action in this sense and offer guidance as to our judgments. There are many examples of the ways in which religions call us to account, but let us illustrate this point with two. Firstly, an indirect example already mentioned of Viktor Frankl who survived Auschwitz. At one point during a typhus epidemic in the camp, he and a fellow inmate had an opportunity to escape. As the doctor this would mean leaving his patients and he felt uncomfortable about this decision and in the end decided not to go. Upon making his decision to stay with his patients, the unhappy feeling left, and he writes "I had gained an inward peace that I had never experienced before."[24] This is an example of action that impacts on history following a judgment that was deeply informed by an ethical concern about his patients, a concern which, in Frankl's view, is inherent to the human condition but which is in complete alignment with the injunctions of Judaism. While it is clear that he did not act in this way because his religion said that he should, nevertheless he acted in accordance with what his intuition told him to be right and so indirectly performed the injunctions of the Judaic tradition that makes demands upon us to relinquish personal satisfaction for the sake of the other.

But it is not always clear what the right thing to do is and we cannot always judge the consequences of our actions. Religions serve to guide judgment and the actions that follow judgments are beyond our control. When Abelard and Heloise became lovers and then secretly married they could not know that this would result in their separation and leading monastic lives with Abelard's castration by Heloise's uncle Fulbert and his kinsmen, who punished him "where he sinned,"[25] after which Abelard sought the peace and silence of the cloister of Saint Denys' monastery. Their act of love had severe consequences and further, positive consequences in the impact (admittedly small) they had on the history of Christianity and on others in their letters which in due course became public.

Another example, this time textual rather than historical, comes from the Hindu scripture, the *Bhagavad Gita*. Here the hero of the story Arjuna is reluctant to fight in a great battle over succession to the throne because he will be killing his kinsmen. The charioteer Krishna, who turns out to be an incarnation of God, persuades him otherwise partly on the grounds that he should fight because it is his own personal responsibility, his own duty (*svadharma*) to do so.[26] He must act, thereby impacting upon history, as the result of the demands of tradition, which understands Arjuna's life in a much broader context. In these cases the act is answerable and informed by the demands of tradition. The religious imagination, the imagined canopy within which religious persons operate, functions to inform human action.

This religious sense of the moral act, as that which impacts on history through the body, can be theorized in terms of a philosophy of action. In an important work, *Towards a Philosophy of the Act*, Bakhtin develops an account of action that has ramifications for understanding religious action and meaning. In this book he presents a distinction between the world of culture (which contains various theoretical frameworks such as philosophy, sociology, and politics) and the world of life, the world in which we live our lives and die. Within this world we accomplish actions that are once and for all and never repeated, which Bakhtin calls the unrepeatable act of being. This is his first and important point. Being is an unrepeatable act and a human life, my life, might even be seen as a single, complicated act of being. What is characteristic of such an act is that it is answerable. That is, we have moral responsibility for our actions which must be understood as answerable rather than in abstract terms or in terms of formal ethics. The answerable act is itself "the actualisation of a decision – inescapably, irremediably, and irrevocably."[27] An act is accomplished once and for all (and only once) as being is unrepeatable action (Being-as-event).

This idea is echoed independently by Merleau-Ponty, who speaks of any appeal to universal history as cutting off the meaning of the specific event, it "renders effective history insignificant, and is a nihilism in disguise."[28] Aesthetic theory is incapable of grasping such a once and for all occurrence because it constructs or forms action in an objectified way. Such theory, along with other kinds of theoretical thinking, can give an account of the sense or content of an act in an abstract realm, but this is removed from "the historical actuality of its being, the actual and once occurrent experiencing of it."[29] The act expresses a judgment in the historically unique moment; the judgment which expresses the ought "gains its validity within the unity of my once-occurrent answerable life."[30] The act is the unrepeatable event which penetrates the world of life and is therefore distinct from the world of culture (which might represent the act, its sense, and content in terms of sociology or psychology or other human abstractions). On the one hand we have the world of culture which frames the ways human beings function and act and which forms the fabric of our day to day living. On the other hand we have the world itself in its temporal and spatial modalities which lies outside of culture but which can only ever be articulated through culture. The world is the necessary horizon within which all cultural forms operate and which constrains those cultural forms.

Bakhtin's articulation of action as once and for all being as event is pertinent to our understanding of religious action, but action as once and for all event is not enough for us to develop an account of religious action; we need to develop the idea of repeated action or "routine." For Merleau-Ponty, repeated acts or routine form a praxis or the embodiment of meaning; a regular and regulated structure of behavior that is rule-governed. In his discussion of praxis, Denys Turner develops the point with an example of the kiss in relation to how actions "speak"; "you cannot kiss without understanding what it is to do so," which means that it is a meaningful action that is rule-governed. "A person who knows how and when to kiss is a person who understands the differences between a formal kiss of greeting and the kiss of sexual passion; and anyone who understands that difference understands the different connection there is between one kind of physical gesture and what it says and another kind of physical gesture and what that says ... Now such connections are rule-governed in the sense that they can be grasped and understood publicly as being given to those who engage in the behaviour."[31]

What we can take from Bakhtin is that religious action is a penetration of being-as-event not restricted to the world of culture but is the only practice and discourse that attempts to penetrate, order, and make sense of world of life. This world of life is a synonym for the strangeness of the world and the continuity of time. Religions are arguably quests and orientations towards the world of life that are not restricted to the world of culture because of their penetration of the world of life and their claims to transcendence. From Merleau-Ponty we can take the idea of routine; that while religious actions are once and for all marks on the world of life, they can be routinized behaviors or praxes that express a meaning. This is not to say that they become mere routines blindly followed (although they can become that), but 'rather that the routines of religious practice, particularly ritual, are taken into action at each repeated performance. As Turner says, "it is only an understanding of the 'meaning' which a praxis incarnates which makes any repetition possible."[32] If meaning is enactment, an action that impacts upon history as direct, immediate, pure act, then the site of this enactment is the body. It is through the body that I perform the unrepeatable act and through the body that I perform routine actions. Both kinds of religious action, the moral act and the routine, ritual act, are grounded in the body and the human experience of the interaction of body with world and other bodies.

Ritual and the Body

The emphasis on the body has been de rigueur in the social sciences for many years now,[33] an interest that partly stems from Marcel Mauss' famous essay "Techniques of the Body" ("Les techniques du corps") where he draws our attention to how the body is trained. We learn our behavior and the body becomes an instrument, a technique which is an "action that is effective and traditional." Before instruments "there is an ensemble of techniques of the body,"[34] an ensemble of techniques that is trained and social. Mauss writes: "The constant adaptation to a physical, mechanical or chemical aim (e.g. when we drink) is pursued in a series of assembled actions, and assembled for the individual not by himself alone but by all his education, by the whole society to which he belongs, in the place he occupies in it."[35] This bodily attitude and technique Mauss referred to as the *habitus*, the social or cultural habits which vary between societies and which are the "techniques of collective and individual practical reason." Mauss gives examples; thus the English child holds in his elbows at table after a meal whereas a French child would not; English troops were unable to dig with French spades; and Europeans cannot squat whereas Australians can. There is also gender differentiation regarding this and Mauss cites, perhaps a dubious, example of women making a fist with the thumb on the outside and men with the thumb inside. These techniques are learned by both children and adults generally from those in authority and are often a fusion of biological necessity, such as the need to eat, with transmitted social form. The body is shaped by the social situation and tradition, and is thus a technique for achieving particular ends. We see this with walking, jumping, climbing, weaning infants, and in techniques of care for the body such as washing. The body is a mechanism for an instrumental or practical rationality to achieve particular, socially sanctioned goals.

Although underemphasized by Mauss, these techniques of the body are intimately linked to power in a society and gender and age difference. The bodily *habitus* inevitably reflects a power differentiation that other social scientists in the footsteps of Mauss have developed, particularly Pierre Bourdieu's extension of Mauss' idea of the *habitus* as "systems of durable, transposable, dispositions" that results from particular social conditions. Such a *habitus* is not the organization of an agent or "conductor" but is rather "collectively orchestrated" without a conscious aim or mastery.[36] We are all subject to the *habitus* which is, in a sense, the precondition of action in the world; the techniques of the body enable people to achieve their goals and this is true of all cultural practices from tying a shoelace to going to mass. Mauss ends his essay with a reference to Granet's study of the techniques of the body in Taoism, particularly breathing methods, to achieve mystical experience of some kind, which are also known from India; "at the bottom of all our mystical states there are techniques of the body" which, Mauss suggests, "are biological means for entering into 'communion with God'."[37] These observations are important and relevant to us in so far as the practices of religion are in and through the body, including mysticism and methods of prayer, meditation and asceticism.

Talal Asad even goes so far as to say that Mauss' brief remarks "carr[y] what are perhaps the most far reaching claims for an anthropological understanding of ritual," in so far as embodied practices "form a precondition for varieties of religious experience. The inability to enter into communion with God becomes a function of untaught bodies."[38] Religions are enacted and the primary focus of their concern is the teaching of the body, the control of the body and developing techniques of the body, and Asad is surely right in emphasizing Mauss' contribution here. We see the focus on techniques of the body in Moslem prayer where a particular bodily habit is cultivated from childhood, in Christian liturgy where Orthodox children are reared to take communion from infancy, or in Hinduism where there is great emphasis on body posture and breath in yoga.[39]

The techniques of the body, the somatic *habitus*, are central to understanding religious action and therefore religious meaning. The meanings of ritual are performed and enacted in the body and in the interaction of bodies. Even when alone, the body performs the religious *habitus* as part of something much broader, as part of a tradition and wider cosmos in which the practitioner's body participates along with all other bodies.[40] The body is inextricably associated with ritual and religious ritual is no exception. In some ways, this is an obvious point, but it is Mauss' influence that has led sociologists and anthropologists to thematize the *habitus* and stress the importance and centrality of the body in social practice. The implications of this for religion are great, as it means we need to understand religions not so much in terms of belief and cognition but primarily in terms of socially sanctioned action or praxis and in terms of training the body.[41] Religions are ways of life, ways of behaving, of performing ritual, and of acting in the world. We have an interactive, community focused, bodily experience as the basis of religious formation which not only serves as a process of socialization but which functions to address fundamental human concerns. Clearly ritual as the formal organization of action has a social function; it serves to negotiate transitions in life in rites of passage, it functions to cure the sick, and it functions to legitimate political and social power. It also functions, prototypically, in a transformative capacity to reveal the ways in which the invisible is enfolded within the visible; to relate individuals and communities to transcendent power and to imaginatively perform religious goals. Religious experience is predicated upon the body trained in a particular way.

Roy Rappaport defines ritual as "the performance of more or less invariant sequences of formal acts and utterances nor entirely encoded by the performers."[42] This definition entails the body as the locus of experience which unites human beings in the sense that the body and its movements are a presupposition of my being in the world. The body is the precondition for understanding and through the body the invisible is encountered in the world of culture, in the visible. As Mauss convincingly shows, the body can be understood as a technique but it is also more than this as the precondition of experience. Merleau-Ponty observes: "The superficial pellicle of the visible is only for my vision and for my body. But the depth beneath this surface contains my body and hence contains my vision."[43] The body experiences the encounter with transcendence and through the body, the subtle interface of the visible with the invisible is explored.

A Rite of Affliction

To illustrate these points we need to turn to specific examples. Let us examine a possession cure, sacrifice, and the meanings of death. Our first example is a ritual taken from the work of Victor and Edith Turner who worked among the Ndembu of Zambia. Victor Turner recorded their fieldwork in *The Drums of Affliction* (1968) and other texts such as *The Forest of Symbols* (1967). In what Turner calls "rituals of affliction" the Ndembu associated misfortune in hunting, women's reproductive disorders, and other illnesses with the activity of the dead. The spirits (*mukishi*, plural *akishi*) of deceased relatives sometimes possess their descendants because they have been "forgotten" and offerings of beer and food have not been made to them. There are three kinds of spirit that can afflict people, the spirit of a hunter who causes his kinsman to fail in hunting, the spirit of a woman who may cause reproductive difficulties such as a miscarriage, and both male and female spirits who can cause an illness of "wasting away," "sweating and shivering," or "pains all over the body." These three kinds of possession illness are cured by three distinct types of ritual which Turner calls hunting cults, fertility cults, and curative cults.[44]

One of the curative rites is the *ihamba* tooth ritual. The *ihamba* is an incisor of a hunter, particularly a man who hunts with a gun. Upon the death of such a hunter, his two incisors are removed and inherited by his relatives, who are initiates of the gun-hunters' cult. These teeth are kept in a white pouch with cowrie shells for "eyes" which see game. From time to time such a tooth is believed to escape from the pouch and enter a person, thereby requiring a rite of exorcism. The sick person is believed to have been bitten by the tooth of the dead hunter if the hunter (symbolized by the tooth) is neglected. The tooth is believed to enter the body and can be seen beneath the skin to travel along the veins "biting" as it goes, and causing a special kind of illness. The affliction occurs because of some moral fault or transgression of custom. The tooth is removed by cupping two horns and extracting it through a lengthy ritual procedure.[45]

Some years after Victor Turner's death, Edith Turner returned to Zambia with the anthropologist Bill Blodgett, and witnessed two further tooth rituals, one in which she participated, and wrote up her observations in *Experiencing Ritual* (1992) offering a detailed, thick description of the two rites she witnessed. An elderly woman, Meru, was sick with the tooth/spirit of a deceased elder in the community, Kashinakaji, for reasons of family resentment and anger going back into the past in which Meru's aunt had been the victim of anger by a male relative, "the revenge of neglected males on women that head lineages."[46] Meru's family was in disarray and she had experienced the death of her grown up daughter and her grandchildren and been taken away by their father. During the ritual she declared that her "dead" children (dead to her because she had no contact with them) were in her liver and that she wanted to die because there was nobody to look after her. An incision was made by the doctor in Meru's back so that it bled and two horns cupped over the wound. The doctor, Singleton, would attempt to withdraw the tooth from her body through the wound. Through an elaborate process of drumming, singing and talking, the possessing spirit was identified and named, the witchcraft was seen to be "dancing in her," and eventually, after changing the ritual positions of the participants, she fell into a trance. Edith Turner herself was part of the process of clapping and encouraging the tooth spirit to come out and; in her own words:

> Quite an interval of struggle elapses while I clapped like one possessed, crouching beside Bill amid a lot of urgent talk, while Singleton pressed Meru's back, guiding and leading out the tooth – Meru's face in a grin of trance passion, her back quivering rapidly. Suddenly Meru raised her arm, stretched it in liberation, and I *saw* with my own eyes a giant thing emerging out of the flesh of her back. This thing was a large gray blob about six inches across, a deep gray opaque thing emerging as a sphere. I was amazed – delighted . . . Singleton had it in his pouch, pressing it in with his other hand as well. The receiving can was ready; he transferred whatever it was into the can and capped the castor oil leaf and bark lid over it. It was done.[47]

A little after the successful completion of the rite Singleton produced a tooth from the pouch: "It was the *ihamba*."[48]

This is a remarkable account given by Turner that affected her very profoundly. The anthropologist here becomes part of the ritual process. In Mauss' terms, techniques of the body developed through the chanting, drumming, swaying, and interacting of the doctor and other participants developed to a successful conclusion of the rite and Meru was "cured." The whole experience was focused on the body, but not simply the body of the possessed woman; the whole community became involved and the ritual became a kind of collective expression for family antagonism and problematic events in the past. In terms of the Turner's terminology, this was a *communitas* event, a ritual in which social barriers were broken down accompanied by a heightened sense of communion. It is only through and in the body that a knowledge could be gained about the *ihamba* rite; the whole body as an organ of perception

Now from the perspective of a hermeneutics of suspicion we would assume that such supernatural events do not occur and that there would need to be some other explanation. Clearly the *ihamba* ritual has a social function. Victor Turner observes that the rite has only been introduced into Ndembu society in more recent years, post-Second World War, and spread where hunting has declined and the population increased. By frequently performing the *ihamba*, Turner observes, "the Ndembu maintain in fantasy the values, symbols and trappings of a highly ritualized activity that is rapidly losing its economic importance."[49] But on this occasion Edith Turner, the anthropologist, witnessed an event that she could not account for in explanatory terms outside of those of the ritual practitioners. It could have been a hallucination, but what is interesting is that the event was witnessed by others and the tooth was "seen." There was intersubjective agreement that the *ihamba* ritual had been a success and the tooth successfully extracted.

This is a rich, multileveled example of ritual that resists explanation purely in socio-economic terms, although these are clearly important and partially explanatory. Leaving to one side for the moment the question of truth and the conflicting claims to truth that such an event evokes, we can draw from this an illustration of the way in which ritual "means." In the *ihamba* we have an intensification of meaning, a semantic density produced through the techniques of the body. The rite is saturated with meaning in the sense that the symbolic action of withdrawing the tooth is also an action of curing family tension, of expressing the anxiety of the elderly patient, and of ensuring good relationships in the future. The *ihamba* is a popular and regularly performed ritual, almost a routine, with clear intention and purpose and flexibly adapted to the particular situation of the afflicted person. The rite has a social function and an explanation in terms of the decline in hunting in the region and the affirmation of Ndembu identity in the face of modernity, but this does not exhaust explanation of the event. The account of the rite from within Ndembu cosmology might be unacceptable as objective truth by the social scientist but in this example the anthropologist underwent an experience outside of a social scientific frame of reference, and there are other examples in the anthropological literature.[50]

From this account we can make a number of observations. Firstly that social science does not exhaust the explanation of the *ihamba* rite and secondly that the body is central and is the primary locus of experience. Through the body, the world of the Ndembu cosmology is opened and the body becomes an instrument, a technique, or in Merleau-Ponty's terms, an organ of perception for experiencing that world.[51] The experience of embodiment is set in a complex relationship to the structures of tradition in so far as Ndembu cosmology is inscribed onto the body through the tooth spirit. In the *ihamba* ritual, the body, the flesh, becomes both the method or technique for experiencing a world and the experienced world itself. Through the event the invisible is rendered visible and the rite takes the participants into a kind of bodily, visceral knowledge which breaks open another world for the participants and shows that the invisible is enfolded, as it were, within the visible. Through ritual a rational community is permitted to experience an event at the limits of reason in a controlled way.

There are, then, two descriptions of the *ihamba* event, one an internal description where explanation is purely in terms of indigenous categories which are reinforced by somatic experience, and the other an external description which accounts for the rite in terms of a catharsis for a community and in terms of socio-economic conditions which provide the background for the ritual. As Edith Turner observes, the two ways of accounting for the rite seem to be mutually exclusive and in shifting into the analytic mode from the experiential she would have "had to be a different person from the one that saw the spirit form."[52]

This is an interesting and important observation, with implications for how we explain religious phenomena. We will return to this presently, but perhaps it should be said here that these two ways of accounting for the Ndembu rite articulate a deep problem in the explanations of religion. We see in Edith Turner a tension between the external social scientific account and the internal, experiential account, both of which can be seen to have their validity. The Ndembu practitioners will adhere to the indigenous explanation of the *ihamba* which is rational within their frame of reference. The social scientist will seek an explanation in external, social, and historical factors. These are not necessarily exclusive accounts although the explanation of such events is problematic as we will see. For our second example let us turn to sacrifice.

The Meaning of Sacrifice

In the 1972 film *Apocalypse Now* we are presented with a shocking image towards the end of the film of a buffalo being sacrificed; hatchets violently cutting along its back and neck, an image juxtaposed with the killing, and by implication sacrifice, of Kurtz. With the dominance of Christianity followed by the rise of secularism, the West has been shielded from this kind of event and literal sacrificial blood for some time although the metaphor of sacrifice continues in our culture – we speak of mothers sacrificing their careers for children and, perhaps more literally, soldiers sacrificing their lives for their country. The act of sacrifice and the language of sacrifice are at the heart of religion. Christianity is focused on the sacrifice of Christ to end all sacrifice, sacrifice was central to Judaism until the destruction of the temple in AD 72, Islam sacrifices goats during the Hajj, and Hindus practice sacrifice in Nepal, for example, for auspicious beginnings to enterprises and sacrifice is at the very root of that religion.[53]

On our account of religions as cultural forms that mediate the encounter with mystery, sacrifice has been one of the most important sites of this encounter. Through sacrifice we have faced a transcendent reality, through sacrifice we have appeased angry gods, and through sacrifice we have bonded with each other in the primordial act of sharing a meal of the offered meat. While in the West we easily cast a cynical eye upon and make moral judgments about sacrificial cultures, we could say that the West still practices in a sublimated way the bloody sacrifice of animals in their mass industrial slaughter each day for meat. This raises the question about what sacrifice is and why people perform ritualized killing which then becomes a fundamental metaphor at the heart of stories we tell about ourselves. Sacrifice is appropriated to meaningful narratives in plausible and not so plausible ways.

There is no straightforward answer to the question "what is sacrifice?" and why people perform it. Why have people continued to make offerings to the gods again and again when they receive nothing in return, as a long history of Greek writers observed?[54] But in spite of this, gift-giving to a god has been fundamental to religion, as Burkert points out, and the encounter with the invisible has been a communication through gift exchange in which the god accepts the offering by the person or community and in exchange gives a gift of grace.[55] Religion has always been eminently practical. I need help in my life and so I make an offering to a god for supernatural aid or simply to appease the deity, to keep the deity away from my family and cattle, as a hymn in the *Rig Veda* asks of Rudra.[56] The gods are powerful and dangerous and we need to keep them happy if they are to be on our side. On this view, sacrifice is fundamental to the well-being of society and sometimes in ancient Greece and the Middle East the gods even depend upon it.[57] We are a long way here from metaphysical speculation and high theology which understands God as self sufficient and without need.

Sacrifice is arguably the earliest kind of worship; a model which simply comprises making an offering, a gift, and receiving a blessing in return. This fundamental pattern of offering and blessing is found throughout the history of religions. The central act of Hindu worship, *pūjā*, is simply making an offering – usually vegetal offerings – and receiving a blessing, although this basic structure can be elaborated into a complex process and series of actions. Although the relationship between *pūjā* and earlier Vedic animal sacrifice is not precisely clear, the model would seem to be the same, substituting vegetal offerings for an animal. Even in Christian liturgy, which disparages animal sacrifice, the model of offering and blessing remains, instead of meat and blood, "glory" is offered and, finally, the bread and wine of the Eucharist in place of the sacrificial lamb. Theologies of religions develop different understandings of this practice, of course, and sacrifice comes to be reinterpreted or overlaid with secondary elaborations. The Upanishads internalize the sacrifice of Vedic religion such that the true sacrifice is the sacrifice of the breath to a higher knowledge or wisdom of the self; Christianity substitutes bloody sacrifice for the sacrifice of Christ re-enacted in the liturgy; Confucians offer sacrifice to earthly and celestial gods and understand this in moral terms as upholding virtue and order in the cosmos.[58]

There is some debate about the origins of sacrifice, whether those origins lie in Paleolithic hunting cults or Neolithic farming communities. But by the time of the earliest records of religious practice, sacrifice is a key element, found in Hesiod's *Theogeny* dated before the seventh century BCE, in Mesopotamian documents of the third millennium BCE, and in the ancient Indian Veda of around 1200 BCE. Sacrifice is still current and important in religions although the term covers a range of meanings and practices from beheading a chicken to offer to a local Goddess in Kerala, to the once in a lifetime slaughter of a goat at the Hajj, to offering a goat or cucumber to the supreme spirit among the Nuer, and to the mass slaughter of prisoners among the Aztecs. It would seem then that we are dealing with a range of practices or a "family of sacrifice"[59] that are not all identical but which share the common action of making an offering and receiving a blessing, even a negative blessing of appeasement, simply keeping the deity away. Through this simple act we should not underestimate the power of sacrifice and its cultural importance. Indeed, as we shall see, some have argued that sacrifice is the key to understanding human societies and even to understanding the origins of culture itself. But before we move on to those abstract accounts, let us clarify further what we mean by sacrifice and what it entails by looking at a couple of examples drawn from ethnography.

A Phenomenology of Sacrifice

Both Bataille and Girard present functionalist arguments, seeing sacrifice in terms of an economy of consumption and power.[60] But we could argue that sacrifice needs to be understood less in causal terms, explaining one cultural phenomenon by a lower level one, and more in terms of transformations undergone by human persons. Sacrifice orders life and ways of seeing the world in many sacrificial cultures; it functions to order the human world in relation to a divine realm and fosters a social stability that becomes repeated, admittedly by a minority, through the generations. We can develop a phenomenology of sacrifice which maps out sacrificial belief and practice for the social scientific observer as many anthropologists have done. In all of these examples we see less a cathartic release of tension and more a ritual engagement that structures the world and relates the community to its transcendent source, mediated through the body.

A contemporary example of sacrifice is the *teyyam* dance possession rituals of Kerala studied by Rich Freeman.[61] A ferocious Goddess who displays some degree of violence towards her devotees during the *teyyam* dance, is appeased through offering her blood (from a sacrificed chicken) and alcohol. It is not inappropriate to understand the *teyyam* sacrifice in terms of gift – the gift of the sight of divinity (*darshanam*) in return for the gift of blood and strong drink. There would also seem to be an element of catharsis in this rite, the expression of violent force, but arguably more importantly, we have an enactment of a way of ordering the world and an enactment of a kind of transcendence which draws on a rich heritage of "higher level" philosophy and theological speculation. In accepting blood and alcohol, the *teyyams* are gods accepting the human refusal of things which have a cultural, practical, and economic value outside of the ritual context. The world is endowed with meaning for the participants and the rite negotiates the relationship between the visible and the invisible; the gods come down to earth, become visible, and the community sees divinity in the world; the gods have taken on form to receive their gifts and in return give blessing by walking or dancing among the people.

Of course we should not assume the phenomenon of sacrifice is everywhere the same, but taking the *teyyams* as an example, we might claim that it resists explanation purely in functionalist terms in an economy of exchange or purely in terms of social-psychological catharsis of violence that has built up in a society. Rather, we must understand sacrifice not so much in causal terms, as functionalist explanations tend to do, but in terms of indigenous meanings which point to powers or power beyond the community that informs the community in semantically rich ways and which become visible during ritual. Making a more general claim, rather than catharsis we might see sacrifice as being about the formation of meaning, about making sense of the strange world in which we find ourselves, about structuring life in relation to transcendence, and about the refusal of nothingness. In short, sacrifice provides people with a cosmos and must be understood in cosmological terms.

Charles Taylor is insightful in speaking about destruction as divine (as with Kali and Shiva) and the importance of purification through the renouncing of what gets destroyed. "Wild destruction is given a meaning and a purpose. In a sense it is domesticated, becomes less fearful in a way, even as it acquires part of the terror of the numinous."[62] The terror of the numinous revealed in sacrifice, which we can certainly see in the *teyyam* example, cannot be reduced to an economy of gift exchange or the catharsis of violent, excess energy in a society. Rather it must be understood in terms of human meaning and intentionality towards transcendence and the invisible; sacrifice places human beings in a cosmos and structures the world in meaningful ways; ways in which refusal or renunciation at one level is thought to lead to a higher human flourishing at another.

The phenomenology of sacrifice shows us that it has not merely a cathartic function but it is an attempt to locate human reality in a meaningful cosmos, to affirm life over death, and an attempt to transcend the present moment by focusing on ritual details that point to the future. Sacrifice is fundamentally about transcendence and the human drive towards living in a meaningful cosmos; it is about the deepest human motivations and defying of nothing-ness. As such we might claim that sacrifice is the enactment of a metaphor about the transformation of the world and of human subjects, and so is fundamentally the expression of human hope and a resistance to death and darkness.

The Meanings of Death

Closely related to sacrifice is human death. The traditional Hindu belief is that if one dies in the holy city of Benares one goes to liberation with no need to return to the world to work out one's karma. Liberation is the highest purpose of life in Hinduism, the fourth human purpose after duty, pleasure, and worldly success. If a devout Hindu dies in Benares or Kashi, then he has fulfilled his final goal and supreme meaning. While the idea of liberation at death in Kashi is common, precisely what liberation is differs according to different people. Thus one of Parry's informants, a funeral priest, maintained that after death you become a star which eventually disintegrates into the five elements, while another claimed that there were four different degrees of liberation, living in the same world as God, acquiring the same form as God, close proximity to God, and union with God "as water mixes with water."[63] Liberation is guaranteed for all, no matter what caste one belongs to and even to a dog, insect, or foreigner.

When a person dies in Kashi they are cremated the same day, traditionally on open funeral pyres although today mechanized crematoria are becoming popular. There is procession through the street to the site of cremation, accompanied by a band and an element of good cheer if the death is a good one of an old person, although funeral processions are solemn if death has been premature. The corpse is cremated at the funeral ghat and the chief mourner, usually the son of an old person, is supposed to crack the skull of the corpse half way through the procedure to release the soul, although this cannot happen in mechanized crematoria. After the wood has burned down, the chief mourner with his back to the pyre tosses a pot filled with holy Ganges water over his head onto the remnants and walks away, not turning back, the relationship with the deceased having thus been dissolved.[64] In Benares, the remnants of the pyre, including what is left of the bones, are swept and washed into the Ganges. Cremation is regarded as "the last sacrifice" (*antyeṣṭi*) and so, argues Parry convincingly, the cosmic event of creation and destruction is continually replayed because the universe was born through sacrifice. There is a homology created through ritual between the body and the universe.

This is another example of the way in which religion creates meaning through ritual. Examples could be recapped from other cultures throughout the world but the Hindu example is a particularly good one of the way in which death becomes integrated into human meaning. Death, an apparently or potentially meaningless event, is brought into the realm of human meaning through ritual. It is not the case that religion arose in response to death – early religions had a very thin notion of the afterlife, as John Bowker shows us[65] – but religion appropriates death and if, as I have argued, religion brings people into the present, into history through action, then death becomes integrated into history, into the stories humans tell about themselves, and into the universe of which they are a part. Death is given meaning through religion; certainly for those left behind and possibly for the deceased as well (I think this is certainly the case during the dying process).

In these examples we see how the body is both a technique and the locus of experience. While each rite is culturally and historically specific, they illustrate the body as "flesh," as the existential ground of culture-specific experiences. They differ in terms of what is to be achieved and also differ in terms of underlying metaphysics and cosmology. The Ndembu worldview is centered on the symbol of hunting and negotiates complex social relationships through witchcraft accusations; for Hindu examples there is a hierarchical cosmology of different levels. In presenting these examples we see how meaning is realized in and through the body; the body becomes the vehicle for exploring and experiencing the interface between the invisible and the visible. What is invisible is rendered experientially visible through the techniques of the body. The centrality of the body as both locus of experience and symbol system is a claim about meaning in ritual. When we are dealing with the body we are dealing with meaning as the concern for understanding how and where the human subject is located in the universe.[66]

Conclusion

The body is the flesh that "captures the lines and force of the world." In Merleau-Ponty's terms, the body has two sides, one phenomenal and the other objective.[67] In the examples of ritual discussed here we see the phenomenal body, the I-body, which is part of the continuous fabric of the visible, encountering the non-visible realities of different ritual traditions. Ritual intensifies somatic experience and is one way in which the religious imagination impacts upon the world. The habitual and repeated acts of ritual are intentional and performed and make claims upon the rest of life and the broader narrative of one's existence. We shall see this in more detail with regard to the pragmatics of scriptural reception, but even in the examples we have described here, ritual allows the practitioner or community to become located within a cosmos. This in turn affects action outside the ritual sphere and affects the meaning of life – the meaning of my life – in that action as the result of judgment is informed by attitudes and experiences undergone in the ritual body. Human action entails narrative, and narrative in Ricoeur's terms entails "signs, rules, and norms."[68] We see this with the *ihamba* rite which healed social relationships, we see this in the Hindu funeral which marks an end of a particular set of social relationships and sets those within a cosmic setting, and we see this in the sacrifice of fowl to the ferocious goddesses.

We are left with a sense that even if we accept the general argument here that the body entails meaning and the body in ritual is both technique and locus of experience, then this is simply the beginning of inquiry. We still have not adequately dealt with what ritual is and what religious ritual is in distinction from any other kind of ritual. All animals behave ritually and how religious ritual differs from any other kind is an important question. Nor have we dealt with the question of ritual truth. From the perspective of social science there must be skepticism towards the reality of Edith Turner's experience of the *ihamba* tooth, but does asking the question of "objective truth" outside of the religious imagination somehow miss the point of the ways in which religions mean? We shall turn to this vexed question when we examine rationality, but for now we need to continue our inquiry into meaning and religious practice in the idea of life as a spiritual journey.

Notes

1. Taylor, Charles, *A Secular Age* (Cambridge, Mass., and London: Harvard University Press, 2007), p. 25.
2. Solecki, Ralph S., *Shanidar: The Humanity of Neanderthal Man* (London: Allen Lane, 1972), pp. 175–8. In Shanidar IV at least seven species of flowers were identified by the pollen. It is also worth mentioning Shanidar I, who was crippled with a useless right arm amputated below the elbow and who lived to an old age by Neanderthal standards. He may also have been blind in the left eye. He must have been cared for by the community to live for so long. See Bowker, J., *The Sense of God* (Oxford: Clarendon Press, 1973), pp. 57–8. Richard Southwood gives an eloquent account in the context of a broader history of evolution; see T.R.E. Southwood, *The Story of Life* (Oxford: Oxford University Press, 2003), pp. 226–7.
3. Levinas, cited in Batnitsky, Leora, *Leo Strauss and Emmanuel Levinas: Philosophy and the Politics of Revelation* (Cambridge: Cambridge University Press, 2006), p. 5.
4. Foley, William A., *Anthropological Linguistics: An Introduction* (Oxford: Blackwell, 1997), p. 5.
5. Tillich, Paul, *Dynamics of Faith* (New York: Harper & Row, 1957), pp. 1–4.
6. Luckmann, Thomas, "Shrinking Transcendence, expanding Religion?" *Sociological Analysis*, 1990, vol. 51 (2), pp. 127–38. This lecture provides a good general summary of his thinking.

7. Berger, Peter, *The Sacred Canopy* (New York: Anchor, 1990 (1967)), p. 45.
8. Luhmann, Niklas, *Funktion der Religion* (Frankfurt-am-Main: Suhrkamp, 1982); *Religious Dogmatics and the Evolution of Societies*, trans. Peter Beyer (New York and Toronto: Edwin Mellen, 1984). For a bibliography see the interesting and useful article by Rudi Laerman and GertVershraegen, "The Late Niklas Luhmann on Religion: An Overview," *Social Compass*, vol. 48 (1), 2001, pp. 7–20. I have been greatly helped by this article in my reading of Luhmann.
9. Milbank, John, *Theology and Social Theory: Beyond Secular Reason* (Oxford: Blackwell, 1990), pp. 139–40.
10. Heelas, Paul, "The Model Applied," pp. 39–63, in Paul Heelas and Andrew Lock, *Indigenous Psychologies: the Anthropology of the Self* (London: Academic Press, 1981), pp. 39–63. R. Godfrey Lienhardt, *Divinity and Experience: The Religion of the Dinka* (Oxford: Clarendon Press, 1987 (1961)). Leinhardt writes: "The Dinka have no concept of the 'mind' as mediating and, as it were, storing up experiences of the self ... the memories of experiences ... appear to the Dinka as exteriorly acting upon him" (p. 149).
11. Hollis, Martin, *Models of Man: Philosophical Thoughts on Social Action* (Cambridge: Cambridge University Press, 1977), 65–6.
12. Milbank, *Theology and Social Theory*, p. 102.
13. Luhmann, Niklas, *Social Systems*, trans. John Bednary with Dirk Baelber (Standford, CA: Stanford University Press, 1995), p. 59.
14. Luhmann, *Social Systems*, p. 63.
15. Luhmann, *Social Systems*, p. 65.
16. I am indebted to Oliver Davies for this insight and the development of this idea. See his "Introducing Transformation Theology" (www.oliverdavies.com; accessed July 15, 2010).
17. Eliot, T.S., *Four Quartets* (London: Faber and Faber, 1972 (1944)), pp. 50–1.
18. Frankl, Victor, *Man's Search for Meaning*, trans. Ilse Lasch (London: Rider, 1959 (2004)), pp. 105–6.
19. Geertz, Clifford, *The Interpretation of Culture* (New York: Fontana, 1973), pp. 86–125.
20. Scheckner, Richard, *The Future of Ritual* (London and New York: Routledge, 1993), p. 229.
21. Ricoeur, P., "The Model of the Text: Meaningful Action Considered as a Text," pp. 203–6, in *Hermeneutics and the Human Sciences*, trans. John B. Thompson (Cambridge: Cambridge University Press, 1981), pp. 197–221.
22. For a succinct summary, see Andrew Bowie, *Introduction to German Philosophy: From Kant to Habermas* (Cambridge: Polity, 2004), pp. 24–7.
23. Bakhtin, M., *Towards a Philosophy of the Act*, trans. Vadim Liapunov (Austin: University of Texas Press, 1993), pp. 28–9: "The answerable act or deed alone surmounts anything hypothetical, for the answerable act is, after all, the actualization of a decision – inescapably, irremediable, and irrevocably ... The performed act constitutes a going out once and for all from within possibility as such into what is once-occurent."
24. Frankl, *Man's Search for Meaning*, p. 68.

25. "... on le punissait par où il avait péché." Gilson, Etienne, *Héloise and Abélard* (Paris: J. Vrin, 1938), pp. 83–4.
26. *BhagavadGītā* 2.31, 33.
27. Bakhtin, *Towards a Philosophy of the Act*, p. 28.
28. Merleau-Ponty, Maurice, *In Praise of Philosophy*, trans. John Wild and James Edith (Evanston: Northwestern University Press, 1963), p. 53.
29. Bakhtin, *Towards a Philosophy of the Act*, p. 2.
30. Bakhtin, *Towards a Philosophy of the Act*, p. 5.
31. Turner, Denys, *Marxism and Christianity* (Oxford: Blackwell, 1983), p. 21.
32. Turner, *Marxism and Christianity*, pp. 21–2.
33. A good account can be found in Thomas Csordas' introduction to Csordas (ed.), *Embodiment and Experience: the Existential Ground of Culture and Self* (Cambridge: Cambridge University Press, 1994). But also see from an earlier generation the work of Ted Polhemus (ed.), *Social Aspects of the Human Body* (London: Penguin, 1983) and Bryan Turner, *The Body and Society* (Oxford: Blackwell, 1984). Interest in the body in the social sciences is also reflected in philosophy. See for example DonnWelton (ed.), *The Body* (Oxford: Blackwell, 1999). For the impact of the body in the study of religions, see Sarah Coakley (ed.), *Religion and the Body* (Cambridge: Cambridge University Press, 1997), Elaine Scarry, *The Body in Pain: The Making and Unmaking of the World* (Oxford: Oxford University Press, 1985), and Paula M. Cooey, *Religious Imagination and the Body: A Feminist Analysis* (Oxford: Oxford University Press, 1994). Also Tweed, T., *Crossing and Dwelling: A Theory of Religion* (Cambridge, Mass.: Harvard University Press, 2006), pp. 98–103; Knott, Kim, *The Location of Religion: A Spatial Analysis* (London and Oakville: Equinox, 2005), pp. 15–20.
34. Mauss, Marcel, "Techniques of the Body," p. 83, trans. Ben Brewster, in Nathan Schlanger (ed.), *Techniques, Technology and Civilization* (London: Routledge, 2006 (1935)), pp. 77–96.
35. Mauss, "Techniques," p. 83.
36. Bourdieu, P., *The Logic of Practice*, trans. Richard Nice (Cambridge: Polity, 1990), p. 53.
37. Mauss, "Techniques," p. 93.
38. Asad, Talal, *Genealogies of Religion: Discipline and Reasons of Power in Christianity and Islam* (Baltimore: Johns Hopkins University Press, 1993), p. 76.
39. I have written on this in a particular Hindu tradition. See my "Techniques of Body and Desire in Kashmir Śaivism," *Religion*, vol. 22, 1992, pp. 47–62.
40. On this point the ascetic theologian Peter Damian claimed that even when practicing alone, his monks were participating in the broader tradition. See Flood, Gavin, *The Ascetic Self: Subjectivity, Memory, and Tradition* (Cambridge: Cambridge University Press, 2004), p. 190. Virtually the same point is also made by Rappaport, Roy, *Ritual and Religion in the Making of Humanity* (Cambridge: Cambridge University Press, 1999), p. 121.
41. There is no place to develop this here, but the issue of the primacy of belief over behavior is contentious. The general orientation of much academic study of

religion has been away from belief, that embodiment and behavior are more important to understand religion. But nevertheless it could be argued that all behavior is based upon a particular view of the world, i.e. a set of beliefs. On an engaging defense of the importance of belief, see Godlove Jr., Terry F., "Saving Belief," in Nancy K. Frankenberry (ed.), *Radical Interpretation in Religion* (Cambridge: Cambridge University Press, 2002), pp. 10–24.

42.   Rappaport, *Ritual and Religion in the Making of Humanity*, p. 24.
43.   Merleau-Ponty, M., *The Visible and the Invisible*, trans. Alphonso Lingis (Evanston: Northwestern University Press, 1968), p. 138.
44.   Turner, Victor, *The Forest of Symbols: Aspects of Ndembu Ritual* (Ithaca: Cornell University Press, 1967), pp. 10–11.
45.   Turner, *The Forest of Symbols*, pp. 362–77. See Fiona Bowie, *The Anthropology of Religion* (Oxford: Blackwell, 2000), pp. 166–72.
46.   Turner, Edith, *Experiencing Ritual: A New Interpretation of African Healing* (Philadelphia: University of Pennsylvania Press, 1992), p. 139.
47.   Turner, *Experiencing Ritual*, p. 149.
48.   Turner, *Experiencing Ritual*, p. 150.
49.   Turner, *Forest of Symbols*, p. 365.
50.   One fascinating account by an anthropologist who becomes personally involved in a tradition is Karen McCarthy Brown, *Mama Lola: A Vodou Priestess in Brooklyn* (California: California University Press, 1991).
51.   See Csordas, Thomas J. (ed.), *Embodiment and Culture*, pp. 8, 12.
52.   Turner, *Experiencing Ritual*, p. 150.
53.   Stroumsa, G. G., *The End of Sacrifice: Religious Transformations in Late Antiquity* (Chicago: Chicago University Press, 2009).
54.   This point is made by Walter Burkert, *Creation of the Sacred: Tracks of Biology in Early Religions* (Cambridge, Mass.: Harvard University Press, 1996), pp. 141–2.
55.   Burkert, *Creation of the Sacred*, p. 144–5.
56.   *Rig Veda* 1.43, 1.114, 2.11, trans. Wendy Doniger (London: Penguin, 2005).
57.   Burkert, *Creation of the Sacred*, p. 144.
58.   Yao, X., *Introduction to Confucianism* (Cambridge: Cambridge University Press, 2000), pp. 193–204.
59.   Burkert, cited by Heesterman, Jan, *The Broken World of Sacrifice* (Chicago: Chicago University Press, 1993), p. 9.
60.   Bataille, G., *The Accured Share*, trans. Robert Hurley (New York: Zone, 1990); Girard, R., *Things Hidden Since the Foundation of the World*, trans. S. Bann and M. Meteer (London: The Athlone Press, 1987 (1976)).
61.   Freeman, Rich, "The Teyyam Tradition of Kerala," in Flood, G (ed.), *The Blackwell Companion to Hinduism* (Oxford: Blackwell, 2003), pp. 307–26.
62.   Taylor, *A Secular Age*, p. 647.
63.   Parry, C., *Death in Benares* (Cambridge: Cambridge University Press, 1994), p. 26.
64.   Parry, *Death in Benares*, pp. 178–84.
65.   Bowker, J., *The Meanings of Death* (Cambridge: Cambridge University Press, 1991), p. 32.

66. Frits Staal has developed an interesting and important argument that ritual is 'meaningless'; it has no semantics but does have a syntax, a structure. He has developed this thesis with reference to ancient Indian sacrificial rituals known as the solemn rites. There is no place to develop this here, but while Staal's argument might work with the Vedic material, it does not seem to be so convincing with the kind of rituals I have described, very much focused on the body and moments of the intensification of significance. See *Rules Without Meaning* (New York: Peter Lang, 1988), pp. 65–70.
67. Merleau-Ponty, *The Visible and the Invisible*, p. 137.
68. Ricoeur, Paul, *Time and Narrative*, vol. 1, trans. Kathleen McLaughlin and David Pellauer (Chicago: Chicago University Press, 1984), p. 57.

3

The Inner Journey

A common metaphor in religions is that life is a journey, an odyssey towards the transcendent and for many towards God who is both goal and origin. This journey is often conceptualized as an inner journey although it can be exteriorized as pilgrimage or the restless wandering of an ascetic. The metaphor of the journey and its development is also the cultivation of a kind of inwardness which highlights subjective experience and the inner connection between the person and transcendence, between the invisible and the visible. This cultivation of inwardness or intensification of subjectivity which occurs in the major religious traditions of human history, we might call "spiritual practice" which is often accompanied by narrativization of one's life, although we must be aware that the adjective "spiritual" comes out of a particular Christian history from the "spiritual exercises" (*exercitia spiritualia*) of Ignatius Loyola (1491–1556) and the term "spirituality" has a distinct history.[1]

The main connotation of spirituality is the cultivation of the inner life of a religious community, particularly a monastic community, although in recent years the term has come to denote an individual, private experience, linked with the economic and political conditions of modernity, which is sometimes contrasted with formal, institutional "religion."[2] It is the former connotation that we need to begin with, integral to the structure and nature of religions. If my claim is that religions are cultural forms which penetrate the world of life and mediate the encounter with mystery, then spiritual practice along with its narrative context is central to this enterprise. Indeed, according to many traditions spiritual practice brings the person into the fullness of life and is the conduit for connecting self to transcendence or the development of spiritual

The Importance of Religion: Meaning and Action in Our Strange World,
First Edition. Gavin Flood.
© 2012 Gavin Flood. Published 2012 by Blackwell Publishing Ltd.

practice is regarded as treading the path itself. We might say that spiritual practice is the heart of tradition, the basic foundation upon which political, artistic, and "external" practices are based. The image of the meditating Buddha is a sign for an interiority which is the goal of tradition from which the entire edifice of Buddhist institutions – monasticism, education system, and doctrine – stems. The idea of spiritual practice not only indicates a set of techniques of the body such as prayer, meditation, pilgrimage, and asceticism, but also indicates the development of subjectivity or intensification of subjectivity expressed in the language of inwardness or interiority.

What is now referred to as "spirituality" fell within the semantic range of the category "mysticism." Mysticism itself has a fascinating history and has been associated with consciousness and experience that is out of the ordinary. The term "mysticism" develops from Christian "mystical theology," direct knowledge of God or knowledge of God through experience, in contrast to dogmatic theology – knowledge of God through revelation – and natural theology – knowledge of God through reasoning about the universe.[3] There has been some debate during much of the last century about whether "mystical experience" was at the heart of religions as a "common core" or whether there were different types of such experience, and what the relationship is between language and mystical experience.

On the one hand, the "universal" or "common core" view maintained that there is an essential unity to mystical experience that can be identified independently of different interpretations. That is, although interpretations of the experience vary, the experience itself of unity with the divine is fundamentally the same in all religions throughout history. This view is linked to Aldous Huxley's peyote- and mescalin-fuelled idea of perennial philosophy, although the origins of perennial philosophy can be traced to Schleiermacher's "feeling of absolute dependence" and to William James' study of religious experience. Mystical experience is the losing of self-distinction characterized by a sense of union or oneness with the world or with a transcendent power. On the other hand, we have the view that mystical experiences are linked to specific traditions and can only be understood in particular linguistic and historical contexts and that experience cannot be so easily separated out from interpretation, a view put forward by Steven Katz in a number of publications.[4] A position between relativism and universalism is put forward by R.C. Zaehner and also by the phenomenologist of religion Ninian Smart, who claims that we can identify mystical or contemplative experience in which the mystic becomes one with a transcendent reality, numinous experience, or the apprehension of transcendence outside of the self which overwhelms the self, and "panenhenic experience," a term coined by Zaehner, in which the mystic experiences a unity with the world or with nature; the self is "being in all."[5]

A detailed discussion of this issue cannot be undertaken here, but we do need to say that universalizing general categories outside of particular historical contexts is limited in terms of description and explanation because it must inevitably remain at a very general or abstract level. The comparative study of mysticism is dogged with epistemological problems, not least the very identification of "mysticism" in non-Abrahamic religions, but there have nevertheless been excellent tradition-specific studies. The study of mysticism in Christianity, where it arguably finds its natural home, has developed apace, especially with the publication of Bernard McGinn's four-volume history. In Jewish mysticism Gershom Scholem deserves mention as the foremost scholar of the twentieth century, who combined meticulous scholarship with a theory of mysticism as a stage in the development of religions characterized by a solitary quest of the mystic in search of God, but who returns to society to communicate his experience and give shape to his vision.[6] In Islam we have the exemplary work of Annemarie Schimmel, who maps the development of Sufi traditions,[7] and Henry Corbin on Iranian mysticism.[8]

These debates about mysticism have somewhat fallen into abeyance in recent years, as the broader culture has moved on and postmodernity has complexified the possibilities of cultural analysis; but the issues remain unresolved. Is there a common core of mystical experience? Can we separate experience from interpretation? I cannot engage directly with these epistemological questions but wish point out the difficulty with the term "experience." Firstly, it is not clear that the term denotes the same thing to all people, and when combined with the adjective "mystical" has the connotation of a state of consciousness out of the ordinary and disruptive of day to day living. While this might be the case in some instances – Aldous Huxley or Stanislav Groff's hallucinogen induced mystical states, for example – it is far from the case that mystics regard their experience as separated from the totality of their lives. Secondly, the term "experience" implies an encounter with the world through the senses and many mystical experiences are regarded as being outside of the body (and therefore beyond the senses).[9]

Given what we have seen regarding the centrality of the body and the human need for understanding at a visceral level, we need to approach spirituality and mysticism from a slightly different angle and to argue that rather than a common core of experience we have a complex of language and bodily practices that have analogues across different spiritual traditions. This is to move away from an essentialist understanding of experience to locate a diversity of human experience in time and therefore in the way that experience is narrated. Indeed if we substitute the term "experience" with "narrative" or even "subjectivity," we can offer an account of spiritual experience in terms of a sense of our continued existence through time and a shared structure which is filled out with tradition-specific contents at different historical times. As Michel de Certeau has observed, with mysticism we have a narrativization of one's life in which autobiography, for St Theresa for example, becomes a way of "ordering one's soul."[10] To illustrate this we need to offer some description of spiritual languages in different traditions and to develop an account of subjectivity that is central to the existential understanding of religions I am developing. I intend to move therefore from the language of spirituality (and the absence of language), to, most importantly, the body and the body's *habitus*, and thence to an account of spiritual subjectivity.

Languages of Spirituality

Spiritual experience is intimately connected with language and yet paradoxically claims to be beyond language. On the one hand language, particularly sacred language, the language of revelation and the liturgical language, is seen as the vehicle for divine communication and the interface between culture and transcendence, between the invisible and the visible or the place where culture meets the world. In Christianity this comes in the form of the paradox that God expresses himself in the written word and yet he is outside of being as the creator of being. This is the language of prayer. On the one hand prayer designates the language of address to a transcendent other which disrupts and breaks with ordinary speech, on the other prayer designates silence and wonder, standing before the mystery of the invisible. There is then a paradox at the heart of mystical language, namely that it cannot express transcendence and yet does so often with great eloquence. This distinction between silence and the word is reflected in other spiritual traditions but for the moment let us stay with Christianity where we see how the language of prayer pushes language to its limit and reaches into silence.[11]

One of the themes in the history of Christian spirituality has been the relationship or tension between language seen as the vehicle for divine communication, the interface between culture and transcendence, between the visible and the invisible, and the idea of God outside of being who is beyond language, beyond meaning, and who is signified only by silence, whose very absence becomes a sign of his presence. Here prayer becomes the limit of the sayable and opens out onto that which is unsayable. As McGinn observes, in highlighting negative language that God is ineffable, the medieval mystics were prophetic in signaling the contemporary idea of the absence of God, although for them the real God they wished to contact "becomes a possibility only when the false gods (even the God of religion) have vanished and the frightening abyss of total nothingness is confronted."[12]

The "abyss of nothingness" that McGinn mentions is a vitally important theme in the history of religions. With the retreat of language from expressing

transcendence it is a short step to proclaiming the absence of transcendence
and non-being as underlying human language and subjectivity. As previously
mentioned, we see this in the history of philosophy from Hegel through to
Nietzsche and Kierkegaard.[13] This issue is particularly relevant for us in that
it highlights one of the central claims of this book about the importance of
religion, namely that religion is a cultural form but also a sign of something
beyond it. We see this particularly in the language and practice of prayer,
which pushes language to its limits and reaches into silence. As this tension is
not simply parochial but paralleled in the contemplative traditions of other
religions, it is worth exploring.

The western mystical tradition developed two forms of language, *apophasis*, the language of negation that emphasizes the total unknowability of
God, and *cataphasis*, the language of affirmation that emphazises the
qualities of God, such as love, being the creator, being omniscient, and so
on. It is the language of negation that is particularly important and impressive in the history of Christian mysticism, flowing from at least the fifth
century where it finds strong articulation in the Syrian monk Dionysius the
Pseudo-Areopagite or the Pseudo Denys as he is sometimes called, through to
a modified "Christian" *apophasis* in Simone Weil in the twentieth century.
The languages of spirituality are generally affirmative of doctrinal content –
as with the *Cloud* which accepts the general theological framework of
mystical theology – although such language can disrupt doctrine and threaten
ecclesiastical authority. Mystics have therefore sometimes been regarded
with some suspicion by the hierarchs of religious institutions as undermining
tradition, as in the case of Marguerite Porete in the fourteenth century,
whose persistence in propagating her views that the self is annihilated in God
cost her life, or Al Halaj's claim to be one with God which similarly cost him
his life.[14]

But generally the language of negation is not restricted to the mystics who
wish to challenge tradition but is central to the mainstream language of
Christianity, being emphasized by Orthodoxy and the mystical dimensions of
Catholicism, although negation has been generally played down by Protestantism with its emphasis on the word and suspicion of subjective experience.
De Certeau argues that the language of negation enters Christianity from the
Greco-Roman tradition which emphasized silence and "departs in the
direction of an unknown god (*agnostos theos*) who silences all thought
because he is beyond being."[15] It took a long time, argues de Certeau, for this
mystical language to work itself out to its full expression in the sixteenth
century, when we see the creation of a technical language of mysticism.
We do, however, have a trajectory of the language of negation from
Dionysius in the fifth century. As McGinn points out, Dionysius emphasizes
the language of darkness, silence, and the cloud as metaphors to speak about
attaining the hidden God.[16]

This tradition develops through the medieval period, particularly in the western, Latin tradition in contrast to the emphasis on the light of God in mystical theology of the Orthodox Church, a conflict which comes to a head with Gregory Palamas and the debate with Barlaam.[17] One particularly important and shining example of the language of negation is the *Cloud of Unknowing*, which develops and reinterprets the apophatic language of Denys. The *Cloud* is written in Middle English at a time when Latin, although still the professional language of theology and the language that united medieval Europe (as Sanskrit in south and southeast Asia), was being supplemented by texts in vernacular languages, particularly mystical texts. So in France we have women mystics called the Beguines, such as Marguerite Porete, writing in Middle French and in Germany Meister Eckhart writing in Middle High German.

The *Cloud of Unknowing* is an anonymous text written in English around 1370, probably by a contemplative priest to his young, twenty-four year old disciple. Indebted to the apophatic language of Dionysius, it is guide book for prayer. The author acknowledges his debt to Dionysius, whom he calls St Denys, and is an exposition of spiritual exercises as a way of apprehending the total incomprehensibility of God. Setting himself clearly within the apophatic tradition, the *Cloud* reads Denys through the lens of a thirteenth-century theologian Thomas Gallus, especially in his emphasis on *affectus* rather than *intellectus*, on emotional understanding rather than reason.[18] The Latin term *affectus*, Denys Turner observes, refers to "want" but without the connotation of something lacking or something needed. He suggests "love" to be the best translation.[19] Thus with the *Cloud* we have an emphasis on the darkness of God and ineffability, but this cannot be grasped by the intellect or rational mind; rather, only through love can the vast unknowability be understood even a little. Turner also shows how with Gallus there is a reinterpretation of the apophatic tradition such that the intellect, which previously had been identified as the faculty for apprehending the unknowability of God, is replaced with the *affectus*. That is, love as a form of knowledge takes up where the rational intellect stops: "apophasis begins where *intellectus* ends."[20] The cloud of unknowing is the highest sign of God that is "known" only through love and, indeed, "want."

Of the two kinds of Christian life, the active and the contemplative, the contemplative for the author is higher. In Luke's Gospel, when Jesus is visiting the house of Martha, she is busy preparing a meal while her sister Mary Magdalene sits enraptured at Jesus' feet; the *Cloud* tells us that the active life of Martha is good but the contemplative way of Mary is best, absorbed in "the supreme wisdom of his Godhood." Mary is in the "highest and holiest state of contemplation we can know on earth," "there she sat, completely still, with deep delight, and an urgent love eagerly reaching out into that high cloud of unknowing that was between her and God."[21]

The text makes a distinction between the "godhood" of Jesus and his "manhood" or humanity and the contemplative life being a movement from the latter to the former. The first part of the active life is exemplified by Martha preparing the meal, the second is concerned with the beauty and voice of Jesus' manhood which is also the first stage of the contemplative life, with the second stage of contemplation going beyond this to absorption in the cloud of unknowing. God is a dark "cloud of unknowing" who cannot be understood through reason but only through prayer and practice of longing love. Yet although God is incomprehensible, he is immanent in all things, and so the soul is not totally separated from him because being created in his likeness and image, it has "some affinity with him."[22] In prayer the young monk must contemplate the dark cloud and try to pierce it with darts or arrows of longing love. In due course, after patient practice, the light of God's love will shine upon him. The "method" or spiritual practice that the *Cloud* advocates is patient waiting, focused in an act of will upon the cloud of unknowing. In the words of the *Cloud*:

> Do not give up but work until you feel longing. For the first time when you do it you find but a darkness and, as it were, a cloud of unknowing, which you do not know what it is except that you feel your will as a naked intent upon God. This darkness and this cloud is, whatever you do, between you and your God, so that you may not see him clearly by light of understanding in your reason, nor feel him in the sweetness of love in your affection. And therefore be determined to abide in this darkness as long as you can, evermore crying after him who you love; for if ever shall you feel him or see him, as it may be here, you must always be in this cloud and in this darkness.[23]

Through longing love that transcends intellectual understanding, the monk stands before the cloud of unknowing until such a time as the grace of God shines through to bless the disciple. This is a simplified model of the self that somewhat goes against the traditional understanding of the person as possessing memory, understanding, and will, putting in its place an understanding of the person in terms of the two powers of loving and knowing[24] of which love is the power and kind of knowledge that gives us spiritual progress. In this text we have downplaying of imagination and the traditional language of interiority and ascent to God that developed in Christian spirituality from Augustine, as Sarah Coakley shows, and a stripping down of the person alongside the development of an individuality which is a precursor of later developments.[25]

The *Cloud*'s language of spirituality is a development of Christian apophasis, speech of denials that is paradoxically the affirmation of a transcendent reality. The invisible that is just out of reach behind appearances, is confronted through prayer and prayerful longing and a patient dwelling in the darkness of God. As we see in the passage just quoted, for the *Cloud* prayer is a practice in which the intention of the one who prays is directed towards the God who remains hidden by the cloud of unknowing. In due course God will be apprehended through his grace and the adept experience the sweetness of prayer. In practical terms the text tells us that the adept should take a single, one syllable word such as "love" or "God," "fasten this word to thy heart" and hammer the cloud with it.[26] The text must thus be seen in a ritual context, the context of a practice or *habitus* of regular prayer.

Here prayer is a speech act through which the disciple hopes to penetrate the boundary separating him from God. By repeating this one word all thoughts are suppressed in the "cloud of forgetting" and the soul stands before the cloud of unknowing, a method not dissimilar to mantra repetition in Buddhism and Hinduism. The language of the text is therefore an interesting combination of the idea that transcendence is outside of all language and apprehension, God is beyond human understanding, along with longing love and also the technique of repetition. The *Cloud* advocates a kind of devotional meditation directed by the will that emphasizes not rational understanding but immediate affective encounter or knowledge of the unknowable. The prayer of the *Cloud* is an understanding which is a non-understanding directed by the will, only minimally using language if at all. Indeed, the repetition of a single word disrupts ordinary speech, which is pushed into the cloud of forgetting in order to free the mind from the trammels of ordinary life to stand before the mystery of God's darkness. This theme is developed within the history of Christian spirituality, not least by the Beguines, especially Porete, and by Eckhart, who develops a distinctive "apophatic anthropology" to use Denys Turner's phrase.[27]

While this language of darkness is set within the history of Christian contemplation, it is tempting to see a style of language, a style of denial, which can be found in other traditions. Although we must not lose sight of its specificity and historical location, we can speak about prayer and contemplation in general terms which cuts across traditions. Although this is complex, we should not be skeptical about arriving at some general understanding, and we need to locate contemplation and the language of spirituality in the understanding of religion as an intensification of subjectivity or inwardness, and also in terms of ritual and skilful action. By way of contrast, and to bring out what I see as the essential elements in languages of spirituality, let us take another example, this time from Buddhism, where the language of negation is given centre stage.

The kind of discourse that might be called "mysticism" in the sense of personal testimony of experiences intertwined with doctrinal claims, as we saw with the *Cloud*, is generally absent from Sanskrit Buddhist and Hindu traditions of the classical and medieval periods. While some personal testimony of a parallel kind to the West is found in devotional poetry in vernacular languages, authors of Sanskrit religious texts tend to limit their statements about personal experience to the introductions to their commentaries and treatises or to colophons.[28] The texts might well reflect experience, and certainly the experience of liberation (*mokṣa* and *nirvāṇa*) is a central theme in theological and philosophical discourse, but the emphasis is on correct interpretation, argument, and refutation of other positions. Direct, sustained reference to personal experience is generally absent.

Let us take an example from the Madhyamaka school of Mahayana Buddhism where we find a developed language of negation. The ultimate reality is empty (*śunyatā*) of essence or own-being (*svabhāva*), and the goal of spiritual practice is to wake up to this understanding. Form is emptiness and emptiness is form. There is even emptiness of emptiness, in that emptiness itself is empty of own-being. The texts, meditation practice, and the monastic order are all geared towards this fundamental, liberating insight and wisdom (*prajñā*). While the edifice of Buddhist philosophy and practice is complex and vast in its history, there is a certain simplicity in the paradoxical language of the root texts of the tradition. The goal of practice is to become a Bodhisattva, a being who has put of his own final enlightenment out of compassion for all beings, in order to help beings, whose truth is that he is just as ephemeral as all phenomena and language that tries to fix reality is doomed to failure. Let us take one example from the famous *Heart Sutra*. Here the Buddha is addressing his disciple Sariputra:

> Therefore, O Sariputra, it is because of his non-attainmentness that a Bodhisattva, through having relied on the perfection of wisdoms, dwells without thought-coverings. In the absence of thought-coverings he has not been made to tremble, he has overcome what can upset, and in the end he attains to Nirvana. All those who appear as Buddhas in the three periods of time – fully awake to the utmost, right and perfect enlightenment because they have relied on the perfection of wisdom . . . Therefore one should know the prajñāparamitā as the great spell, the spell of great knowledge, the utmost spell, the unequaled spell allayer of all suffering in truth – for what could go wrong? By the prajñāparamitā has this spell been delivered. It runs like this: Gone, gone, gone beyond, gone altogether beyond, O what an awakening, all hail.[29]

In the *Cloud* we saw that God can only be apprehended as a darkness in a state of unknowing. Here in the *Perfection of Wisdom* we have the idea that the ultimate truth of the world is an emptiness that cannot be known but only expressed in ways that disrupt ordinary language. It seems to me that the metaphysics behind the two texts are quite distinct – for the Christian *Cloud*, God is the creator of the world even though ineffable and dark, for the Buddhist Wisdom Tradition (*prajñāparamitā*) emptiness is not a creator but the true condition of self and world that we need to understand, even though ultimately no truth (*dharma*) has been indicated and there is nobody to grasp it anyway. But there is a parallelism between the nothingness of God and the nothingness of ultimate reality. Both truths cannot be understood by the rational mind but both can be existentially understood – the darkness of God realized through *affectus* in the *Cloud* and emptiness realized through meditative insight in the *Perfection of Wisdom*. And both advocate a method, the longing love focused in a single word for the *Cloud* and the perfection of wisdom mantra in the Buddhist text.

The idea of emptiness was to have immense impact on the traditions of Asia and Zen Buddhism – developing in China before being transposed to Japan – and provides perhaps the best example of the importance of emptiness in the Buddhist tradition. Enlightenment is understanding how things really are, beyond language and beyond cultural particularity, directly experienced in the awakened state of *satori* achieved through the Zen meditation practice of "just sitting." Buddhahood is in all beings and the goal of practice, the goal of religion, is to wake up to this. In Chinese and Japanese Buddhism, the paradoxical language of the *Perfection of Wisdom* is developed to an extreme, and we have the *koan* such as "what is the sound of one hand clapping?" (to which, of course, there is no rational answer) and the "dialogues" (*mondo*) such as the following cited by Suzuki:

> The venerable Yen-Yang of Ksin-hsing, was asked by a monk:
> "What is the Buddha?"
> "A mass of clay."
> "What is the dharma [the teaching]?"
> "The earth moves."
> "What is the Sangha [the monastic community]?"
> "One who eats gruel (*chou*) and rice (*fan*)."[30]

Such dialogues express the idea that the experience of the ultimate reality cannot be articulated in coherent language and furthermore that the language itself can be a trigger for a sudden awakening. Again, the cultural particularity of such language is not easily reconciled with the language of the Christian mystical tradition, and yet as Pattison observes, the parallels over the concept of nothingness and inexpressibility of an ultimate reality are compelling[31] and indicate some shared understanding of the limits of language and paths that the languages of spirituality can draw the disciple along. The languages of spirituality confront us with the limits of being and with our own nothingness.

The kind of meditation practice that emphasizes immediate awareness and the awakening experience of liberation in the here and now is called insight meditation (*vipaśyāna/vipassana*) in Buddhism. This is contrasted with a kind of meditation in which calmness (*śamatha, samatha*) is stressed and the development of stages of awareness in which consciousness develops through a hierarchy of levels called absorptions (Sanskrit *dhyāna*/Pali *jhāna*).

In this practice the meditator develops spiritual qualities of applying thought to an object of concentration (*vitarka*) and keeping it there (*vicāra*), which is accompanied by a feeling of joy (*pīti*), contentment (*sukha*), and one-pointedness (*ekāgratā*). As meditation develops, these qualities fall away leaving only one-pointedness or complete absorption in the object of meditation, particularly a mental object or sign (*nimitta*), arising in the mind's eye; an inner photic image that becomes the focus of meditation. Here we have a distinct kind of practice which may have existed before the Buddha, which emphasizes an ascent of consciousness to higher levels in which experience of this world of desire (*kāma loka*) disappears and we experience more refined states and their accompanying world of experience (*dhyānaloka*). These two styles of practice emphasize, on the one hand, the immediacy of awareness here and now and, on the other, the idea of a hierarchy of stages in which consciousness leaves this world behind. There was some debate within the tradition as to whether the meditation that emphasized the graded hierarchy was necessary, as liberation could be attained by insight meditation only, but there seems to be consensus that *samatha* is a prerequisite, a grounding, that suppressed the hindrances to allow insight to arise.[32]

The style of meditation that emphasizes ascent in contrast to that which stresses here and now awareness is paralleled non-Buddhist traditions. In Christianity we have texts such as the *Cloud* which stress praying to God and remaining in the darkness in immediacy of the present moment, reacting against mystical texts which have emphasized inner ascent to higher states of being. This mystical ascent emphasized in medieval mystical literature is simultaneously a return and a going deeper into the self, a penetration of the Ground of being through which we return to God.[33] Many examples can be drawn here from Augustine's truth dwelling in the inner man, to Bonaventura's journey into the mind of God, even to Dante's journey through the cosmos.

In an Indian context we find innumerable examples of a spiritual journey as inner ascent. An example is the sixteenth century Shaivayogin Jnanaprakasha, who wrote a short treatise describing the ascent of the self through the different levels of the cosmos to the realization of Shiva. This journey is also a journey through the body beginning, in this text, with the heart and rising up the central channel of the body through the throat, to the palate, the top of the palate, the centre between the eyes, to the crown of the head, and then beyond to Shiva located "twelve fingers" above the crown, a realization which takes the form of the master (guru) dancing, who manifests the qualities of Shiva. This realization is also that the self is equal to the Lord (*śivatulya*). Each of these stages is associated with a particular deity and a particular realization of God which is increasingly refined. The final state is the realization that the self is identical with God – "I am He" (*sohamasmi*).[34]

We see in these brief examples languages of spirituality, which are distinct and particular to tradition. It is not possible or desirable to posit some objective reality to which the levels of cosmos and body refer and which are given different descriptions or terminologies. The density and complexity of the material from the traditions needs a more sophisticated and respectful approach. Knowledge of Shiva cannot easily be assimilated to the *Cloud*'s unknowing nor Bonaventure's journey into the mind of God easily mapped on to the yogin's inner journey through body and cosmos. But nevertheless we can attempt some generalizations about the nature of pre-modern religions and the limits of language.

Firstly, the examples I have presented are all from medieval or classical Christianity, Buddhism, and Hinduism. These traditions present hierarchical cosmologies which are not only cosmologies but conditions of being within interiority. That is, the levels of the universe are thought to exist within the self and, particularly in the Indian traditions, within the body. The cosmos is located within: the macrocosm within the microcosm, to use one kind of language. Secondly, the spiritual journey is a solitary journey of the practitioner from a state of limitation (bondage, sin, impurity) to a state beyond limitation that is direct experience or apprehension of a higher state of existence, an apprehension or vision of God. We might make the generalization, then, that pre-modern religions tend to be cosmological, that the cosmos is hierarchically ordered with the lower levels being more solidified than the higher, and that the spiritual journey is an ascent to higher levels through the cosmos which might also be conceptualized as a journey through the body. These traditions tend to be esoteric and have flourished within the context of pre-Reformation monasticism and in renunciate institutions in the Indic religions. Thirdly, we can say that in parallel to the hierarchical model of the cosmos, pre-modern religions offer a language about the limits of language and the direct, non-verbal apprehension of a reality that is designated as ineffable. Such a realization is spoken of in terms of a here-and-now understanding that while it might be communicable, is essentially unsayable and outside of usual linguistic constraints.

The Spiritual Habitus

The two kinds of spiritual languages that I have described, namely languages of unsayability and languages of inner ascent, are not merely intellectual curiosities or leftovers from a past that we have gone beyond after the retreat of religion from cosmology with the rise of science. They are still with us in contemporary traditions, albeit in altered ways, and we can trace trajectories of these languages into modernity, particularly in poetry and philosophy. But what both styles of spirituality share is, firstly, that their spiritual languages point to something beyond which is brought into human narration and, secondly, that they are focused on the body. While a spiritual tradition might display a language of ascent and transcendence of the body – an idea that Plato expressed in the phrase *soma sema*, the body is a tomb – these traditions are themselves rooted in body-based practices. Even Martin Luther, Norman Brown reminds us, had the Protestant illumination "while seated on the privy."[35] But apart from singular, religious experiences, all spiritual traditions develop a *habitus*, a form of repeated behaviors that are conducive to the tradition's goals and which are intimately linked to spiritual languages of evocation and address or of instruction. In the jargon, this is to say that spiritual languages are illocutionary – they are verbal actions that have effects, as in the repetition of the Jesus Prayer – and they are perlocutionary – they have effects on their audiences when integrated into a manual of instruction or story of a life.

That spiritual traditions develop a habitus is almost commonplace. The *Bhagavad Gita* tells us that to practice yoga the yogi must go to a clean place and with body, neck, and head erect he should gaze at the tip of the nose and, with his mind concentrated, should meditate upon the Lord.[36] The *Cloud* tells us that the student should pray sitting quite still, as if asleep or sunk in sorrow, and in this position repeat the short words of his prayer such as "sin" or "God";[37] and the Hesychasts of Greek Orthodoxy adopted a particular bodily posture sitting on a low stool, with head bowed onto their chests and, like yoga, emphasized the control of the breath while repeating the Jesus Prayer.[38] There are many, many examples of the use of the body and the development of bodily focused devotional or spiritual methods, and we need only be reminded of the standard forms of religious ritual, Christian Eucharist, Moslem prayer, Zen meditation, pilgrimage, dietary and sexual restriction in all religions.

The body is central for developing a spiritual habitus, creating an orientation towards transcendence, and making one's life conform to the constraints of tradition.[39] It is here that we see experience in terms of narrative and subjectivity. We cannot generally speak of isolated "experiences" but rather the whole of the practitioner's life, his narrative and inwardness, are suffused by the practices of his tradition. There is constancy to spiritual practice which remains the same, or with little variation, through the generations and through the duration of a single lifetime as the body develops, ages, and dies. Throughout we have spiritual languages thoroughly integrated into spiritual practices, which are integral to their performance, and which serve to inspire and instruct others.

We might argue that the emphasis on the body in spiritual traditions shows us that religions are not so much concerned with leaving the world, with the negation of the physical, but are more concerned with bringing practitioners into the world. Through the development of spiritual *habitus* the practitioner performs repeated actions in the world that affect his subjectivity and broadly all those in the community around him. Each of the religions focuses on the body through repeated series of actions, through posture, through the control of food and sex, and through the control of the breath, although some traditions thematize or emphasize the body more than others. Within Christianity we have the rejection of an anti-matter Platonism with the idea, central to the religion, of bodily resurrection that, while complicated (some would say compromised) by the Greek idea of the immortal soul, can be traced from its earliest foundations. Norman Brown particularly emphasizes Protestantism in this regard and what he appositely calls "body mysticism," exemplifying the Christian hope of life over death. In contrast to mysticism understood as flight from the material world, as exemplified in what he calls the "popularisers" of his day, such as Evelyn Underhill and Huxley, Brown observes that in the West there is "another kind of mysticism, which can be called Dionysian or body mysticism, which stays with life, which is the body, and seeks to transform and perfect it."[40] Brown identifies three trajectories of body mysticism, the Christian idea of the spiritual body, the Jewish idea of Adam's perfect body before the Fall, and the alchemical idea of the subtle body. All of these, says Brown, come together in the work of the Protestant mystic Jacob Boehme and parallel developments can be seen in oriental traditions, particularly Taoism as mapped out by Needham, and yoga as mapped by Eliade.[41] From Boehme we can trace a development through to Blake,[42] and according to Brown to Novalis, Hegel, Goethe, Berdyaev, and Rilke,[43] and one might include Brown himself. We might also trace this development into the popular esotericism of the twentieth century, particularly theosophy and anthroposophy.[44]

While this is not the place to trace this trajectory or critically review Brown's work, it seems to me that his emphasis on body mysticism and delineating its particular historical trajectory is highly pertinent. Spirituality in religions tends not to be a flight from the world – even where there is a rhetoric of ascent – but brings practitioners into the world through the development of the *habitus* and underlines material causation in the body. In speaking about the body we are inevitably speaking about the gendered body, even though human perfection by many mystics, such as Boehme, was thought of in terms of bodily androgyny. Languages of spirituality and the emphasis on bodily practice tend to be orientated towards the male in the histories of traditions (but then up until fairly recent times so have most cultural practices). For both men and women, communities of practitioners undergo regimes of bodily control accompanied by speech acts such as prayer or the repetition of mantras in order to transform life and open up the possibilities of life to something greater than everyday expectation, to an openness to what life shows and reveals to us, which is simultaneously an openness to transcendence, an openness to the depth of the world. Spiritual traditions are examples par excellence of the ways in which religions must be primarily understood as modes of being and modes of bodily awareness which are fundamental to human life. We might say that the spiritual *habitus* is the body's longing for the infinite in practice.

The centrality of the body in spiritual practice is bound up with subjectivity and so with narration. Certain kinds of bodily regime, such as repeated prayer, long vigils, fasting and other kinds of asceticism, are conducive to a deepening of human understanding and an intensification of subjectivity, which is understood as being central to a person's life story. Religious experience, we might say, is a particular kind of intensification, although there could be other forms of inwardness which are not particularly religious, developed through reading or writing poetry, for example, or through music or through being in love. But even with secular forms of inwardness, we have an encounter of person and community with the limits of the knowable and the limits of the sayable.

To speak about the body is to speak about action, and to speak about action is to speak about meaning in so far as our acts display both sense – they have a meaning in relation to each other – and reference – they refer or point to something outside of themselves.[45] Spiritual practices are clearly like this, having both sense and reference. Religious actions such as prayer, fasting, and meditation, point to and open out through imagination possible worlds for religious practitioners, and this opening out of possible worlds is at the same time the bringing the practitioner into this world through involvement in material causation. In the spiritual *habitus* the practitioner performs repeated actions and says repeated utterances (performs illocutionary acts) which serve to give meaning to life and to create a particular kind of subjectivity in which the story of a life is made to live within the story of tradition. The story of my life, my persistence through time and narrative identity (again to refer to Ricoeur)[46] become an index of tradition and the bodily *habitus* becomes a vehicle for a transformed subjectivity. The illocutionary act of speaking a spiritual language along with a bodily practice, as we have seen with the *Cloud*, serve to connect me with transcendence and the story of my life with a much broader, longer life of tradition, and so, tradition teaches, with the story of the universe itself.

We have seen this in the examples already given. In the *Cloud*, the subjective experiences of the one who prays can be intense and overwhelming. But these experiences are the development, through practices of the body, of a certain kind of medieval Christian subjectivity. The *Cloud*'s disciple desires to "recover the cleanness lost through sin" and to do this through patiently abiding in contemplation of God as the cloud of unknowing.[47] The disciple's subjectivity is thus formed through the teachings expressed in the text. The Buddhist seeks enlightenment through insight meditation and following the moral practices of the tradition. In both cases the practice seeks to transform the ordinary sense of self or of the "I," the everyday or "indexical-I," to conform to the "I" implied within the tradition and even within the texts of tradition. We might even say that the goal of spiritual practice is for the indexical-I to be overwhelmed by the "I of discourse," in Greg Urban's terms.[48] Furthermore we might say that such practices are well winnowed through the generations and successful in their bringing the practitioner to a spiritual awareness and sense of self. My inner experiences do not simply belong to me, but practices developed over long periods of time serve to shape and direct my experience as part of a greater, collective project of tradition. The mystic's language serves both to inspire or instruct and to map the inner journey, to show how my life is part of a larger story, and to show how the meaning of my life is more than I can understand. Perhaps more simply, we might say that the practitioner makes tradition his or her own; the seed of longing born within us is nurtured through the practices of tradition.

Conclusion

The overwhelming entailed in spiritual states points to the limit of what can be explained and what can be said. In spiritual languages and spiritual practices we see how the invisible is contained within or "folded into" the visible (to use Merleau-Ponty's phrase), and these languages always exist uneasily at the interface of what can be said and what cannot be said, of the story of my life and that which is beyond it, of the "I" and the "not-I" that might overwhelm it. While clearly there are few agreements at doctrinal level among religions through their histories, and even ethics vary, there is a shared area of concern with the way language reaches into the infinite and the way in which such language finds a place within spiritual practice, which is to say within the story of my life and what I do within a community of religious actors. But in the end, the practices of tradition and their spiritual languages reach into silence and mystery. It seems that all spiritual traditions could be in agreement here that, in the words of the enigmatic E.M. Cioran, "after having suffered on the heights of despair, in the supreme hour of revelation, you will find that the only answer, the only reality, is silence."[49]

Notes

1. See Dupuy, Michel, "Spiritualité," pp. 1142–3, in M. Viller et al. (eds), *Dictionaire de Spiritualité* (Paris: Beauchene, 1990), vol. 14, pp. 1142–73. See also Hadot, Pierre, *Exercises spirituels et philosophie antique* (Paris: Albin Michel, 1993), pp. 21–74.

2. See Heelas, Paul and Linda Woodhead, *The Spiritual Revolution: Why Religion is Giving Way to Spirituality* (Oxford: Blackwell, 2005). Also see King, R. and J. Carrette, *Selling Spirituality: The Silent takeover of Religion* (London: Routledge, 2005).

3. For a good account of mystical theology, see McIntosh, Mark A., *Mystical Theology* (Oxford: Blackwell, 1998), pp. 18–23.

4. For an excellent survey of this scholarship, see McGinn, Bernard, *The Foundations of Mysticism, Origins to the Fifth Century* (New York: Crossroad, 1997), pp. 291–326. For mystical relativism, see Katz, S. (ed.), *Mysticism and Philosophical Analysis* (Oxford: Oxford University Press, 1978), *Mysticism and Religious Traditions* (Oxford: Oxford University Press, 1973), and *Mysticism and Language* (Oxford: Oxford University Press, 1992). On a more recent version of the perennial philosophy, see Forman, Robert, *Mysticism, Mind, Consciousness* (Albany: SUNY Press, 1999), and on a comparative psychological view of mystical states, founded on Jung and empirical studies with LSD, see Stanislav Grof, *Realms of the Human Unconscious* (New York: Souvenir, 1996). For an argument on the distinction between experience and interpretation, see Ninian Smart, "Understanding Religious Experience," in Katz, *Mysticism and Philosophical Analysis*, pp. 10–21. On mystical language, see Katz (above). On gender and mysticism, see Janzen Grace, *Power, Gender and Christian Mysticism* (Cambridge: Cambridge University Press, 1995).

5. See Smart, Ninian, *Dimensions of the Sacred: An Anatomy of the Worlds' Religious Beliefs* (London: Macmillan, 1996), pp. 169–70. Smart is an important figure in understanding "religious experience" in a broad sense. For a comprehensive overview of Smart's oeuvre, see Shepherd, J. (ed.), *Ninian Smart on World Religions*, 2 vols. (London: Ashgate, 2009).

6. Scholem, Gershom, *Major Trends in Jewish Mysticism* (New York: Schocken Books, 1941).

7. Schimmel, Annemarie, *Mystical Dimensions of Islam* (Chapel Hill: The University of North Carolina Press, 1964).

8. Corbin, Henry, *Spiritual Body and Celestial Earth: From Mazdean Iran to Shi'ite Iran* (Princeton: Princeton Univesrity Press, 1977).

9. See McGinn, *Foundations*, pp. xvii–xviii.

10. de Certeau, M., *The Mystic Fable* (Chicago: University of Chicago Press, 1992), p. 120.

11. On this topic, see Oliver Davies and Denys Turner (eds), *Silence and the Word* (Cambridge: Cambridge University Press, 2002).

12. McGinn, *Foundations*, p. xviii.

13. For tracing this history of nothingness, see George Pattison, *Agnosis: Theology in the Void* (London and New York: Macmillan and St Martins Press, 1996).

14. For a discussion of Porete in this context, see my *The Ascetic Self: Subjectivity, Memory, and Tradition* (Cambridge: Cambridge University Press, 2004), pp. 196–9.

15. de Certeau, *The Mystic Fable*, p. 114.

16. McGinn, *Foundations*, p. 175.

17. On divergent views of the self implied by these theologies, see Sarah Coakley, *Powers and Submissions* (Oxford: Blackwell, 2002), pp. 73–86.
18. Minnis, Alistair, "Affection and Imagination in *The Cloud of Unknowing* and Hilton's *Scale of Perfection*," *Traditio*, vol. 39, 1983, pp. 323–66.
19. Turner, Denys, *The Darkness of God: Negativity in Christian Mysticism* (Cambridge: Cambridge University Press, 1995), p. 187 n. 5.
20. Turner, *Darkness*, p. 191.
21. *Cloud of Unknowing*, p. 17. Phyllis Hodgson (ed.), *The Cloud of Unknowing and the Book of Privy Council* (Early English Text Society, Oxford University Press, 1944), p. 47. Clifton Walters' modern English translation, *The Cloud of Unknowing and Other Works* (London: Penguin, 1961), p. 83.
22. *Cloud of Unknowing*, 4, p. 18.
23. *Cloud of Unknowing*, 4, pp. 16–17. I have followed Denys Turner's practice of citing the original but have made some orthographic changes to make the text more readable for the modern reader. The original reads:

> Lette not therefore [do not give up], bot travayle [work] therin tyl thou fele lyst [longing]. For at the first tyme when thou dost it, thou fyndest bot a darknes, and as it were a cloude of unknowing, thou wost never what [you do not know what this is], saving that thou felist in thi wille a naked entent unto God. This darkness and this cloude is, howsoever thou dost [whatever you do], bitwix thee and thi God, and letteth thee that thou maist not see him cleerly by ligt of understanding in thi reson, ne fele him in swetnes of love in thin affeccion [nor feel him in the sweetness of love in your affection]. And therefore schap [determine] thee to bide in this darknes as longe as thou maist, evermore criing after him that thou lovest; for if ever schalt thou fele him or see him, as it may be here, it behoveth alweis to be in this cloude and in this derknes.

24. *Cloud*, 4, pp. 18–19.
25. Coakley, *Powers and Submissions*, p. 73.
26. *Cloud*, 7, pp. 28–9.
27. Turner, *The Darkness of God*, p. 139.
28. For example, Utpaladeva (early tenth century) writes in his introductory verse to his *Verses on the Recognition of the Lord* (*Īśvarapratyabhijñākārikā* 1.1) that he has in some way attained the state of a servant of God.
29. Conze, E., *Buddhist Wisdom Books* (London: Allen and Unwin, 1982), pp. 93, 101.
30. Suzuki, D.T., *Essays in Zen Buddhism*, third series (London: Rider, 1953), p. 354.
31. Pattison, George, *Agnosi*, pp. 108–37.
32. Shaw, Sarah, *Buddhist Meditation* (London: Routledge, 2009), pp. 39–58.
33. McMahon, Robert, *Understanding the Medieval Meditative Ascent: Augustine, Anselm, Boethius, Dante* (Washington: Catholic University of America Press, 2006), p. 9.
34. Michael, Tara (ed. and trans.), *Le joyau du Śiva-yoga Śivayogaratna de Jñānaprakāśa* (Pondichery: Institut Français d'Indologie, 1975), p. 46.

35. Brown, Norman, *Life Against Death* (London: Routledge & Kegan Paul, 1959), p. 206.
36. *Bhagavad-gītā* 6.11–14.
37. *Cloud*, sections 39–44.
38. Ware, Kallistos, "The Body in Greek Christianity," p. 106. In Coakley, Sara (ed.), *Religion and the Body* (Cambridge: Cambridge University Press, 1997), pp. 90–110.
39. There is a large body of literature here that particularly developed in the 1980s and 1990s and has continued. For a general orientation and a good collection of essays, see Coakley (ed.), *Religion and the Body*; the review article by Richard Roberts "Religion and the Body in Comparative Perspective," *Religion*, 2000, vol. 30, pp. 55–64; and Csordas (ed.), *Embodiment and Experience: the Existential Ground of Culture and Self* (Cambridge: Cambridge University Press, 1994).
40. Brown, *Life Against Death*, p. 310.
41. Brown, *Life Against Death*, p. 310.
42. See the interesting book by Désirée Hirst, *Hidden Riches: Traditional Symbolism from the Renaissance to Blake* (London: Eyre and Spottiswood, 1964); Northrop Frye, *Fearful Symmetry: A Study of William Blake* (Boston: Beacon Press, 1947), p. 153.
43. Brown, *Life Against Death*, chapter 6 ("The Resurrection of the Body"). See also Robin Waterfield, *Jacob Boehme: Essential Readings* (Wellingborough: Crucible, 1989), pp. 39–50.
44. See Partridge, C., *The Re-Enchantment of the West: Alternative Spiritualities, Sacralization, Popular Culture and Occulture* (London: T.&T. Clark, 2006).
45. This understanding of action as having sense and reference is indebted to Ricoeur, "The Model of the Text: Social Action Considered as a Text," in John B. Thompson (trans. and ed.), *Hermenutics and the Human Sciences* (Cambridge: Cambridge University Press, 1981), pp. 204–5.
46. Ricoeur, Paul, *Oneself as Another*, trans. Kathleen Blamey (Chicago: Chicago University Press, 1992), pp. 2–3, 118–19.
47. *Cloud*, p. 29.
48. Urban, Greg "The 'I' of Discourse," in Benjamin Lee and Greg Urban (eds), *Semiotics, Self and Society* (Berlin and New York: Mouton de Gruyter, 1989); Urban, Greg, *Metaculture: How Culture Moves through the World* (Minneapolis and London: University of Minnesota Press, 2001), pp. 108–9. Also see de Certeau, *The Mystic Fable*, pp. 160–4.
49. Cioran, E.M., *The Heights of Despair*, trans. I. Zarifopol-Johnston (Chicago: University of Chicago Press, 1992), p. 123.

Part Two
Speech

The wealth and diversity of speech genres is boundless because the various possibilities of human activity are inexhaustible, and because each sphere of activity contains an entire repertoire of speech genres that differentiate and grow as the particular sphere develops and becomes more complex.

M.M. Bakhtin, "The Problem of Speech Genres," p. 60.
Speech Genres and Other Late Essays, trans. Vern McGee
(Austin: University of Texas Press, 1986)

4

The Reception of the Text

In ninth-century Kashmir, the sage Vasugupta had a dream that Shiva had inscribed the *Shiva Sutras* on a stone at the top of Mahadeva mountain which he then retrieved and recorded; and Moses likewise returned from a mountain with ten "words," the words of the Ten Commandments. Religions prototypically claim to be revelations of something previously concealed or unknown, something transcendent to human life. This revelation is often articulated in a text set aside as sacred or expressed in the life and presence of a particular individual. Thus the Torah is revelation for the Jewish people, the Veda is revelation for the Hindus, the *Qur'an* for the Moslems, and Jesus Christ, witnessed by the New Testament, is revelation for the Christians. The theologies of traditions are reflections on these revelations.

By "revelation" I mean a tradition's account of a display or showing of something about the nature of the world and/or the nature of transcendence that could not otherwise be known. These revelations could be regarded as without author (as in the case of Vedas for some schools) or a theistic reality could be regarded as the source. But all are attempts to show human beings something about what the tradition regards as truth about the world and what lies beyond and behind it; texts with semantic density that make significant claims on those who attempt to follow their teachings and that through following their teachings the full nature of what is shown as life can come to light. Indeed, religions as kinds of showing probably go back many thousands of years to shamanic practices, although we know so little about them other than suggestive hints, for example representations of shaman-like figures on cave walls.

The Importance of Religion: Meaning and Action in Our Strange World,
First Edition. Gavin Flood.
© 2012 Gavin Flood. Published 2012 by Blackwell Publishing Ltd.

The revelations of religions are preserved in text, both oral and written, and are passed through the generations with great care and a strong sense of their importance. The preservation of knowledge thought to be revealed is vital to religions, a knowledge that points to transcendence, points to a future, and points to corrective ways in which human beings should live their lives. Indeed, the preservation of revelation is intimately linked to mimetic action or the repeated acts of ritual, ritual habitus, and calls forth a response in action. Revelation is preserved and is encoded in human behavior and the ethical codes of communities.

Routes to the World of Life

The importance of religion, I have argued, lies in the way it meets human needs to live a meaningful life, and central to this meaning is text set aside as sacred. In this chapter we need to examine the centrality of text for religion and the ways in which it is enacted. Our task here is to present an account of sacred text as a living entity for a community of reception. Sacred texts are generally ancient compositions received by a community within a ritual context or context of religious reading. The relationship of a text believed to be revealed from a non-human source to a community who receives it as sacred is complex and there is often a gap between what a tradition claims about its revelation and what modern scholarship tells us to be the case. Religions might claim that their revelation came to human beings in a pristine state but scholarship shows that these texts were often composed over a long period of time; this is the case with the Veda, whose origin can be located in particular tribal communities in what is now north India. Likewise, the Torah has a long history of composition. The source text cannot be separated from the tradition that carries it and interpretations of the text are incipient from their formation. Traditions of revelation claim to show something important about reality and point to routes to the real; their meanings are generally not locally restricted but are keys to understanding the strangeness of the world. In Bakhtin's terms, we might say that religions' scriptures offer routes to the world of life, to the transcendence of the world of culture, and claim to point to the invisible or to point to light that is the precondition of the visible. Furthermore, they claim that such transcendence is crucial to human well-being and to understanding the world.

"Text" is a category fundamental to culture. Paul Ricoeur defines it as something inscribed by writing.[1] But we do not need to be so restrictive, for there are many texts outside of literate cultures, and unwritten texts have been handed down through the generations often with great accuracy, as with the Veda among the Nambudri Brahmins of Kerala, for example. In ancient India, writing was thought to be a polluting activity and there was a clear understanding that sacred text should not be committed to writing but rather taught orally. Indeed, not only the Vedas but Hindu narratives were handed down orally, the stories told and retold until we have the great epics of today. Similarly philosophy and science were created without the use of literacy, as Staal observes.[2] The link between text, writing, and reasoning seems to be a predominantly western phenomenon: rationality exists without written text as the south Asian examples demonstrate. But text, broadly understood to incorporate oral composition as well, is central to religious meaning and provides the justification for and the reasoning behind certain kinds of action that we would call religious, both ritual and ethical. Fundamental to religions are texts that have been set aside, made sacred, preserved, and revered through many generations.

These texts are often thought to be a revelation from a non-human source and were mostly composed well before the modern era, with some exceptions such as Joseph Smith's *Book of Mormon*, or the writings of the Bahula for the Bahais composed in the nineteenth century. Religious action is fundamental to these texts, as it is through action that the texts are made alive for a community and through action their impact is felt. We might argue that religious action is characterized as the expression of a certain kind of textuality; a textuality that is defined by claiming its source to be outside of the human and in making claims upon the realm of human action. The sacred text tells people what to do and how to behave both in ritual and in everyday transactions, from washing to arranging a marriage.

Religious action can be understood as a kind of textual reception. By this I mean that the text is enacted in both a ritual and a moral space. The Christian sacrament of Holy Communion can be understood in terms of the reception of a revelation textually mediated through the New Testament to a community. The community of reception receives its sacred texts and the messages they contain primarily in a ritual form. The Orthodox Holy Communion is saturated by the text of the Bible. The book itself is revered, processed, and readings from it follow a pattern determined by the liturgical year. While there is solitary reading of the text, it primarily has a ritual function. Even Protestant churches perform the text, although in a less liturgically complex way. The Bible is used as the source of prayers, for preaching, and its recitation is the expression of belief in the non-negotiable word of God. Indeed, in the Protestant churches we have the idea of *sola scriptura*, that the scripture is self-interpreting, that there can be no interpretation of it other than itself. In the Chinese Taoist context, Kristofer Schipper describes how written texts are read during ritual performances which differentiate the classical rites of the *tao-shih*, the "black head" Taoist masters, from the vernacular rites of the *fa-shih*, the Taoist masters of the law who do not read texts but recite them from memory.[3] In both cases the sacred text is integral to the rituals. Similarly Islamic prayer enacts the injunctions of the *Qur'an* and mantras found in the Veda are performed in daily worship.

As I have developed elsewhere, this performance of the text in a ritual setting has three components: the realization of the text, the internalization of the text, and the externalization of the text.[4] In brief summary, a community's sacred text or texts is enacted in ritual, people identify with its message and the stories it tells, and then take that message and those stories into their daily life. In a slightly longer version, the realization of the text is its actual performance: the construction of a sphere of ritual within which the sacred text is brought to life or realized by a particular community within the present. Indeed, the bringing to life of the text can only be done by a community of reception for whom the text is revelation. Through this enacting the text the community participates in the authority of the revelation and the past is brought into a present realization. Textual reception in the religious act thus entails a collapse of time from the past into the present, such that the past is brought to life, ever new in the present. Through religious action or ritual there is a reconfiguring of time; a collapse of the past origin of the revelation into the present and a collapse of the future orientation or goal of revelation into a present realization. Everyday time is in a sense distinct from liturgical time.

This realization of the text in the ritual present is accompanied by the internalization of the text in the subjectivity of the community of reception. This internalization is a kind of transformation, the awakening of the text within the practitioner through the intensity of the liturgical act. The sacred text makes claims upon its community of reception and a shared inwardness is formed through reading or recitation and through liturgical action mediated by the tradition. Furthermore the realization of the text and its internalization in the subjectivity of practitioners impacts upon the extra-ritual world. Thus there is a further stage in that the enactment of the text determines extra-textual and extra-ritual patterns of behavior or ways of life. The text and its liturgical expression constrain events and ways of behaving in the larger world of culture, and nourish life.

The text and its liturgical expression thus have an ethical, legal, and political dimension. Moses, for example, received the Ten Commandments, communicated them to the human community who internalize them and enact them in social life and politics. Through laying claim to action outside of the ritual sphere, the text lays claim to all kinds of human interaction, and so to politics broadly understood. Indeed, this structure of religious action as the realization of the text, the internalization of the text through ritual, and the externalization of the text in ethical, legal, political, and even artistic action, resists explanation purely in terms of socialization, or in terms of the protection of the genes in the thesis of evolutionary boundary protection. The unique nature of religion lies in religious action characterized as a kind of textual reception. We might say, then, that moral action flows from the ritual recapitulation of tradition. Rather than moral action being antithetical to ritual (as sometimes thought), ethics flows from ritual understood as the reception in action of the sacred text. Good speech flows from ritual speech; good deeds from ritual deeds.

Religious action in the three modes of realization, internalization, and externalization of the text penetrates the world of life, to use Bakhtin's phrase, or is itself an interpretation and an attempt to give order to our strange world. Religions as text mediated through action are orientations towards the world of life which give life meaning through reference to something beyond us, either in the future or outside of space and time. There are, of course, other kinds of things that give life meaning – love, a job, a passion for art, sport – but religions are effective structures that open out experiences of transcendence. In penetrating the world of life, religions point to a goal outside the world. They claim to show us something through the repeated, non-identical acts of ritual, and through moral behavior that responds to what life demands of us.

These two kinds of action are linked but distinct. Indeed in the ancient pre-axial religions, ritual action and ethical action were the same. For the Mimamsakas, the performance of *dharma*, duty or virtue, is the performance of correct ritual; for Orthodox Judaism, the performance of correct ritual is the expression of Torah. Yet there is also a pattern in the history of religions in which ritual action has been critiqued by moral action. The Buddha rejected Brahmanical ritual, claiming that the true Brahmin is not one who keeps to ritual purity but someone who is morally upright and acts ethically. John Wesley rejected elaborate liturgical action in favor of the exhortation of the word to act ethically in the world. Yet both kinds of action, ritual and moral, are integral to religions and express, to use another of Bakhtin's phrases, the answerability of life.

The symbolic actions of ritual provide us with a sense of who we are, a sense of identity and social belonging,[5] but they also address fundamental existential questions. Traditionally religions provided people with a total meaning within which to live their lives, but although this is reduced in the secular world, even now religious action provides a framework within which to live and an orientation to the future. All this is understood within the body; religious ritual is fundamentally somatic, and in the field of the body the world of life meets the world of culture. A Roman Catholic's weekly attendance at church is an act that serves to reinforce Catholic behavior outside of that context and gives life a sense of purpose beyond the ordinary. One might also say that the fundamentalist who desires to impose his view through violent means is likewise externalizing the text through what he believes to be its legitimate performance in articulating a specific political end. This is not to equalize kinds of religious action but it is to point to a shared process or structure.

We will defer the problematic relation between "reasonable" religious action (i.e. within law) and "unreasonable" religious action (disruptive of law), but it is germane to point out that both the suicide bomber and the regular attendee at mass enact the heart of their religion in the liturgical moment and both translate that moment into the broader sphere of cultural and political action. Through the ritual realization of the text, through the repeated actions of liturgy, and in the internalization of the text and its externalization in ethical codes and political practices, religious people face the world in a way that allows them a sense of transcendence and a sense that their lives are constrained by a non-material power or powers which can have profound impact on the world, not only in the existential particularity of a life but on global politics and civilizations.

To sum up so far, I have sketched an argument that religious communities are formed by the reception of their sacred texts. People enact, recite, read, and sing their scriptures. The enactment of these texts helps the practitioner to absorb them and this informs other aspects of life. Thus a good Moslem expresses the Qu'ranic text in prayer and performs its injunctions in other areas of life. The Christian liturgy is an enactment of text; the Christian narrative of Jesus' death and resurrection. The Theravada monk's recitation of the *pratimokṣa* is the ritual enactment of the monastic discipline that guides and structures the monastic's life on the way to enlightenment.

Theories of the Text

In previous chapters I have argued that one of the distinguishing features of religion that marks it out from other cultural practices is bringing the community of believers into the world of action through ritual and injunction to act in moral ways. Another way of looking at this is from the perspective of the text, to see religious action through the lens of the text or the text as metaphor for action. To develop this idea and the distinctive quality of religious text, we need a more robust understanding of textuality. What then is a text and what is a *sacred* text?

Texts have been with human beings for a very long time and we might even take text to be a defining feature of human culture. The Bible is arguably the foundation text of western civilization – although Homer or Virgil might also be contenders– and for thousands of years people have been speculating about what it means. The Veda can be taken to be the foundation texts of south Asian civilization, however little understood it is. And along with texts we have their simultaneous interpretation, which begins with their production. There are long histories of the interpretation of texts in Chinese, south Asian, Middle Eastern, and European civilizations down to the present day.

Some of the contemporary problems concern the "correct" and "incorrect" interpretation of texts and how we can distinguish between them.

So far I have been speaking about the idea of a text in vague terms, attempting to generalize the internal perspective of religions, but there is also the question of external, scholarly, and critical accounts. Is interpretation enough or should we not also have critique, especially from socially critical perspectives that have sought to lay bare the power discourse innate within textual traditions and expose the inequalities they espouse? Modern critical discourse can expose power difference or reveal occluded voices of gays and women, for example. If critique exposes the socio-historical conditions of narrative and even the act of interpretation itself, then it stands outside of interpretation. But does it necessarily stand outside of tradition? Can there be a genuine Christian feminist reading of the Bible or a Marxist Hindu reading of the Upanishads? I think that this certainly stretches the boundaries and probably stands outside the liturgical-narrative tradition, although clearly such readings have an important place in contemporary interpretation. And if interpretation is so central to tradition, how can we establish correct from distorted interpretations, if not by appeal to some external, true reality? But in this case, how do we have access to that reality?

If interpretation cannot appeal to "true reality," then it can only establish a coherent picture and then the question arises as to what the criteria of judgment are between competing interpretations. This is a complex question that we shall revisit in Chapter 6. When religious texts or teachers make empirical claims, they are liable to be tested against "true reality," but when the claims are not empirical we simply have competing interpretations. These are well winnowed problems and the history of interpretation has developed different response to them. Charles Taylor (again) has a useful definition of interpretation. He writes:

> Interpretation ... is an attempt to make clear, to make sense of, an object of study. This object must, therefore, be a text, or a text-analogue, which in some way is confused, incomplete, cloudy, seemingly contradictory – in one way or another, unclear. The interpretation aims to bring to light an underlying coherence or sense.[6]

Interpretation on this view is a task of clarification and is an intellectual discourse to be distinguished from textual enactment of the kind I have outlined above. This clarification involves understanding which itself entails "prejudice" in Gadamer's terms, or "forestructures" in Heidegger's terms, of "forehaving" (*Vorhabe*), "foresight" (*Vorsicht*), and "foreconception" (*Vorbegriff*). An interpretation is "grounded in something we grasp in advance – a foreconception."[7] Gadamer develops Heidegger's understanding of hermeneutics in that once free from scientific notions of objectivity we can do justice to the historicity of understanding. He writes:

> A person who is trying to understand a text is always projecting. He projects a meaning for the text as a whole as soon as some initial meaning emerges in the text. Again, the initial meaning emerges only because he is reading the text with particular expectations in regard to a certain meaning. Working out this foreprojection, which is constantly revised in terms of what emerges as he penetrates into the meaning, is understanding what is there.[8]

This is the hermeneutic circle; the meaning is gradually illumined by repeated readings. This implies that the text is a totality, a complete entity, and it is this completion that functions as a constraint upon interpretation. There is an "anticipation of completeness" (*Vollkommenheit*) and this understanding is part of interpretation, which is necessary for any understanding at all: there could be no passive reception of the text and meaning occurs because of preconception. Thus a revealed, sacred text breaks open its meaning for the practitioner in the act of interpretation. On this view, according to Gadamer, truth is arrived at through tradition-constrained understanding in contrast to a "method" of the objectivist sciences.[9] Culture (*Bildung*) is more important to understanding than method. A more extreme version of this view is that of deconstruction as practiced by Derrida. As there is no inherent relationship between signifier and signified, all that we have is a differential network of meaning: signifier becomes divorced from signified and we are left with a network of texts and their interconnections; a network of meanings without access to some external criteria of truth.[10]

The trouble with this view is that it opens up the category "text" to include almost anything; any cultural practice could be considered as a text – tattoos on the body, or a fashion show. We need a narrower understanding to distinguish text from other cultural productions. Although I am making a claim that ritual action can be understood as "entextualization," this is not to confuse action or even body with text itself. We need to maintain a clear notion of text in order to understand what is being internalized by practitioners and what is being externalized in daily life. Religious action is suffused by the text, but is itself text only by analogy. The realization of the text that I have spoken of above is the reception of the text as text within the present ritual situation. This involves reading (for those who can) and more importantly its aural and ritual reception by the community: a reception which is always communal even when a ritual is performed alone. Gracia is helpful in clarifying the idea of text from non-text. He defines text as "a group of entities, used as signs, which are selected, arranged, and intended by an author in a certain context to convey some specific meaning to an audience."[11] That is, a text is not simply any event that can be interpreted but a specific kind of entity within language. Furthermore we need to distinguish, says Gracia, between "text" and "work." The work is the work itself and the text the actual instances of it. Thus *Moby Dick* is a work with particular textual instantiations some of which are slightly different – a Spanish translation is a different text of the same work, for example. This distinction is implied in philology in establishing a critical edition where manuscript sources are "witnesses" to the work. This is, however, a controversial distinction and some scholars have rejected it on the grounds that it is too Platonic: each text is in fact a work.[12]

The Reception of Sacred Texts

There are problems with this distinction. If a work develops over time in different and expanded versions such that the original is far removed from what it eventually becomes, are we dealing with one work in different versions or do the newer versions become a new work? These are difficult questions but the work/text distinction is nevertheless important. For our purposes we can take a religious scripture to be composition in language, relatively fixed or established, handed down through the generations in oral or written form, that is set aside as having a particular quality. Thus the *NetraTantra* was handed down through a line of scribes. This quality we might call "sacred," but to avoid the connotation of the term being in distinction to "secular," it is perhaps clearer to call this quality "semantic density," a term now generally in use in theology but first coined by Nelson Goodman in relation to aesthetics.[13] The semantic density of a text allows it to be read and re-read and always be enriching. While in theory any text could be a sacred text if understood and enacted in that way by a community of reception, in practice only semantically rich texts, which are well winnowed through the generations become established in this way. Thus the *Lotus Sutra* and the Bible are liturgical, semantically dense texts that are set aside and received by their communities of reception as sacred, whereas Yann Martel's *Life of Pi*, for all its merits, could probably never become a text like this. Thus the sacred text is not simply constructed by the community of reception but by the very nature of the text itself.

This quality of semantic density, the propensity to be read and re-read repeatedly without semantic exhaustion, might be shared by other texts, such as great poetry for example. It is then, the combination of semantic density along with liturgical reception that defines a text as sacred. The same text, of course, could exist simply as semantically rich text without a liturgical reception. The Bible can be and is read by thousands of people simply as literature or read philologically by the critical historian with no sense of, or attempt at, liturgical reception. Indeed the same person could read the Bible as literature on one occasion and then receive it as sacred in Christian liturgy on another occasion. Griffiths has referred to two kinds of reading, religious and consumerist,[14] although I would not wish to concede that the "consumerist" mode of reading is somehow morally inferior, although it is clearly different. To receive or read the text religiously is to allow the text to come to life in ritual, to make it live and be relevant to the present moment and to bring the community of reception into the here and now, into the world. To read the text as a scholar is to keep it at a critical distance. To read the text as literature is more ambiguous, as literature penetrates the world of life but in a non-liturgical mode. To read the text as a religious practice is to collapse the distinction between self and text. A single person could arguably read the same text in all three modes.

The liturgical reception of sacred text is an intensification of the present moment for a community. This also involves the quality of temporal collapse: that is, time is condensed into the present in the reception of sacred text. The text embodies a voice from the past that is vivified and made to live for some community or person. The realization of the text is just this temporal collapse, which also looks to the future and enacts a future salvation or liberation. Thus the Christian liturgy gives expression to the voice of the text from the past, which simultaneously looks to the future and the coming of God's kingdom. The Moslem call to prayer embodies the voice of the *Qur'an* that in its collective participation also looks to the future judgment. A service or *pūjā* in the ShriVaishnava (*śrīvaiṣṇava*) temple of ShriRangam enacts the Pancaratra (*pāñcarātra*) texts, the priest enouncing the texts' mantras, which looks to the future state of quiescence in the being of the Lord Narayana (*nārāyaṇa*), a form of Vishnu. The Theravada Buddhist meditation group recapitulates the story of the Buddha's enlightenment in the very act of sitting and practicing mindfulness of breathing and so looking to the future end of suffering. Examples could be multiplied.

The collapse of the past into the present in the reception of sacred texts, which is the realization of the text, also entails the temporary eradication of agency. In the liturgical act agency is handed over to the tradition in a kind of asceticism. My life conforms to the life of the text and tradition, and my will becomes one with the will of the text. Any Kantian autonomy is given up to a heteronomy of the ritual act. Furthermore, this is expressed in bodily imitation in ritual. The practitioners make their bodies conform to the dictates of the ritual tradition in repeated acts in which individual will is made to conform to the collective will of the tradition. Indeed, it is through this conformity to tradition and to the master (Christ, the guru, the priest) that transformation occurs. One of the reasons why religions do not die out is because they feed people in this way; they give meaning beyond the individual and satisfy the need for meaning through the act of self-erasure. The bodies of practitioners recapitulate tradition in imitation through the generations, and the communities of reception receive meaning and enrichment by this process. This process is so important that people are willing to die for it.

Once the ritual is over, once the meditation is finished, people go to their homes, but the process of liturgical reception is not complete. The text, realized in the liturgical act, is again recapitulated in the moral behavior outside of the ritual setting. The Buddhist tries to be a good Buddhist, the Christian a good Christian. This is to give life meaning by locating oneself within a broader cosmos and to bring text and action together into close proximity. In understanding ritual action as the enactment of text, we are in a sense understanding action in a way analogous to text. Ricoeur made this move many years ago in his consideration of meaningful action considered as a text. Part of his project was to claim that if social action displays some features constitutive of a text, then the human sciences are akin to the social sciences with regard to their object. This argument is relevant to the thesis presented here about ritual act expressing text because of the parallel implied between text and act.

Sacred Text and Act

Ricoeur's thesis is that the human sciences may be said to be hermeneutical in so far as their object (social action, society, etc.) displays some features constitutive of a text, and their method develops the same procedures as text interpretation. Two questions arise from this thesis, namely to what extent is text a good paradigm for the object of the social sciences, and to what extent may we use the method of text interpretation as a paradigm for the interpretation of social action and for the human sciences in general? Ricoeur makes a distinction between written and spoken discourse in so far as the latter contains non-textual elements such as intonation and gesture; the dialogue between two people refers to the shared situation in which they find themselves. The written text therefore frees its meaning from the particular situation, from ostensive reference, as its meaning is not confined to the dialogical speech situation of actual conversation. Because of this, writing is also free from the author's intention. Spoken discourse has ostensive reference because it can be understood only by the speakers who are sharing in the particular situation and any misunderstanding can be remedied by the speaker through clarification or intonation. Written discourse, by contrast, entails that any lack of clarity is remedied through interpretation. There is no ostensive reference in written discourse (except direct speech situations within the text but not within the world), and it is addressed to anyone who can read, not simply the second person of direct address.[15]

To what extent then, asks Ricoeur, can we say that the object of the human sciences conforms to the paradigm of the text? If the object of the human sciences is meaningful behavior, as Weber stressed, then to what extent can we replace meaningful behavior by "readability characters?" In response to these questions, Ricoeur argues that meaningful action may become the object of the human sciences in so far as action is like a speech act. It has propositional content (as in the statement "Brutus killed Caesar," which can be understood outside of any context whether or not Brutus killed Caesar) and it has illocutionary force as in a speech act which promises something or threatens. An action, once performed by an agent, goes beyond the agent and develops consequences of its own. Thus, as a text becomes detached from its author and has unintended effects, so an action becomes detached from its agent. An action is like a speech act. Completed actions go beyond the immediate environment of their occurrence and can have wider consequences. It is in this sense that acts become historical. "History," writes Ricoeur, "is this quasi-'thing' *on* which human action leaves a 'trace', puts its mark."[16] An action can exceed ostensive reference and go beyond the social conditions of its immediate production, and, like a text, address an indefinite number of possible "readers."

Drawing this parallel between action and text is very suggestive in our context. The meaning of the ritual act exceeds the intentionality of the actors and so the meaning can be detached from the event as the meaning of a text can be detached from authorial intention. But what is interesting here is that in the liturgical act, in the ritual moment, the sacred text and ritual action become one. The meaning of the text is completely intertwined with the meaning of the action. For example, Hindu tantric ritual involves a preliminary rite of the purification of the body or more precisely, the purification of the elements of the body (*bhūtaśuddhi*). In this rite the body becomes entextualized: the sacred text is mapped onto the body in a hierarchical sequence and mantras from the text uttered at each stage of the purification process.[17] The text and the rite are fused together and the rite exceeds the intention of the ritual agent in the sense that he participates in the broader tradition and his textualized action is marked as non-identical repetition. The singularity and unrepeatability of the act itself is yet repeated each day but, inevitably, never exactly the same. The consequences of the act go beyond the agent's intention because he cannot foresee how this act will affect others, nor anticipate the unseen consequences (the purification and building up of merit).

If by sacred text we mean a text realized in the present moment through action, then action becomes entextualized. Developing this idea we might also say that the location of action becomes entextualized and by extension, other sacred locations. The forming of a sacred geography, the forming of a cosmology, is in a sense a textual formation of the landscape. To what extent this could be true for prehistoric peoples is difficult to say; the sacred geography of stone and wood circles, barrows, and hill forts on southern

England's chalk downland might be the mapping out of a textuality that is long forgotten. Certainly the network of pilgrimage sites in India is closely linked to the texts and narratives they contain. The sacred sites (*pīṭha*) of the goddess are places of semantic density justified textually by the myth of the death of Sati. The goddess married Shiva but his father in law, Daksha, disapproved of him. Daksha organized a large sacrifice but did not invite Shiva, his daughter's husband. Sati was distraught, and in her distress self-combusted through the power of her yoga, burning herself to death in protest. Shiva, on hearing of this, danced a frenzied dance carrying the corpse of his wife above his head. The other gods fearing the destructive energy of the dance would destroy the universe asked Vishnu to cut up her body with his discus which he duly did. Where different parts of her body fell, there is a sacred pilgrimage site. These form a network of place for the enactment of the religion.[18]

Conclusion

I have argued that sacred texts need to be understood as enacted and so their reception is not simply a cognitive act but is a bodily act that shares in our gestures, postures, and expressions within a community. By way of summary we might say that the voice of the sacred text, the community's revelation, is received by a community of reception and brought to life in the ritual act. Through the realization of the text in the present moment the past is enlivened. This reception of text is not restricted to reading, as most religious practitioners through history have probably been illiterate. Furthermore, this enlivening of the text entails its internalization in the practitioners and the externalization of the text in daily life and ethical behavior. The sacred text is made my own and my life made to conform to tradition. We now need to examine more closely the idea of language and look at the claim of universalism implicit in my account.

Notes

1. Ricoeur, P., *Hermeneutics and the Human Sciences*, trans. John B. Thompson (Cambridge: Cambridge University Press, 1981), p. 145.
2. Staal, Frits, "The Independence of Rationality from Literacy," *European Journal of Sociology*, vol. 30, 1989, pp. 301–10.
3. Schipper, Kristofer, "Vernacular and Classical Ritual in Taoism," *Journal of Asian Studies*, vol. 45 (1), 1985, pp. 21–57. *The Taoist Body*, trans. Karen C. Duval (London, Los Angeles, Berkeley: California University Press, 1993), pp. 49, 55–60.
4. Flood, Gavin, "Dwelling on the Borders: Self, Text, and World," *Temenos*, vol. 44 (1), 2008, pp. 13–34.

5. Although I do not pursue this angle, social identity theory, that individuals identify with the groups to which they belong, is relevant to the general framework presented here and its findings could well be applicable to religions. See Tajfel, H. and Turner, J. C., "The Social Identity Theory of Inter-group Behavior," in Jost, T. and J. Sidanius (eds), *Political Psychology: Key Readings in Social Psychology* (New York: Psychology Press, 2004), pp. 276–93.

6. Taylor, Charles, "Interpretation and the Human Sciences," in *Philosophy and the Human Sciences: Philosophical Papers II* (Cambridge: Cambridge University Press, 1985), p. 15.

7. Heidegger, Martin, *Being and Time*, trans. John McQuarry and Edward Robinson (Oxford: Blackwell, 1962), p. 191.

8. Gadamer, Hans-Georg, *Truth and Method*, second edition, trans. Joel Weinsheimer and Donald G. Marshall (London: Sheed and Ward, 1993 (1975)), p. 267.

9. Grondin, Jean, *Introduction to Philosophical Hermeneutics*, trans. Joel Weinsheimer (New Haven: Yale University Press, 1994), p. 109. This is certainly a good account of interpretation by religious communities of their texts, although on this account there is no way of telling whether incomprehension is the fault of the reader or the text. This is why, arguably, to circumvent this problem we need some idea of phenomenology as descriptive and revealing structures of the text itself through philology.

10. Derrida, J., *Of Grammatology*, trans. GayatriSpivak (Baltimore and London: Johns Hopkins University Press, 1974), pp. 10–18.

11. Gracia, Jorge J.E., *A Theory of Textuality: The Logic and Epistemology* (Albany: SUNY Press, 1995), p. 38.

12. For a good discussion, see Greetham, D.C., *Theories of the Text* (Oxford: Oxford University Press, 1999), pp. 44–51

13. Goodman, Nelson, *Languages of Art: An Approach to a Theory of Symbols* (Indianapolis: Hackett Publishing Company, 1976). pp. 252–5. Cited in Giovannelli, Alessandro, "Goodman's Aesthetics," *The Stanford Encyclopedia of Philosophy* (Summer 2010 Edition), Edward N. Zalta (ed.) (http://plato.stanford.edu/archives/sum2010/entries/goodman-aesthetics/; accessed August 17, 2010).

14. Griffiths, Paul, *Religious Reading: The Place of Reading in the Practice of Religion* (Oxford University Press, 1999), pp. 44–5.

15. Ricoeur, Paul, "The Model of the Text: Meaningful Action Considered as a Text," p. 201, in *Hermeneutics and the Human Sciences*, pp. 197–221.

16. Ricoeur, "The Model of the Text," p. 207.

17. See Flood, Gavin, "Text Reception and Ritual in Tantric Scriptural Traditions," in J. Schaper (ed.), *Der Textualisierung der Religion* (Tubingen: Mohr Siebeck, 2008), pp. 241–9.

18. On the importance of place and space see Knott, Kim, *The Location of Religion, A Spatial Analysis* (London and Oakville: Equinox, 2005) and Tweed, Thomas A., *Dwelling and Crossing: A Theory of Religion* (Cambridge, Mass: Harvard University Press, 2006).

5

Tradition, Language, and the Self

In Book 7 of the *Republic* Plato tells the famous story of the cave through a dialogue between Socrates and his friend Glaucon. Imagine, says Socrates, humans living underground in "a cave-like dwelling, with an entrance a long way up." The people have been there since childhood fixed in their place by bonds which do not enable them to turn around. Behind and above them a fire provides light and all the prisoners can see are shadows cast by the fire dancing on the wall before them. They take these shadows to be reality. If one of these strange prisoners were to be released from his bonds, turn around, and be dragged into the sunlight he would be dazzled by what he saw. The world of the cave is the visible world in which we dwell; a prison. The fire inside the cave is like the power of the sun (although not the sun) and the path out of the shadows into the sunlight is the path from this world to the intelligible world or higher world where the forms exist, the pure essences of the universe particularly truth, the good, and beauty.[1] This is a fine image for the idea of mystical ascent that we saw in Chapter 3, which contrasts the unreality of our world of shadows with the bright intensity of the real world outside the cave. Many religions are like this in claiming to guide people from relative darkness and ignorance into the true light.

This image conveys the idea that there are objective, universal truths, in particular the truth of the sun, the source of everything, and that the shadows on the cave walls are but reflections of that truth. Freedom lies in freedom from the bondage of shadows and the journey into the light. While this is an image of the spiritual journey from darkness into light, from ignorance into knowledge, it is also an image for truth as undivided and almost monolithic. The sun is the real, the true, to which everything owes its

The Importance of Religion: Meaning and Action in Our Strange World,
First Edition. Gavin Flood.
© 2012 Gavin Flood. Published 2012 by Blackwell Publishing Ltd.

appearance and all language, in the end, points to it. Indeed, on this view there are universal forms that constrain all human beings and were we able to turn our eyes to that source we would be free. This is also a metaphor for the inadequacy of language to convey the splendour of the true but we are left in no doubt that there is such a truth and that the world we experience is but a grey shadow of it.

With this rich metaphor we have a number of interpretations. The most obvious is the one provided by Plato himself, that spiritual progress entails moving from the world of shadows or the imagination to faith or belief, to thought, and thence to understanding (*noesis*) when we see the sun. This interpretation might extend into language itself where we have a variety of human languages all of which express, albeit inadequately, the truth of the ideas or referents behind the words. There are universal semantic units that are expressed in particular languages. Thus on this view we might see various religious languages in different traditions as ways of conveying the same, unitary truth of a transcendent reality represented by the sun. Plato believed that we all share or have access to universal, common ideas in a world beyond the material, outside of the dark cave, and that these universal forms constrain or determine their expression in the world.

While the metaphysical claims of Plato have been largely rejected in philosophy, the issue of whether there are human universals, particularly of language, is still very current. This question is highly relevant to our problem of religion. If, as I have argued, human beings are meaning-constructing and meaning-needing beings, and if religions seek to address spiritual need, the desire for cosmic meaning which is shared by human beings, then this question is intimately linked to the question of human universals. We have seen how religions are inseparably connected to the body, how they produce particular kinds of bodily habitus, and how, while religious doctrines are themselves extremely diverse, repeated patterns of somatic gesture and posture along with the internalization of texts and narratives are shared across cultures. The other side of the coin, as it were, is language. Alongside human action – the movement of the body and bodily orientation in space – we have language and the use of language in concrete situations. In the context of spiritual traditions, we have seen that language has its limits and spiritual languages reach into silence. But long before we get there, the vast range of human language and the human competence to speak are obvious grounds for seeking shared meaning and common structures of thinking that are relevant to my claim that religions are expressions of and responses to human desire for meaning, and so we need some account of how human beings make meaning – a question intimately linked to language and what we share and do not share.

Underlying this idea of shared meanings, or rather the shared capacity for meaning formation, is a version of the "psychic unity of humankind" doctrine that in earlier Christian centuries was expressed in the idea that there is a common human nature. But before we can make any such claim we need to examine the idea whether human beings share linguistic and cognitive capacities, or whether our linguistic categories and abilities are purely culturally constructed and so historically bound. Whether religion is a shared category will partly depend upon the extent to which we share language capacity. The debate about linguistic universals has been heated at times and not without political dimensions; the claim of universals can be seen in political terms as a backlash against a colonialist and potentially racialist relativism, while the reaction against universals can be seen as a desire to acknowledge the legitimacy and authenticity of indigenous languages and cultures (quite the opposite of any colonialist enterprise).[2] Let us examine this issue and see how it is pertinent to the study of religions. I wish to begin with an account of semantic universals and then to contrast this with examples of the linguistic relativity thesis. We will then be in a position to draw from this a soft relativist argument about the universality of religion.

Linguistic Universals

Although bereft of any religious or explicitly Platonic connotation, in more recent years in linguistics the idea of universals of human language finds its expression in Noam Chomsky's universal structures of language and his idea of competence. Chomsky, reacting against the behaviorism of his day in the 1960s, proposed a model of language or specifically grammar "concerned with discovering a mental reality underlying actual behaviour."[3] This mental reality referred to the competence of speakers, their knowledge of language, which constrains the actual use of language or performance. Chomsky advocated the study of competence before performance in order to create as complete a picture as possible of the structures of language and the universal grammar which underlies performance. Later generations of linguistic anthropologists focused on performance rather than competence, and while accepting the ability to produce language as an innate capacity of human beings, they wished to emphasize the great diversity of linguistic performance and so questioned some of Chomsky's claims. But before turning to this work let us take one more example of a claim to language universals, this time not so much regarding structure as actual semantic and lexical units, that is, universal words and ideas.

Anna Wierzbicka develops what she has called a "natural semantic metalanguage" (NSM),[4] according to which there are common units or semantic primitives across languages: "All types of meanings ... can be rigorously described and insightfully compared in terms of the same set of universal semantic primitives and the metalanguage based on them."[5] This

NSM comprises basic units of meaning or semantic primitives and syntax for their combination. A semantic primitive is a term whose meaning cannot be defined by other expressions and which is universal or found as a lexical item in all natural languages.

Wierzbicka lists a number of these and the number has varied from fourteen in earlier publications to fifty-five, among the most important being the "substantives," I, YOU, SOMEONE, SOMETHING, PEOPLE; the "determiners," THIS, THE SAME, OTHER; and the "quantifiers," ONE, TWO, MANY (MUCH), ALL. There are also "mental predicates," THINK, KNOW, WANT, FEEL, "speech" SAY; and "actions and events," DO, HAPPEN.[6] There is no language in the world in which one cannot say I or YOU even though in some languages, due to politeness, these are expressed indirectly. These semantic universals refer to what Wierzbicka calls the "psychological subject" and which, following Urban, I have referred to in terms of indexicality (see p. 95). By this she means that I and YOU can occur with the mental predicates THINK, KNOW, WANT, FEEL, SEE, and HEAR, and also with the action predicate DO, as in "You/I did something bad."[7]

Some of this work is intuitively not surprising and Wierzbicka presents a strong case for NSM, but actual NSM items remain at a very general and vague level and it is not clear that, for example, the NSM THINK is sufficient to cover the English word "think," which might include within it the semantic range "consider," "reflect," and "contemplate," as well as Sanskrit verbs "to think," derived from the roots *man* (*manyate*), *cint* (*cintayati*), or even "to remember," *smr̥* (*smarati*). The semantic range of *cint* and *smr̥* include meditation or visualization which the English "think" does not. In other words, NSM operates at a very general level and is not sufficiently nuanced to provide much particularly useful culture-specific analysis. Also, in restricting her observations about semantic universals to lexical items, Wierbzbicka glides over significant structural differences between languages which constrain, if not determine, cultural forms and individual behavior. It is to these accounts of the relation between linguistic structures, behavior, and cultural norms that we must turn before we can present some account of universality and relativity in respect of religions.

Linguistic Relativity

In contrast to Chomsky's stress on language competence, universal grammar, and Wierzbicka's search for semantic universals, counterbalancing positions have developed in linguistics and anthropology that emphasize performance and insist on the cultural particularity of linguistic utterances. The turn to performance, in Duranti's terms, "allows us to broaden the analytic horizon of language use,"[8] particularly the emphasis on the potentially infinite generation of sentences from finite rules and the creativity of language speakers, individuals' contribution to particular situations, the way things are said, and the role of the audience in the formation of meaning.[9] In contrast to an emphasis on abstract structure, the turn to performance has allowed the study of language use to demonstrate that the way utterances are made, their context, and who is speaking, has political and social implications.

This stress on performance not only responds to Chomsky but develops a line of linguistic anthropology in the United States from Franz Boas to Sapir and Whorf which stresses the diversity of language and linguistic performance. What became known as the Sapir-Whorf hypothesis, put simply, claimed that the structures of language influence thinking (and so culture). This tradition has developed in more recent years with a revitalization and revision of the linguistic relativity hypothesis that "differences among languages in the grammatical structuring of meaning influence habitual thought."[10] A classic formulation of the hypothesis is stated by Whorf in the following terms:

> We dissect nature along lines laid down by our native languages. The categories and types that we isolate from the world of phenomena we do not find there because they stare every observer in the face; on the contrary, the world is presented in a kaleidoscopic flux of impressions which has to be organised by our minds – and this means largely by the linguistic systems in our minds. We cut nature up, organise it into concepts, and ascribe significance as we do, largely because we are parties to an agreement to organise it in this way – an agreement that holds throughout our speech community and is codified in the patterns of our language.[11]

Thus, users of different grammars are: "pointed towards different types of observations and different evaluations of externally similar facts of observation, and hence are not equivalent as observers but must arrive at somewhat different views of the world."[12]

Whorf argues that language can unite different aspects of reality by giving these aspects similar linguistic treatment. That is, by analogy we identify one area of our experience with another and group events together as "the same" because of this linguistic identification. Whorf gives his famous example of men smoking by empty gasoline drums in the false belief that because the drums are "empty" it is safe to smoke. On the contrary, it is highly dangerous. By analogy they associated the word "empty" with "safe," which has affected the behavior of the workers and led them to smoke by the empty drums.[13] We are predisposed to acting in the world in particular ways because of the linguistic categories that form the basis of our language. Our beliefs are therefore, according to Whorf, influenced if not determined by our language. Furthermore the basic grammatical structure of a language can formulate cultural beliefs and ideas.

He illustrates this by contrasting what he calls Standard Average European (SAE) with the Native American language Hopi. SAE, Whorf, argues, has a three-tense system – past, present, future – in contrast to Hopi which does not, but rather has two basic tenses of now and other. Speakers of SAE treat cyclic events such as the passing of the day, that is, the passage of time, in the same way as they treat other object nouns (such as "chalk," "paper," or "sheep"), namely, as a substance. This is in sharp contrast to Hopi which treats time cyclically in terms of recurrent events and does not treat time as a substance. This grammatical difference, claims Whorf, gives rise to funda-mental differences of worldview. Thus in SAE the three-tense system has allowed for the development of a metaphorical space in which abstractions can be projected, such as the idea of time itself and the notion of history, which contrasts with Hopi which has a cyclic understanding of time and in which one day follows much like the next and so no abstraction and development of "history" would be possible.[14]

The strong version of the thesis that there is a *causal* link between the structures of language and the way we think has been controversial and Whorf's findings have been questioned by some linguistic anthropologists, particularly his understanding of Hopi time categories[15] and, most famously, the critique and counter claim by Berlin and Kay that there are indeed universals across languages, particularly color. They researched into color coding schemes across a wide range of languages.[16] Berlin and Kay argued that all languages operate with a small number of basic color terms which, it can be shown, develop in a sequence such that if the number of color terms in a particular language is known, what those colors are could be predicted. Thus black, white, and red are foundational and common color categories.

This work in turn has been subject to criticism on the grounds, for example, that high saturation color chips were used that would never occur in local, forest, or rural environments of the language communities asked to identify colors, but more particularly the Berlin and Kay data, in Lucy's words, is "characterised by a theoretical vision of a decontextualized 'natural' word-object relationship."[17] Lucy emphasizes the problematic nature of ignoring significant structural differences between languages in favor of an intuitive understanding of the correspondence between lexical items and their referents. This procedure, Lucy argues, is faulty in that from the start it assumes that only the "denotational value of colour terms with respect to hue, brightness and saturation will be considered," and so "all languages will look like English"[18] because structural dimensions of lan-guage and contextual use have been excluded a priori from the analysis. English is tacitly assumed to be "natural" in characterizing objective reality, perhaps one reason for the thesis' having been widely accepted "despite the obvious circularity of the procedure."[19]

In support of a modified version of the linguistic relativity thesis, Lucy compares the performance of English and Yucatek speakers. He tests fairly narrow hypotheses, for example that English speakers attend to the shape and number of objects more than Yucatek speakers, and that English speakers tend to group objects according to a common shape whereas Yucatec speakers group objects according to substance.[20] This more recent support for linguistic relativity has been developed particularly in relation to spatial awareness by Levinson and others. For example, the Australian language of Guugu Ymithirr spoken in northern Queensland contains spatial categories and a spatial awareness that differs significantly to English and other languages. Thus "[i]nstead of notions like 'in front of,' 'behind,' 'to the left of,' 'opposite,' etc. . . . Guugu Ymithirr speakers must specify locations . . . as 'to the North of,' 'to the South of,' 'to the East of,' etc."[21] There is some evidence, then, that basic linguistic categories, such as those of spatial direction, influence or constrain bodily habitus, people's bodily life and experience.

I have presented a fairly lengthy discussion of the issue of linguistic relativity as it is clearly important for understanding religions across cultures if religions are, as I and others claim, cultural forms. In Gumpertz's summary, (1) differences exist in linguistic categories across cultures and (2) linguistic categories determine aspect of thinking. Therefore (3) "aspects of individuals' thinking differ across linguistic communities according to the language they speak."[22] The broad point that the structures of language influence the way we think and more generally our broader cultural horizon and worldview is well made within the linguistic anthropological tradition. Clearly there are meanings in one language which do not have direct equivalents in another and even meanings that cannot be adequately expressed in another. But perhaps we need to be more cautious or nuanced in accepting Whorf's point that the very experience of life itself is determined by the languages we inhabit.

Let us take stock of our discussion so far. The position that grammatical categories affect thinking is not incompatible with the idea of semantic universals. The evidence of careful empirical studies demonstrates how people's understanding and experience of the world is closely related to the linguistic categories they inhabit and anyone with acquaintance of more than one language will be familiar with problems of translation. Languages are relative to cultures and express cultural forms and religions are cultural forms and so closely tied to language (as we have seen).

The problem of universals, the question raised so poetically by Plato, depends upon what we understand to be shared and not shared between cultures and peoples. While language categories influence thought and cultural experience, it is also the case that there are not only lexical items but experiences foundational to being human that, while being culturally mediated, are in some sense shared. I am particularly thinking about the experience of being a body, of being embodied, and the way in which language rests upon or assumes our embodiment. Indeed this is borne out by work in both anthropology and linguistics; for example, in the work of George Lakoff and Mark Johnson, who have underlined the metaphorical use of language, showing how the body is central in this process.[23] There is therefore evidence for a soft relativist position as regards language: linguistic categories influence thought and constrain the ways in which we both classify and experience the world, but language itself is rooted in the shared human experience of being a body in the world.

Language and Religious Experience

How then is this relevant to our understanding of religion? It would seem to be the case that language influences fundamental bodily orientations such as spatial and possibly temporal awareness, but to what extent language influences higher level cognitive functions, particularly religious experience, is not clear. In the 1970s some scholars argued for a strong connection between religious, particularly mystical, experience and language, against an earlier view that there is a common core to mystical experience beyond language or that there are distinct types.[24] It is not my intention here to review this literature but rather to present two examples of the ways in which language informs the bodily habitus of people who inhabit their religions, before moving on to a more general discussion. The first example is from an ethnography of Mexican immigrants in Los Angeles, the second from an ethnography from Kerala.

In a study of Mexican immigrants in California, Baquedano-Lopez describes how the identities of teachers and students are formed within a shared narrative of tradition. In religious doctrine classes, stories of individual lives are understood within the context of religious teachings and "a traditional religious narrative becomes not only a story to live by, it affirms and contests the community's past, present, and possible stories."[25] A popular story tells of a Mexican peasant, Juan Diego, who had a vision of the Virgin Mary at Mount Tepayac near Mexico City in 1531.

The Virgin Mother appeared to him in the form of an Aztec woman and addressed him in the Aztec language Nahuatl. A shrine was built on the site and Diego spent his remaining seventeen years in attendance giving the Virgin's message of hope in the face of colonial oppression.[26] The important point is that a Mexican Indian became the recipient of an important divine message rather than the high, Spanish-speaking, Church officials, and the story has been used throughout its history to affirm or define a national, Mexican identity. The vision or texts bearing witness to the vision thus become political tools and the vision itself a political event. The way in which the story is used in doctrina classes fits in with other practices of socialization recorded in other ethnographies from Samoa to American churches in which Bible lessons have the effect of introducing children to linguistic registers which reinforce their sense of cultural and linguistic identity. In the doctrina classes, teachers link the particular experiences of the students with the narrative of the Lady of Guadalupe.

Doctrina classes had been taking place in Mexico since the sixteenth century, originally in the native language but since 1680 and through Church degree in 1770 in Spanish, with a view to eliminating the native tongue. Doctrina classes were thence conducted in Spanish and continued to be so taught in Mexican immigrant communities. Ironically, there was a movement in Los Angeles in 1996 to eliminate Spanish as a language of instruction, in order that doctrina classes should conform to the English-speaking, dominant church culture; but this seems to have failed. And while catechism classes are conducted in English, doctrina classes continue to be conducted in Spanish, although, apparently, Spanish is slowly being eradicated as the language of instruction. Through a close linguistic analysis of classroom interaction, particularly the use of the imperfect tense, Baquedano-Lopez shows how narrative activity in the classes socializes children to identify with being Mexican and to identify with a colonial history narrated by the teacher. The Virgin, so the story goes, appeared in Mexico to look after the Indians who were oppressed by the Spanish and to liberate Mexico from oppression. Throughout the narrative, there is a blurring of the Indian past with the Mexican present, particularly linked to skin colour; the dark skin of the Virgin and the Indians being reflected in the present dark skin of the class participants. This is a good example of socialization through language and the importance of language in forming religious and cultural identities. The vision of the Virgin of Guadalupe is made to be highly relevant to the present situation of the children, and their own stories of being "Mexican" highlighted. The voice of the vision still speaks to the present community and religion serves to express the meaning and purposes of the community.

Similar processes of socialization occur in other cultural contexts. My second example is from the *teyyam* tradition of Kerala in southwest India studied by Rich Freeman. Each year in Kerala there is a religious festival season which celebrates local deities called *teyyam*, a name possibly derived from the Sanskrit term for "god," *deva*. Throughout the year these local deities, deified culture heroes or temple guardians, and, often ferocious, goddesses, are housed in small shrines without iconic representation, in pots, swords, or shields. Once a year they are taken out from their shrines and installed in a living dancer who becomes ritually possessed by the *teyyam*.

Each deity is performed and the festival at each shrine lasts about two days. The *teyyam* dances around the shrine to the accompaniment of vibrant drumming, giving her vision (*darshanam*) to the local community, and is finally appeased by offerings of alcohol, a tall receptacle (*kalasham*) of palm wine, and blood in the form of sacrificed chickens who are decapitated and their blood placed in a bowl which is then offered to the goddess by being poured out on the ground in front of her as an offering (*bali*). The *teyyam* might also function in a prophetic or advisory capacity for the community.

The low caste dancers perform a series of *teyyams* in elaborate costumes for twelve to fifteen hours at a time, performing one deity after another, and the ceremony can become very intense and emotionally charged. At Nileshvaram in northern Kerala, for example, one of the deities is Muvalamkulicamundi, a ferocious goddess who in her legend was invoked to protect a Nambudri Brahmin against another who was magically attacking him. The attacking Brahmin trapped the goddess through the power of his mantra, placed her in a copper vessel, sealed it, and buried it. The goddess became so angry that she burst out of the pot and hole, and chased the Brahmin who ran terrified to the local Shiva temple for protection. Here she calmed down on condition that she could be installed in the temple beside Shiva, which duly happened. This story is told by the *teyyam* dancer in front of her shrine before the possession sequence. Indeed, the violence and anger of the goddess is expressed by the dancer.

Although usually a controlled possession, the dancer interacts with the audience – particularly the young men who chase after her – in often quite boisterous ways. Reflecting the myth, the *teyyam* dances out from the shrine to the local Shiva temple where she knocks at the door but is refused entrance. She then returns to her own shrine. The analysis of the *teyyam* phenomenon can be complex, as low caste groups (at Nileshvaram, the Vannans and Malayans) perform the *teyyam* for the higher status Caliyars, themselves still much lower than the high caste Nambudri Brahmins. The performers are always men, although they often perform female deities. What is interesting in terms of language is that the *teyyam* songs are sung before the shrine first of all in the third person, praising the god indirectly, then in the second person, the language of direct address, and finally in the first person, during which time the dancer gazes into a mirror and the possession is complete.

There is a shift from third to first person and an accompanying shift in the status of the dancer from human to divine. In the linguistic terminology we have developed above, the indexical-I of the dancer becomes overwhelmed by the "I of discourse," the deity as an "I." The dancer becomes the deity, identifies himself with her, and it is this which is culturally important. The inner state of the dancer would seem to be irrelevant to the performance – and indeed there is a range of responses with regard to the question of the inner state of the dancer. It is not so much the inner state of the dancer that is important but the socially sanctioned possession as a performative act.[27] This socially sanctioned performance is furthermore reflected in linguistic performance, where the dancer's usual indexicality is overwhelmed by the indexicality of the *teyyam*. We see that this is the shift of language from the detached third-person voice, to direct address, to the personal voice identified with the deity.

Both of these contemporary examples are from very different cultural worlds, one a Christian context in California, the other a Hindu context in Kerala, yet both share a common process – admittedly with great variation of intensity – of the ways in which language structure and categorization informs experience of the world in the body and serves to convey cultural knowledge through the generations. In the first example, Juan Diego's vision of the Virgin Mary is itself part of the broad history of Catholicism adapted and articulated in local conditions, through a vernacular language. This vision continues to directly influence and form the cultural and religious identities of the children in the doctrina class. In the second example, the *teyyam* phenomenon is part of the history of "Hindu" traditions in Kerala, strongly influenced by a tantric understanding of the body, deification, and divinity itself as being a fluid substance that can dwell within different forms (pots, swords, or even persons). The *teyyam*, directly through the language of tradition, reinforces social relationships and cultural identities and gives a glimpse into a transcendent reality: the invisible becomes articulated in the visible in the bodily form and language of the *teyyam*. In both cases we see how personal language – particularly the use of the first-person pronoun – adopts and appropriates the language of the tradition. My story becomes part of others stories for the Spanish American children, my witnessing the *teyyam*, having the *darshanam* of the *teyyam*, informs my identity for the low caste Malayali Hindu. Furthermore, in both cases language structure is linked to a bodily habitus: the children are socialized to behave in certain ways in the classroom, the *teyyam* performs and the community responds in culturally determined ways. Examples could be repeated across the globe for the ways in which language, intertwined with the being of the body and performance, patterns social interaction and religious formation.

Language as a Model of Religion

The evidence from linguistic anthropology shows us a number of relevant things. Firstly, language, its grammatical structures and schemata along with its implicit metaphors, informs and influences all our experience in significant ways. Partly through language there is a patterning or ordering of the body and its interactions through time which, secondly, builds into broader patterns of narrative and mimesis within a culture. These patterns of narrative and imitation of cultural forms – which are kinds of cultural knowledge – are conveyed through the generations as traditions. It is in such cultural forms or traditions, inseparably connected to bodily habitus, inseparably connected to linguistic categories, wherein the importance of religion lies. The story of a person's life, what gives us meaning and purpose, what determines our meaningful relationships with each other, is formed through traditions, and furthermore religious traditions mediate the human encounter with transcendence, with the invisible, an encounter that occurs primarily through the two processes of body or habitus and language. Body and language are intimately connected in the making of general linguistic meaning and in the making of religious meaning.

Given the difficulties of establishing semantic universals at other than a vague and general level we might nevertheless say that the linguistic evidence from anthropology does allow us to make general claims about process and patterns that are shared across language that are not trivial or overly general. On the one hand, language informs and forms our experience of the world (as the examples cited above indicate, particularly our spatial and temporal experience); on the other hand, language itself is rooted in our bodily life.

Mark Johnson and George Lakoff in particular have done interesting work in this area, showing how metaphors in language are rooted in bodily experience and at the same time how metaphor affects experience and concept formation. Briefly, they have argued that metaphor is fundamental to language and itself is based on human, bodily experience, which in turn significantly contributes to the formation of concepts and cultural categories. Cultural values and concepts are intimately linked to the metaphors of language, particularly spatial-orientation metaphors (up and down, inside and outside, central and peripheral), and the container metaphor cut across all languages.[28] Of particular importance is the "up–down" orientation which organizes our concepts where "up" is associated with good and happy, "down" with bad and sad, and so on. We can see this operating within religions where, I suspect universally, "up" is associated with moral good and virtue, with the other (good) world such as heaven or the realm of the gods, and "down" with the other (bad) world of hell, the realm of devils and demons. This is true in Christianity, where heaven has been conceptualized as above us, and in medieval cosmology, where it was understood more literally as being above us (with hell below). In Hindu and Buddhist cosmology, this basic vertical structure of cosmology is also found, although more complex and elaborated that the Christian model.

Thus in Hinduism the ancient mythological texts called Puranas offer elaborate and ornate accounts of cosmology and temporal processes. We also find the container model very important in religious traditions, particularly contemplative traditions, with the "inside" being identified with intensity of experience and finding truth in contrast to the "outside" of mere ritual or external observation. In the *teyyam* tradition I referred to above, for example, the deity is conceptualized as being outside of the dancer (located in various objects in the shrine) and enters into the dancer in the same way that the deity's power or consciousness can enter into an icon or image. The conceptual, metaphysical structure underlying the *teyyam* tradition, derived from the tantric tradition, also uses the up–down metaphor as fundamental, with the higher worlds located above and the lower below: the gods emanate and become manifest in the lower world from the higher. Furthermore this cosmos is mapped onto the vertical axis of the body and so we have the "in–out" metaphor conflated with the "up–down" metaphor as the expression of this fundamental cosmology.

This understanding of language as fundamentally metaphorical is linked to imagination in the sense that the imagination involves understanding one thing in terms of another. This analogical process is central to the formation of ideas about the world and our place within it. The cosmological imagination of religions operates as a template or structure for the location of meaning, a structure that is generated through language and is rooted in the property of language itself to function through fundamental metaphors shared by human communities. As Lakoff and Johnson observe, metaphors create realities for us and guide future action.[29]

Conclusion

Drawing abstract conclusions from our considerations so far and the examples given, we might say that a religious imagination operates at a number of levels: at a macro-historical level of processes through time, specifically as representation of interpersonal relationships and as personal kinds of subjectivity. While macro-historical processes, the *longue durée*, of religions need to be understood both by theologians and historians of religion, it is the ways in which subjectivity links to them through the languages of religions, through the religious imagination, and through the body, wherein the importance of religion arguably lies. Developing our discussion of linguistic categories and human experience, we might say then that religions function as traditions with long histories that contain fundamental metaphors and imaginaries. It is at this level that the religious imagination conveys cosmologies and soteriologies (a journey back to the One, for example, or a utopian vision of the world). A second level, as it were, expresses an interpersonal realm of tradition, social forms, dietary laws, marriage laws, and so on. And a third level embodies these concerns in the person and subjectivity, in the way the indexical-I embodies the "I" of discourse and in the way the body learns, in Mauss' phrase, communication with God.

But even if we take this account – the centrality of a certain kind of language, the formation of a distinct cosmological *imaginaire* – as a characteristic feature of religion, we are still left with the problem of coherence and rationality. Is it sufficient or even acceptable to modern people simply to take religions as self-sufficient language games or *"imaginaires"* within which people can live meaningful lives? If religions are so intimately connected and formed through language – and they must be if cultures are formed through language in significant ways – then surely we need some criteria of judgment or rationality – which are also properties of language – to test or show the validity or otherwise of religious belief and practice? Is it sufficient simply to show the meaningfulness of religion in people's lives without making judgments about the adequacy of religious accounts of the world? Plato's cave is a metaphor but to what extent are we justified in taking it seriously as an account of reality? This is a question of rationality and the adequacy of religious language, and it is to this question that we must now turn.

Notes

1. Plato, *Republic* VII.516–17. John M. Cooper (ed.), *Plato: Complete Works* (Indianapolis and Cambridge: Hackett Publishing Company, 1997).
2. For a good account see Foley, William A., *Anthropological Linguistics: An Introduction* (Oxford: Blackwell, 1997); Duranti, A.(ed.), *Linguistic Anthropology: A Reader*, second edition (Oxford: Wiley-Blackwell, 2009).
3. Chomsky, Noam, *Aspects of the Theory of Syntax* (Cambridge, Mass.: MIT Press, 1965), p. 4.
4. Wierzbicka, Anna, *Semantics: Primes and Universals* (Oxford: Oxford University Press, 1996), pp. 22–3.
5. Wierzbicka, *Semantics*, p. 426.
6. Wierzbicka, *Semantics*, p. 35.
7. Wierzbicka, *Semantics*, pp. 114–15.
8. Duranti, "Introduction," p. 21, in Duranti (ed.), *Linguistic Anthropology*.
9. Duranti, "Introduction," pp. 21–2.
10. Lucy, John, *Language, Diversity and Thought: A Reformulation of the Linguistic Relativity Hypothesis* (Cambridge: Cambridge University Press, 1992), p. 8.
11. Whorf, Benjamin, *Language, Thought and Reality*, ed. John Carroll (Cambridge, Mass.: MIT Press, 1956), pp. 213–14.
12. Whorf, *Language, Thought and Reality*, p. 221.
13. Whorf, *Language, Thought and Reality*, pp. 135–37. For a clear discussion and useful diagrams, see Lucy, John, *Language, Diversity and Thought*, pp. 48–50.
14. Whorf, *Language, Thought and Reality*, pp. 148, 152–4, 158. Lucy *Language, Diversity and Thought* pp. 31–3, 40–1.
15. e.g. Malotki, E., *Hopi Time: A Linguistic Analysis of the Temporal Categories in the Hopi Language* (Berlin: Mouton, 1983).

16. Berlin, Brent and Paul Kay, *Basic Colour Terms: Their Universality and Evolution* (Berkeley: University of California Press, 1969).
17. Lucy, *Language, Diversity and Thought*, p. 185.
18. Lucy, *Language, Diversity and Thought*, p. 186.
19. Lucy, *Language, Diversity and Thought*, p. 177.
20. Lucy, John, *Grammatical Categories and Cognition: A Case Study of the Linguistic Relativity Hypothesis* (Cambridge: Cambridge University Press, 1992), p. 157. For examples in the linguistic relativity tradition, also see H. Hoijer "The Sapir-Whorf Hypothesis," in H. Hoijer (ed.), *Language in Culture* (Chicago: Chicago University Press, 1954), pp. 106–23.
21. Levinson, Stephen C., "Relativity in Spatial Conception and Description," p.180, in Gumpertz and Levinson (eds), *Rethinking Linguistic Relativity*, pp. 177–202. Also see Levinson, "Language and Cognition. The Cognitive Consequences of Spatial Description in Guugu Yimithirr," *Journal of Linguistic Anthropology*, vol. 7 (1), 1997, pp. 98–131.
22. Gumpertz, John S., "Introduction to part 1," p. 24, in Gumpertz and S. C. Levinson (eds), *Rethinking Linguistic Relativity* (Cambridge: Cambridge University Press, 1996).
23. Lakoff, George and Mark Johnson, *Metaphors We Live By* (Chicago: Chicago University Press, 1980); Johnson, Mark *The Mind in the Body: The Bodily Basis of Meaning, Imagination, and Reason* (Chicago: Chicago University Press, 1987).
24. See the volumes edited by Steven Katz: *Mysticism and Philosophical Analysis* (Oxford: Oxford University Press, 1983), *Mysticism and Religious Traditions* (Oxford: Oxford University Press, 1983), *MysticismandLanguage* (Oxford: Oxford University Press, 1992).
25. Baquedano-Lopez, Patricia, "Creating Social Identities through Doctrina Narratives," p. 365, in A. Duranti (ed.), *Linguistic Anthropology*, pp. 364–77.
26. Baquedano-Lopez, "Creating Social Identities," p. 365, quoting Lenz, R., *Nuestra Señora de Guadalupe/Our Lady of Guadalupe* (Burlington: Bridge Building Images, 1987).
27. Freeman, Rich, "Purity and Violence: Sacred Power in the Teyyam Worship of Malabar" (PhD thesis, University of Pennsylvania, 1991), p. 116.
28. Lakoff and Johnson, *Metaphors We Live By*, p. 30.
29. Lakoff and Johnson, *Metaphors We Live By*, p. 156.

6

Religion and Rationality

During the French Revolution in 1793 the Gothic Cathedral of Notre Dame de Paris was rededicated to the Cult of Reason, an atheistic doctrine intended to replace Christianity. While it might be ironic that Christianity was to be replaced by a "cult," the fundamental idea that reason had or should replace religion as humanity advances is widespread and commonplace as a fundamental, implicit assumption of the secular age. The term "cult" was not used then, of course, in the sociological sense of today but rather in the ecclesiastical sense of *cultus* as a system of devotion; the revolution proclaimed itself to be devoted to reason, which would oust religious faith. In earlier times reason was seen to be compatible with revelation, and even necessary for knowledge about the truths of God, but in the course of time reason or rationality, along with empirical inquiry into the world, came to replace revelation as the primary source of knowledge. The French Revolution's rededication of Notre Dame underlines the strong link between rationality and atheism or anti-religious sentiment that developed in the West during the course of a couple of hundred years. Religion is understood as "superstition" in contrast to scientific reason, and the history of religion as the history of error.[1]

But the history of religions shows us that rationality is not alien to religious revelation and there are forms of reasoning that take place within the "sacred canopy" of religions that are integral to them. The intellectual history of religions is, of course, vast and beyond the scope of a book such as this to offer even an inadequate description, but if the importance of religion lies in its meaningfulness for human subjects, as I have argued, then rationality is inseparable from this enterprise because, as rational creatures,

The Importance of Religion: Meaning and Action in Our Strange World,
First Edition. Gavin Flood.
© 2012 Gavin Flood. Published 2012 by Blackwell Publishing Ltd.

we need good reasons for our practices and endeavors and good reasons for thinking that our practices and ideas are related to truth. The question of the relation between rationality, religion, and truth is as vibrant now as it has ever been. We need to raise the question as to what we mean by rationality, whether rationality is a universal property of human beings, to what extent rationality is compatible with religious claims and practices, and the extent to which rationality questions the adequacy of religious claims. These are highly contested issues and virtually imply the whole history of thought from Plato, the Buddha, and Confucius. For the purpose of the current chapter I wish to support the view that processes of reasoning are shared across cultures but that these processes are not free of a narrative foundation; that reasoning is integral to reflexive religious traditions and to the meanings they expound; and that reasoning develops within traditions of thought, integrated with imagination and with ideas about virtue, justice, and truth.

What is Rationality?

The idea of rationality in the West has been broadly understood as knowledge of truth through inference from valid premises. It has also been associated with the development of logic from Aristotle and the two rules of logic, the law of non-contradiction that a statement (p) cannot be simultaneously true and false – it cannot be the case that p and not p, it cannot be both raining and not raining – and the law of the excluded middle, that for any statement p, it is the case that "either p or not p" is true, either it is raining or it is not raining, where "raining" is understood in exactly the same way in both occurrences. That is, it cannot be both raining and not raining at the same time and in the same place.[2] But we cannot restrict the range of rationality to logical rules, and vagueness is not necessarily antithetical to rationality. We need to understand rationality in terms of human practices that have developed over millennia that involve making judgments in particular situations that are the best means to achieve a particular end. This practical rationality has clearly been practiced throughout history to find food, to hunt, to grow crops, to make shelters. Such practical rationality has also been accompanied by symbolic actions that, from a modern perspective, do not seem to directly contribute to achieving a particular end, such as saying a prayer before hunting, burying a piece of the Eucharist in a field to help the crops to grow, and other magical actions. But leaving aside the dispute about causation, it is almost self-evident that cultures throughout history have expressed a belief in the coherence of action and meaning, and that people in different cultures have practiced reasoning on the basis of what could be known to them.

The debate about rationality has not only been about the application of logical rules to statements, but more broadly about coherence and the degree to which statements correspond to reality. Thus, on the one hand, an argument could be formulated that belief in witchcraft was rational within a non-scientific frame of reference, but, on the other hand, such an argument could be refuted on the grounds that science has proved witchcraft to be false because it misunderstands the true nature of causation. These are difficult questions, but leaving aside the laws of the excluded middle and non-contradiction as rules for the adequacy and rationality of statements, we could claim, minimally, that rationality entails coherence and intelligibility. Whether coherence and intelligibility entail that a culture must adhere to the two laws of logic articulated above is an interesting question. It is clearly possible for people to operate successfully in a society with conflicting or opposed beliefs without too much cognitive dissonance (it is almost a self-evident truth that we each inhabit different worlds or "provinces of meaning", to use Schutz's apposite phrase). But to function successfully in a society we do need to operate within some intelligibility. Each person in a culture needs to make the world and her fellow travelers intelligible and the schema for doing this we might call a culture's rationality. Thus the implicit schema for understanding the ancient Greek world was *dike*, translated as "justice" but implying cosmic order in a way parallel to the Indian idea of *dharma*, translated as "duty" or "virtue" and again implying cosmic order. The schemas of a culture are not necessarily articulated but are, in principle, communicable, although often only a culture's intellectual elites will be in a position to articulate them adequately.[3]

A culture's schema involves a narrative dimension, a story or an account of a series of events, and reflection on that narrative or explanation. As I have written elsewhere, religion has been understood as "story" – a true story for those who stand inside of it – and the explanation of story has been a function of rationality.[4] But it could be argued that the Enlightenment claim to free reason from narrative or myth has never been wholly successful (or even desirable), and there are narrative structures important to reason in the sense that good reasons for practices might be supported by examples from life. Even in Hegel's emphasis on reason, the whole manifesting of the Spirit through history involves a story right up to Hegel's declaring the end of history with Napoleon's entry into Jena. The structure of reason entails a narrative aspect through being articulated in time. That is, reason entails communication and communication often takes the form of narrative. We tell stories to make a point and reflect upon the meaning of those stories (Genette makes a useful distinction between story (*histoire*) or series of events and *narrative*, the discourse about those events).[5] We might also say that rationality entails communication and communicability not necessarily across the boundaries of tradition but certainly within those boundaries.

The schemas which operate within a culture provide some coherence to people's experience of life. Cultural schemas constrain our desires and emotions which, as MacIntyre observes, are norm-governed, and we have to learn what the norms of a society are and both how to express ourselves and read others emotions.[6] One way of understanding culture – and implicitly understanding rationality – has been the philosopher Ludwig Wittgenstein's famous idea of "forms of life," that we live in particular modes of being characterized by "language games" in which the important thing about language is its use rather than any objective referent. Like a game, language is determined by conventions or rules and we need to understand and evaluate statements according to the conventions operative for that particular language. As the moves in a game can only be judged by what is and is not permissible (the rules) and the rules of one game cannot legitimately or even coherently be applied to another game, so language must be understood in terms of the rules or constraints operating upon it in particular circumstances, in a way that extends beyond natural languages to areas of meaning within a single natural language. Thus the linguistic conventions operating at a birthday party will be different to those operating at a business meeting or in the House of Commons in the United Kingdom. One language game is self-contained and closed-off from another. On this line of reasoning, cultures operate in analogous ways to language: they are self-regulating entities that contain their own rules or constraints and we must make sense of cultures in terms of their own frames of reference. Rationality is the ability to follow a rule and the set of rules might be understood as the schema implicit in cultures.

Against universalizing criteria of judgment that fed-in to colonialism and relegation of the West's other to a subordinate status, anthropologists and many philosophers in the post-Second World War era tended to agree with the view of cultures as closed systems or forms of life, along with the idea that there are different kinds of rationality; that rationality is bound by culture. On this view, cultures need to be understood in their own terms as having their own coherence. A philosophical justification for understanding cultures in this way was developed by Peter Winch, influenced by Wittgenstein. Cultures have their own standards of rationality and we cannot judge one culture – one form of life – through the standards of rationality developed in another. In *The Idea of a Social Science and Its Relation to Philosophy* (1958), Winch argued, beginning with Wittgenstein's aphorism that "the limits of my language (of the only language I can understand) mean the limits of *my* world," for the importance of the formation of our experience through language and social context (he does not use the term "culture").[7] The world is not separable from language in the sense that the world is what is presented to us through concepts and so religion and philosophy are attempts to present an intelligible picture of the world to us.

A key part of our understanding the world is being able to follow a rule. Developing Wittgenstein's argument that we can only make sense of the words "the same" through being able to grasp the idea of a rule and to know when it is or is not correctly followed, Winch claims that we can extend this idea to social life apart from language. Action always has a relation to a social context and must be understood as the application of a rule driven by motives and reasons. That is, "I can only be committed to the future by what I do now if any present act is the application of a rule,"[8] and so a person must know what the right and wrong way of doing something is. Thus in voting Labour a person must live in a particular country with a particular political institution and must understand what it is to follow a rule; casting a vote is not simply making a mark on a piece of paper.[9] This extends to all aspects of social life, so "(a) religious mystic, for instance, who says that his aim is union with God, can be understood by someone who is acquainted with the religious tradition in the context of which this end is sought."[10] To live in a society is to be able to act, which is to have reasons for acting within a framework of rules and thereby to know that there is a right or wrong way of doing something. In Weber's terms this is rational action in relation to a goal (*Zweckrational*). For Winch "all meaningful behaviour must be social, since it can be meaningful only if governed by rules, and rules presuppose a social setting."[11]

The implicit or explicit rules which govern social action are relative to particular societies and to follow these rules is to behave meaningfully for people who live within that particular form of life. To understand neurosis among the Trobriand islanders, for example, we would need to understand the Trobriand concept of fatherhood and so on, and not simply import an account of the etiology of neurosis from Freud.[12] For Winch, we need to understand people in their own terms, in their own social contexts, an idea he develops in "Understanding a Primitive Society" where, relying on the account of Evans-Pritchard, he discusses Azande notions of witchcraft. Such practices rather than being judged by the external anthropologist as being irrational, must be understood as being coherent within their social frame of reference and providing a meaningful world that the Azande inhabit. For example, the Azande perform a rite while harvesting their crops which anthropologists have interpreted as a method whereby the Azande try to ensure a good crop return. But Winch argues that understanding Azande culture through the lens of such instrumental rationality is a mistake; rather we must understand the Azande rite as an expressive activity, not an instrumental one. That is, the Azande actions are intelligible not as a kind of technology but rather as an expression of their freedom from dependence on the harvest through actually expressing this dependence. To view the Azande rites as a kind of erroneous technology is to impose European assumptions about instrumentality. To see the Azande belief in witchcraft as erroneous is to assume that science corresponds to reality and this makes assumptions about language corresponding or pointing to a reality outside of itself (a problem to which we will return in the next chapter).[13]

This issue was brought out some years ago in the context of postcolonialism and a debate about the British military explorer Captain Cook, who was killed on Hawaii in 1779. Cook was deified as the god Lono as he so happened to arrive on Hawaii during the god's festival Makahiki and was treated with honor and respect. After a short stay, Cook sailed away but was forced to return because of a problem with the mainsail on one of the ships. He was subsequently killed by the Hawaiians on the beach. But this was no mere killing; it was a sacrifice, claims Sahlins. As the god Lono, Cook received obeisance and respect but upon his return he disrupted cultural expectation and a complex of events eventuated in a cultural improvisation in which he became a sacrifice: "Cook was transformed from the divine beneficiary of the sacrifice to its victim."[14] The sacrifice of the king or deity was a practice not unknown and Cook's body was dismembered exactly in accordance with Hawaiian sacrificial practice. The killing of Cook is coherent within the frame of reference of the Hawaiians at that time. The anthropologist Gananath Obeyesekere argued against this interpretation, claiming that it is a European myth that places the Europeans as rational above the natives, who were still within a mythical universe and characterized by a "primitive" mentality which irrationally took Cook to be their god. On the contrary, the Hawaiians, claims Obeyesekere, performed a practical rationality which is shared by all human beings, rooted in our biological nature, and the Hawaiians were fully aware of the political dimensions of the Cook expedition.[15] Sahlins in turn accused Obeyesekere of a kind of ethnocentrism in viewing the Hawaiians as Europeans.

While Sahlins' deep knowledge and scholarship about Hawaii has the edge, Obeyesekere nevertheless raises important questions about rationality and western hegemony. But these two understandings are not necessarily antagonistic, and cultural coherence does not necessarily entail untranslatability or that there is no shared practical rationality. We have seen the same issue as regards Edie Turner's experience among the Ndembu. The *ihamba* tooth ritual can be understood within the cultural logic of the Ndembu worldview. Magical affliction by the hunter's tooth is a part of the cultural norms of the society. As Evans-Prichard remarked with regard to witchcraft beliefs among the Azande, not to come across witchcraft on a daily basis would be cause of surprise for a Zande; it is simply part of the everyday world.[16]

Yet even understanding the Ndembu or Azande worldview assumes some common ground shared between the anthropologists and their informants; it assumes that intelligibility and coherence are translatable. While it might not be possible, as we saw in the last chapter, to establish semantic universals, there are nevertheless shared processes of linguistic consensus and metaphorical use. It is these processes that we can call rational. It is rational to agree what it is to win a football match because participants know what it is to follow a rule. By extension in the case of the Ndembu exorcism rite, there was agreement as to whether the woman was cured of the witchcraft affliction or not, and an implicit cultural understanding of the rules of exorcism and what constitutes a cure. In the Ndembu case there is a coherence in the belief system and judgments are made and acted upon which are based on that system. Whether such judgments are based on a mistaken understanding of causation is a different question, but in so far as such a belief system is coherent it is arguably rational.

In many ways Winch is a precursor to some postmodern thinking that stresses the particularity of cultural difference as different worlds and these different worlds are formed within language; "there is nothing outside the text" ("il n'y a pas hors texte") in Derrida's famous expression. Winch clearly has a point that to act meaningfully in a particular culture, even to know how to speak in particular social situations, is to follow a rule, to know when the rule has been broken and to understand the concept of "the same." Even within a single society there are many different forms of life which contain different language games; for example, "hello, how are you?" is a form of greeting in American English which could not be used to mark a farewell. The recitation of the opening verses of the *Qur'an* (*fātihah*) is a form of language used in a particular situation of Moslem prayer; in one sense, language games are self-contained and to understand their intelligibility we have to enter into them.

And yet there is a sense in which Winch's argument is limited. Of course we need to understand cultures, religions, and languages in their own terms, but the very idea of making something intelligible entails a shared ground, entails the ability to make judgments, discern intelligibility, and therefore entails shared processes of reasoning. This in turn entails some notion of correspondence between language and reality, and it is here where so many problems lie: one community's correspondence is another's imagination.

If religions are cultural forms that mediate the encounter with mystery, then these forms are coherent in the sense that practices and beliefs create an integrated worldview, an implicit schema, which participants can comprehend; to live within an Orthodox Jewish community is know how to follow its rules, to know how to behave in the synagogue, and to know how to make judgments in particular situations based on the values of that community (such as choices to eat within the limits of kosher in a restaurant). But the question still remains as to whether the same standards of rationality can be applied across cultures. As we have seen, Winch has argued against the view that standards of western rationality can be applied universally, and has argued that rationality within a particular culture must be linked to coherence and the ability to follow a rule. Probing this question further, Taylor has argued that Winch's defense of Azande practices against the accusation of irrationalism on the grounds that they are engaged in "quite a different language game" is not enough. What is needed is not only coherence but the ability to give an account of a practice or idea. That is, an important part of rationality is the ability to articulate an activity and to reflect upon it or to develop a theoretical understanding. Such a theoretical understanding in the Greek tradition is a disengaged perspective linked to contemplation and true knowledge: "we have a rational grasp of something when we can articulate it," which is "why the Greek philosophical vocabulary marks this inner connection between speech and reason...".[17] This ability to articulate reasons is the ability to formulate a theoretical understanding of a social practice and some cultures, suggests Taylor, are theoretical in this sense and some are not. Winch's objection to reading Azande magic in terms of practical rationality is, on Taylor's re-description, an objection to an a-theoretical culture being judged by the standards of a theoretical one. Cultures which theorize their practices are able to articulate them, give reasons for doing what they do, and so Taylor argues are superior in one sense to cultures which do not. This is not to accuse the Azande of irrationality, says Taylor, because to be irrational is to violate the standards of rationality within a particular culture through inconsistency, but it is to acknowledge that standards are different when understood in terms of the expression of a theoretical understanding versus a non-theoretical one.[18]

This distinction between theoretical and non-theoretical cultures is clearly controversial. Is this not simply a covert colonialism or way of claiming the superiority of the West over the third world? Such would be an ungenerous reading of Taylor's point. While all societies are complex, some cultures have a historical density that has brought with it sustained theoretical reflection over a long expanse of time. But this is not enough for Taylor, for what marks out the modern from earlier kinds of rationality is the link to science, empirical knowledge, and the abandoning of "atunement" that saw the meaning of human life integrally linked to the structure of the cosmos. To this important point we will need to return in the next chapter, but the key argument that Taylor presents is that rationality entails not only *coherence* but also *articulation*.

While Winch's claim that we need to understand cultural practices in their own terms is important, Taylor's account of rationality as entailing artic-ulation is attested by the histories of civilizations in Asia, Europe, and the Middle East, which developed sophisticated accounts of their cultural and religious practices and a range of theoretical reflection on the human encounter with mystery. These theoretical reflections were often at odds, but all illustrate Taylor's principle. Buddhism, for example, expressed in texts and traditions from the fifth century BCE made headway into central Asia, China, and southeast East Asia in due course, and now into the West.

Rationality would seem to entail not simply cultural coherence or intelligibility for a community, but also articulation and communicability. It is possible to learn other languages, to learn others' rules, and to learn to live within other ways of life. Geoffrey Lloyd, for example, has shown how ancient China and Greece shared techniques of persuasion,[19] and one might add that ancient India too developed such techniques. Indeed for religions that had a missionary goal, namely Buddhism, Christianity, and Islam, such communicability of rationality was central to their very nature: the ability to render themselves intelligible was essential to the communicative acts that marked them. As Donald Davidson has argued, the ability to translate others' concepts into one's own language entails that we live in the same world.

Davidson's famous principle of charity offers a generous view of communication that we should optimize agreement and in so doing optimize the meaning of others' statements. That is, the beliefs attributed to others come out as largely true. A distinct although related thesis is Davidson's "radical interpretation" that works out the meaning of linguistic utterances without prior knowledge of grammar or speaker's mental states through working out the meaning from the context of linguistic use. This is in fact to recognize the cohesiveness and truth of the speaker.[20] This method is intended not to eradicate disagreement but "to make meaningful disagreement possible" and assumes a foundation in agreement.[21] For Davidson meaning entails a theory of truth according to which, following Tarski, the meaning of a sentence is given by providing it with truth conditions. Furthermore, radical interpretation is needed to link utterances to evidence and so Davidson defends a version of the correspondence theory of truth; that "truth can be explained by an appeal between language and the world."[22] Through speaking sentences we can say what is true. On this view not only coherence is important for truth and rationality but correspondence between language and reality is too. Thus "s is true if and only if p" – "'it is snowing' is true if and only if it is snowing." Sane and insane understandings of the world have been judged by criteria of the correspondence between statements and reality, but even here, as philosophers of social history such as Foucault have pointed out, what is judged sane by one culture or one period of history – such as witchcraft accusations – might be judged insane by another.

The more relativist position of MacIntyre and Milbank argue against Davidson on the grounds that cultural languages have to be mastered on their own terms without "translateability,"[23] and there are rival positions that are incompatible with each other. But evidence from the human sciences suggests that human beings are, as Brandom claims, "normative" beings with the ability to commit ourselves to particular statements and courses of action and to articulate those commitments, and "rational" beings with the ability to rationally navigate difference and to understand the reasons to undertake a commitment. We have the ability to make explicit what is implicit in our language.[24] The important point for our purposes is that ideas and beliefs can be communicated and even though we can enter into different social worlds, those different social worlds are translatable.

Our discussion so far has indicated that rationality has two characteristic features: it needs coherence and it needs articulation (and so is communicable). Good reasons for particular practices entail a coherence of acts with each other, coherence between thought system and action, and the ability to communicate practice and express that coherence. If cultures are rational in this sense as forms of life containing particular rules, beliefs, and repeated kinds of action (a *habitus*), then they are communicated in two ways, temporally through the generations (over long expanses of time), and spatially between people and between communities. Indeed, the effective communication of religions through the generations is essential to their survival. Communication is communication *of* something *for* a community. We have seen this in respect of sacred text, a text set aside and communicated through time for a community of reception. We might say that this generational communication, this "chain of memory," as Hervieu-Léger had described the process,[25] is the communication of how an encounter with mystery takes place. In this sense religions are forms of knowledge that communities hold to be important and that need to be preserved, transmitted, and brought to life in each generation. Traditions of practice and thinking are forms of rationality that are coherent and can be articulated and so entail intelligibility.

The criterion supported by Davidson that rationality expressed in language entails correspondence with reality is more problematic. When making statements about the objective world (such as "it is raining"), such statements can be corroborated, but when it comes to non-empirical statements, such as many theological statements ("God is love"), they cannot be empirically demonstrated. This has led some philosophers and scientists to regard such statements as meaningless. But rather than condemn large sections of the global community as irrational, we need to understand rationality in terms of practices of reasoning. Such practices are, of course, constrained by the world and the laws of physics, and so on, but they are nevertheless culture- and community-specific; and while such practices might regard themselves as corresponding to reality, an externalist view must rather understand them in terms of coherence and the ability to be articulated.

Rational Religious Communities

Cultures are rational to the degree that they are coherent and to the degree that cultural judgments can be articulated. Within a community an act is rational if the judgment that precedes it is coherent in the context of other actions and the world picture that allowed that judgment to be made. This entails its being able to be articulated. Coherence and communicability are the hallmarks of rationality and communities are rational in which these processes occur. This does not mean, of course, that a rational culture is more ethical – look at the Aztec, which was clearly rational but whose mass sacrificial culture was unethical when judged from the perspective of the West (not that this justified the mass extermination of that civilization by Europeans). While it might be difficult to make judgments of different cultures based on ethics, it could be argued that an ethical understanding is integral to the world itself and while particular judgments might be brought into question, the fact of ethical judgment as shared points to such a conclusion.

In spite of some alternative descriptions (such as Kierkegaard's "I believe because it is absurd"), religious communities are rational communities; forms of life that are coherent, communicable, and ethical. Alisdair MacIntyre in particular has developed historical philosophical accounts of moral rationality in relation to these traditions. Modernity lost the idea of virtue, which had been preserved in the Aristotelian-Thomistic tradition, when moral reasoning and any claim to universal morality were rejected after the Enlightenment, particularly with Nietzsche and genealogical thinking. Modernity and post-modernity have lost an important kind of discourse that needs to be retrieved for the collective good.

On this account, religious rationality is an important dimension of meaning; being located within a cosmos and being part of a larger structure which gives life coherence is a moral source which itself is rooted in and expresses God. Charles Taylor's description of the Renaissance world in which "atunement" to the cosmos was a central feature of understanding is an illustration of this. Science breaks the link between understanding and atunement[26] and so puts a strain on the maintaining of religious meaning in modernity.

So far we have argued that humans share rationality in the sense that we attempt to make sense of our strange world and offer intelligible and consistent accounts of it that are communicable. Religions are rational in this sense. They offer accounts of the world, particularly the origin of the world, they offer accounts of the meaning of human life and death, they offer ways of negotiating the difficult boundaries of life, and they offer an ultimate meaning in liberation or salvation. We can also concur with Taylor that there are theoretical and non-theoretical cultures, which does not necessarily map onto literate and non-literate but maps onto philosophical and non-philosophical practices of reasoning. Ancient India was a self-reflexive theoretical culture, although predominantly oral in its earliest phases, that developed rational forms of knowledge and developed scientific approaches to the world (particularly the science of language, but also mathematics and astronomy[27]). Theoretical cultures, as Taylor argues, have a strong account of rationality, and these cultures developed to a high degree in China, India, Europe, and the Middle East.

The German existential philosopher Karl Jaspers first drew our attention to the idea of the Axial age during the first millennium BCE that marked the rise of new developments in world history with the Buddha and sages of the Upanishads in India, with Confucius and Lao Tzu in China, with the Hebrew Prophets in the Middle East, and with Socrates in Greece.[28] The rise of these new religions, or new forms of older religions, marks a shift from an orientation from magical manipulation of supernatural forces towards a rational ethics. Leaving aside the question about the viability of the Axial age concept and the problem of whether there are parallel historical developments in different areas of the world, I take the general point that we can make a distinction between magical practices or popular religion, and religions of salvation that offered an ethical worldview and processes of reasoning. The development of the "Axial revolution," Taylor observes, "reaches its logical conclusion" with an emphasis away from collective, cosmos-related rituals towards individuated religion and devotion in the Middle Ages to the Renaissance. This shift of emphasis he calls "the Great Disembedding."[29] The history of religions might be seen in terms of tension between these two kinds of religion which develops to its logical conclusion with the gradual erosion and disparaging of magical traditions, culminating with the rise of science.

But although there are developed scientific cultures in India and China from an early period, the break between atunement and understanding or explanation only becomes marked during the Renaissance with the rise of humanist scholarship and science. As we will see in the next chapter, one of the contentious issues is the scientific critique of religions as the refutation of empirical claims. When religions make empirical claims they are open to refutation. In pre-Renaissance times the distinction between atunement and understanding was not made and early empirical investigation was not regarded as being incompatible with metaphysical claims. Thus the linguistic philosopher Bhartrihari in sixth-century Kashmir could link the Sanskrit language to a hierarchical cosmology. But reasoning is not restricted to giving accounts of the world in empirical terms and within religions has been strongly linked to the religious imagination and cosmic meaning. The main feature of religious reasoning is locating human beings within a cosmos, which means giving an account of the human person in relation to the cosmos and in relation to revealed truth.

Rationality and Cosmology

There are many examples of the way in which reasoning is linked to religious cosmology. In medieval Europe, as Lovejoy has shown, the universe was contained and although immense was "limited and fenced about"; even in the fifteenth century, men lived "in a walled universe as well as in walled towns."[30] Christianity offered an ornate cosmology within which people lived meaningful lives, that is, lives which could be cosmologically located. As C.S. Lewis pointed out, there were four grades of earthly life in the medieval period, mere existence (as with stones), existence with growth (vegetables), existence and growth with sensation (animals), and these with reason (humans).[31] Similarly, in medieval India we have taxonomies of a vast, but contained, universe in which humans have their place in the hierarchy of beings with plants, insects, and other crawling things, birds, wild and domestic animals, and the various gods and demons who inhabit the multilayered cosmos.[32] Likewise in Islam during the same period we have ornate cosmologies in which humans have a place along with angels and demons.[33] The main feature of religious meaning in pre-modernity is being located within a cosmos or, in Taylor's term, being atuned to the cosmos. Meaning, cosmical location, and atunement are virtually synonyms in this world. Religions have supposed that the universe has a fundamental, dis-coverable order but this chain of being was to be broken with the rise of science (as we shall see) and the discarding of the cosmological image.

Presupposing a cosmology and that the universe has a fundamental order, forms of religious reasoning developed that offered intellectual justification for a particular worldview and particular practice. Reasoning on this view is closely linked to the imagination – reasoning is the consequences of state-ments and the development of ideas that flow from a particular imagination or way in which the cosmos is imaged along with human life within it. Thus a theology developed within Christianity that sought intellectual coherence in the light of its cosmic worldview, often linked to political expediency, as it did in Islam and Judaism. In Indian religions robust debate developed about epistemology, metaphysics, and the nature of revelation, particularly be-tween rival schools of Hindu philosophy and the Buddhists; in China, debates occurred between Taoists, Buddhists, and Confucians. In all of these, practices of reason developed within tradition, assumed the narratives of tradition, and assumed the picture of the universe that tradition passed down. This is not free-floating rationality but ways of thinking that grow out of the imagination and narratives of religions. Christian theology assumes the Christian narrative (which reinterprets the ancient Israeli narrative of Ex-odus); Buddhist philosophy assumes the narrative of Gautama Siddhartha and his quest for enlightenment, and so on. Innumerable examples could be given but let us take three from Islam, Christianity, and Hinduism, to illustrate this idea of tradition-specific reasoning.

Our first example is Al Ghazali (1058–1111 CE), whose hermeneutical work highlights virtue and develops ethics as the heart of his interpretation of the *Qur'an*. Ghazali was perhaps the greatest Moslem philosopher; his scholarship covered a wide range of topics including law, jurisprudence, and mysticism. Virtue, Moosa tells us, was central to Ghazali's understanding of one's inner disposition or *habitus* (*malaka*), which needed to be cultivated to achieve *adab*, "civility" or more specifically "the disciplining of the spirit (*nafs*) so that the spirit may direct the body to perform deeds of merit almost instinctively."[34] Right ethical conduct leads to salvation and ethics needs to be cultivated, particularly through the development of mysticism (*taṣawwuf*), which, together with law (*fiqh*), has the ability to transform the self. These ideas he propagated through his readings of the revelation. For example, in the famous verses on light – "the Niche of Lights" (*Mishkāt al-anwār*, Qur'an 24.35) – Ghazali describes the self. The verse reads:

> God is the light of the heavens and the earth.
> The simile of God's light is like a niche in which a lamp,
> The lamp in a globe of glass,
> The globe of glass as it were a shining star,
> Lit from a blessed olive tree
> Neither of the East nor of the West,
> Its light-giving oil nearly luminous
> Even if fire did not touch it.
> Light upon light![35]

This verse, Ghazali tells us, represents the self through similes, each of which – niche, lamp, glass, tree, and oil – is represented by a spirit (*ruh*). These spirits form a hierarchy, each growing out of the other, so Ghazali interprets the text in the light of his anthropology in which the self forms a graded hierarchy comprising essential existence (corresponding to prophetic spirit, oil), sensory existence (the niche), imaginary existence ("glass"), rationale existence (lamp), and analogical existence (tree).[36] Here reasoning develops from revelation, philosophy from the text, and Ghazali develops an interpretative strategy that places subjectivity at the heart of his thinking.

While Ghazali was teaching Sufism in Tus, his contemporary in Canterbury, Anselm was arguing about ecclesiastical authority with William II and had by then written his *Discourse on the Existence of God*, the *Proslogion*, in which he formulated the famous ontological argument. The ontological argument has been developed by later philosophers, such as Descartes, and refuted by philosophers such as Kant. What is notable is that this argument (one can imagine a being which none greater can be conceived, existence in reality is greater than existence in the mind, therefore a being than which none greater can be conceived must exist in reality) is located in the text between extensive meditations on God. That is, the argument is not intended to convince unbelievers but is rather part of Christian contemplation rooted in the theological, textual tradition. Reasoning is not free-floating but developed within a context of tradition and meditative reflection on the nature of God.[37] This is a textual tradition as well as a contemplative and liturgical tradition in which reasoning is always rooted in text: a free-floating reasoning would be inconceivable to Anselm.

On still a different continent, in Kashmir, Kshemaraja (c.1000–1075 CE), the monistic Shaiva theologian and disciple of Abhinavagupta, again contemporary with Anselm and Ghazali, composed his *Essence of Recognition*, the *Pratyabhijnahrdaya*, a summary of his non-dual Shaiva teachings for those endowed with small intellect but strong desire for liberation. This text is a synthesis of teachings found in the monistic Shaiva revelation of the Tantras and presents the view that there is one consciousness that manifests in different forms, including the doctrines of other traditions. This view is an argument supported by scriptural reference and quotation, which sets itself in opposition to other positions and relegates other philosophies to lower levels of understanding. Kshemaraja's strategy is to colonize the views of opposing schools and to incorporate them within his graded hierarchy of meaning. Like those of Anselm and Ghazali, this is a textually grounded argument in a style that assumes the truth of revelation and the legitimacy of supporting claims with the authority of textual back-up.

In all three figures, reasoning assumes tradition and is a long way from the Enlightenment conception of reason divorced from tradition. The reasoning of these thinkers is an expression of their atunement. Their thinking is not irrational but theological and textually grounded. One suspects that were they to learn each others scholarly languages, Latin, Arabic, and Sanskrit, they might well find shared ground on which to dispute; but one also suspects that it would take a long time to find a shared language and mode of procedure. We do have historical, if short lived, instances of cross-theological dialogue between Islam, Judaism, and Christianity in Moslem Spain, but even here it is not that the thinkers involved were using the language of neutral reason; rather they were developing dialogical encounters from within their own theological traditions. Through these three brief examples, contemporary with each other, I hope to have illustrated the general point about rationality, that reasoning is a process found in the major religious traditions but that this thinking is established within traditions of text and practice. The Encyclopedic mode, to use MacIntyre's phrase, of the Enlightenment which claimed universal, objective reason, has yet to emerge in the history of thought, but clearly we have long traditions of theorizing about transcendence and about the nature of the human person in relation to transcendence. Here we have human reason mediating the encounter with mystery.

Religious traditions have not ceased from this activity. In spite of Enlightenment reason and the spread of scientific rationality, there are still traditions of thought rooted in religious traditions. In Islam, scholarship is not simply an academic activity but is central to political policy decisions in countries such as Iran and Indonesia. We have, again to refer to MacIntyre, three modes of ethical enquiry – the Enlightenment mode of detached reason, the traditional mode of reasoning within tradition, and the genealogical or critical mode that is skeptical of claims to truth.[38]

In the contemporary world it is hardly possible to be a Ghazali or Anselm in the western intellectual environment. Intellectuals who see themselves as standing within theological traditions nevertheless must engage with modernity and the Encyclopedist mindset. One form of such engagement, which attempts reasoning across traditions rooted in texts while engaging modernist reason and is set within the modern academy, is *scriptural reasoning*, founded by Peter Ochs. This is a mode of thinking in which textual traditions of Islam, Christianity, and Judaism encounter each other through the root texts of their traditions. We will end this reflection in rationality with a short consideration of this movement because it challenges predominant modes of secular thinking within the academy while at the same time wishing to go beyond traditional ways of thinking.

Scriptural reasoning assumes that religions are legitimate and not irrational ways of being in the world in modernity. Far from being apologetic, religions have a rightful place in the world and contain modes of reasoning which are legitimate and reveal wisdom and knowledge. Stemming from practices of Jewish reading and textual reasoning, scriptural reasoning has been developed, particularly by Peter Ochs, to become a practice of Jews, Moslems, and Christians studying their texts together in the spirit of friendship. Indeed, from the perspective of scriptural reasoning, secular reason is an impoverishment of the full potential of human thought for deeper kinds of rationality that reflect the very structure of reality. Indeed, this is a modern form of atunement that takes place within the secular academy. As Peter Ochs says, scriptural reasoning is "a response to the inadequacies of modern liberal and anti-liberal theologies."[39] Not dissimilar to the Indian philosophical discourse, scriptural reasoning is less about arriving at consensus, an Enlightenment model, and more about the clarification of difference. In this way scriptural reasoning sets itself against the idea of a universal reason for, as Nick Adams puts it, "[d]espite enquiries by some of the most impressive minds of the last two hundred years, there is no convincing account of universal reason or a satisfactory 'theory' of traditioned reasoning."[40]

Scriptural reasoning is then about the primacy of practice over theory, although there is an emergent theoretical discourse that arises as a consequence of the practice. This theoretical discourse is theological in so far as it takes the theological claims of traditions seriously but cannot arrive at a consensual theology other than in the broad terms of disagreement about theological axioms in the spirit of hospitality. Certain theological claims arrived at through the long histories of tradition, such as the doctrine of the trinity or the seal of the prophet, are, in a sense, non-negotiable in the context of discourse with other traditions. Were these doctrines to be changed, that would have to occur in tradition-specific contexts. But while each tradition has its axioms that people adhere to, there is a vast array of philosophical and practical issues that the texts of tradition can be used to address, from the nature of a human being, to attitudes to gender, to ethical issues such as stem cell research. In some sense, scriptural reasoning might be seen as a response to religion's "cultured despisers" within the academy, but equally a response to literalist, anti-modernist readings of scripture (usually found outside the academy). Reason is compatible with faith.

Conclusion

So far then we have argued that processes of rationality are shared but rationality is always linked to traditions of thought and practice. Religious reasoning has been traditionally associated with institutions that fostered and developed practices of thinking that assumed a particular revelation or sacred cosmos. Monasticism in Buddhist India and then in Europe were particularly important developments in the formation of religious reasoning but also the *yeshivas* and *madrasas*. These forms of religious reasoning can be contrasted with modern, scientific rationality that developed particularly since the Enlightenment in the West, although clearly there was scientific reasoning – arguments based on empirical evidence – from an early period in India and China. Different kinds of rationality therefore govern human cultural actions, although there is probably a spectrum here in that it makes sense to speak of Christian hermeneutics but I am not sure it makes sense to speak of Christian Physics or Hindu mathematics.

I suspect that the more empirical the claims of tradition are, that is, the more open to empirical falsification they are, the less bound by the particularity of culture and language they are, although never wholly free from human tradition. The meaning of religious actions must therefore be understood both in terms of intentionality (reasons for action) and in terms of significance for a community. The intentionality of act, the complex of willing that results in action, is itself based on basic cultural assumptions encoded in language and other cultural institutions (kinship patterns for example). I have argued that what is characteristic of religious acts is that while they are clearly cultural, they articulate or give expression to an aspect of the real that would otherwise remain concealed. The dance-possession rites of Kerala, the *teyyam* rites, are unique to Kerala in style and content (language, gesture, costume, music), but they open out a realm of the real for the participating community. This is similarly the case for the *ihamba* tooth ritual among the Ndembu. In more prosaic examples, one might even say that this structure holds true in Moslem daily prayers and Christian mass. The importance of religion therefore lies in the meaning of religious performance for agents who act in certain ways and the significance of those actions for the community. Sometimes these are small acts – offering incense to Ganesh – sometimes actions spawn a civilization – the Buddha's meditation or Christ's crucifixion.

It is all very well, one might say, that reasoning is within the bounds of tradition – and this can be empirically demonstrated from numerous examples in the history of civilizations, but are these modes of reasoning adequate for assessing human truth? Clearly, as MacIntyre has shown, traditional reasoning, particularly moral reasoning, is within traditions of thinking, but some might wish to argue for the superiority of the Encyclopedist or modernist practices of reasoning on the grounds that social coherence and meaning are not enough for the justification of irrational belief systems. Scientific reasoning gives us truth; religious reasoning gives us falsehood. This is a familiar view from Marx – who saw his thinking as based on scientific, empirical grounds – to Dawkins and the biological reductionists. Even theologians might adhere to this view and claim that religious reasoning needs to stand up to the rigors of scientific truth based on firm knowledge, particularly as derived from science; truth is objective and language needs to be adequate to express it. It is to this issue of the development of science in relation to religion and the adequacy of religious paradigms that we must now turn.

Notes

1. Certeau, Michel de, *The Writing of History*, trans. Tom Conley (New York: Columbia University Press, 1988), p. 23. For a well-written account, see Wilson, A.N., *God's Funeral* (New York, London: Norton and Co, 1999).
2. Lemmon, E.J., *Beginning Logic* (London: Nelson, 1965), pp. 50–2.
3. MacIntyre, Alistair, *Whose Justice? Which Rationality?* (Indiana: University of Notre Dame Press, 1988), p. 22. MacIntyre writes: "Central to every culture is a shared schema of greater or lesser complexity by means of which each agent is able to render the actions of others intelligible so that he or she knows how to respond to them."
4. Flood, G., *Beyond Phenomenology: Rethinking the Study of Religion* (London: Cassell, 1999), pp. 118–23.
5. Genette, G., *Narrative Discourse* (Oxford: Blackwell, 1980), pp. 25–7.
6. MacIntyre, *Whose Justice?*, p. 76.
7. Winch, Peter, *The Idea of a Social Science and Its Relation to Philosophy* (London: Routledge & Kegan Paul, 1958), pp. 14–15. For a good account of the importance of Winch, see Colin Lyas, *Peter Winch* (London: Acumen, 1999). For a critique of Winch, see Robin Horton, *Patterns of Thought in Africa and the West* (Cambridge: Cambridge University Press, 1993), pp. 139–42.

8.   Winch, *The Idea of a Social Science*, p. 50.
9.   Winch, *The Idea of a Social Science*, p. 49.
10. Winch, *The Idea of a Social Science*, p. 55.
11. Winch, *The Idea of a Social Science*, p. 116.
12. Winch, *The Idea of a Social Science*, p. 90.
13. Anthropology has roughly been divided into two camps, the expressivists and the intellectualists. Expressivists, such as John Beattie (*Other Cultures; Aims, Methods, Achievements in Social Anthropology* (London: Routledge, 1964), p. 72), understood ritual in terms of the expression of human need. The "intellectualist" view, on the other hand, emphasizes the instrumental nature of ritual action, e.g. Robin Horton, *Patterns of Thought in Africa and the West*, pp. 108–36.
14. Sahlins, M., *How Natives Think, About Captain Cook for Example* (Chicago: Chicago University Press, 1995), pp. 83–4.
15. Obeyesekere, G., *The Apotheosis of Captain Cook; European Mythmaking in the Pacific* (New Jersey: Princeton University Press, 1992), pp. 74–91.
16. Evans-Pritchard, E.E., *Witchcraft, Oracles, and Magic Among the Azande* (Oxford: Clarendon Press, 1976), p. 64.
17. Taylor, C., "Rationality," in *Philosophy and the Human Sciences: Philosophical Papers*, vol. 2 (Cambridge: Cambridge University Press, 1985), p. 137.
18. Taylor, "Rationality," p. 151.
19. Lloyd, G., *Adversaries and Authorities. Investigations into Ancient Greek and Chinese Science* (Cambridge: Cambridge University Press, 1996), ch. 4.
20. I would like to thank Javier Kalhat for drawing my attention to this distinction.
21. Davidson, D., *Inquiries into Truth and Interpretation* (Oxford: Clarendon Press, 1984), pp. 196–7.
22. Davidson, *Inquiries*, p. 37.
23. Milbank, J., *Theology and Social Theory: Beyond Secular Reason* (Oxford: Blackwell, 1990), p. 342. See also MacIntyre, *Three Rival Versions of Moral Enquiry* (Notre Dame: University of Notre Dame Press, 1990), p. 114.
24. Brandom, Robert, *Making It Explicit: Reasoning, Representing, and Discursive Commitment* (Cambridge, Mass.: Harvard University Press, 1994).
25. Hervieu-Léger, D., *Religion as a Chain of Memory*, trans. Simon Lee (Cambridge: Polity, 2000).
26. Taylor, "Rationality," p. 143.
27. See the papers by Staal, Hayashi, and Yano, in Flood, G. (ed.), *The Blackwell Companion to Hinduism* (Oxford: Blackwell, 2003), pp. 346–92.
28. See Eisenstadt, S.N. (ed.), *The Origins and Diversity of the Axial Age* (Albany: SUNY Press, 1986); Johann Arnason, S.N. Eisenstadt, and Bjorn Wittrock, *Axial Civilizations and World History* (Leiden: Brill, 2005).
29. Taylor, Charles, *The Secular Age* (Cambridge, Mass.: Harvard University Press, 2007), p. 146.
30. Lovejoy, Arthur O., *The Great Chain of Being* (Cambridge, Mass.: Harvard University Press, 1964 (1936)), p. 101.
31. Lewis, C.S., *The Discarded Image* (Cambridge: Cambridge University Press, 1964), p. 93.

32. Flood, Gavin, *The Tantric Body* (London: Tauris, 2006), p. 130.
33. Corbin, Henry, *Spiritual Body and Celestial Earth: from Mazdean Iran to Sh'ite Iran*, trans. Nancy Pearson (London: Tauris, 1986).
34. Moosa, E., *Ghazali and the Poetics of Imagination* (Oxford: Oxford University Press, 2005), p. 210.
35. Qur'an 24.35, quoted in Moosa *Ghazali*, p. 228.
36. Moosa, *Ghazali*, p. 229.
37. On Anselm, see Visser, Sandra and Thomas Williams, *Anselm* (Oxford: Oxford University Press, 2009).
38. MacIntyre, *Three Rival Versions of Moral Inquiry*, pp. 1–8.
39. Ochs, Peter, "Philosophical Warrants for Scriptural Reasoning," p. 121, in David F. Ford and C.C. Pecknold (eds), *The Promise of Scriptural Reasoning*, p. 42 (Oxford: Blackwell, 2006), pp. 121–38.
40. Adams, Nick, "Making Deep Reasonings Public," in Ford and Pecknold (eds), *The Promise of Scriptural Reasoning*, pp. 41–57.

Part Three

World

They said, "You have a blue guitar,
You do not play things as they are."

The man replied, "Things as they are
Are changed upon the blue guitar."

And they said then "But play you must
A tune beyond us, yet ourselves,

A tune upon the blue guitar
Of things exactly as they are"

Wallace Stevens, "The Man with the Blue Guitar,"
Collected Poems, p. 165.

7

The Mystery of Complexity and Emergence

The world is a mysterious place and science has been the human enterprise which has sought to give an account of the mystery in terms of material causation and natural laws. Religion too has sought to give an account of the mystery of the world and the two became competing worldviews in the history of the West, with science trumping religion in terms of causal predictive power and technology. Science clearly improves over time, having increasingly broader explanatory power in a way that religion does not. We might want to speak of progress and development in science, if by that we mean more knowledge and accuracy of procedures in a way that we would not speak of religion. It would not be clear what it would mean to say Buddhism or Judaism have progressed, other than that they have kept up with technological developments. In writing down its scriptures Buddhism in some sense progressed, but we could not claim that Buddhism progressed morally; loving kindness (*metta*) in the fourth century is much the same as in the twenty-first. Science and religion are distinct but have fought over the same ground and there has been a history of antagonism between them in the West, although in recent years some, not only apologists, have advocated the compatibility of religious and scientific claims.

The enterprise of science, if not its success and technical advancement, has been shared by cultures for thousands of years. It is not the prerogative of the West and sophisticated scientific cultures emerged in Chinese, Indian, and later Islamic civilization well before the seventeenth century.[1] But it is in Europe that since the seventeenth century science has developed apace with

The Importance of Religion: Meaning and Action in Our Strange World,
First Edition. Gavin Flood.
© 2012 Gavin Flood. Published 2012 by Blackwell Publishing Ltd.

increasing acceleration. Science has a history. In very broad terms science can be taken to mean systematic knowledge and explanation, although the English term has the connotation of observation, the formation of theory, empirical experiment, the accumulation of evidence, and explanatory conclusions induced from experiment. This reflects the distinction between the "human" and "natural" sciences which was made in the West but not in India or China.[2]

China, as Joseph Needham's *Science and Civilization in China* demonstrates, developed the compass, gunpowder, papermaking, and printing, which had a profound impact not only on Chinese but other civilizations as well.[3] China also developed proto-chemistry in alchemy, geology, astronomy, and medical science. Knowledge systems in India, whose scientific tradition "is as rich as the Chinese,"[4] were not clearly demarcated into the scientific and religious or philosophical, although much Indian thinking is what we would characterize as scientific. Among its earliest achievements are the science of language closely linked to the science of ritual and mathematics. Zero originated in India prior to the seventh century and is known to Aryabhatta who also knew pi and formulated a proof of the Pythagorian theorem independently.[5] From India, mathematics and other sciences were exported to the Middle East where Arabic thinkers took them up (from whence zero enters into European numbering) and into China, although Chinese and Indian science developed independently.

But it was science as found in the history of Europe that comes to have world significance accompanied by the development of medical, agricultural, and industrial technologies – much of which was derived from the East – as well as the growth of commerce and the western economies that resulted in the global capitalism of today. This story generally tells of how science accompanied by an increasing secularization comes to replace religion in explanatory power. Religion is eroded by science, although not completely, as the persistence of religion into late modernity testifies. In this chapter we firstly need to provide some background to the relationship between science and religion in more recent history, and secondly examine the key problems that both science and religion present us with, notably the problem of reductionism and the complexity of systems. While the main thrust of this book is a claim that religions provide people with existential meaning, the data of religion and the interface with science necessitates a further inquiry suggestive of the very nature of reality itself. Science makes claims about the nature of the world and particularly evolutionary biology has something to say to religion, not only in terms of natural selection but also in terms of complexity theory. Religions are integral to the complexity of human life and this complexity seen at the interface of religion and science is suggestive for exploring a second-level phenomenology or ontology of what shows itself in the religious sphere.

A History of Antagonism

The history of religion since the seventeenth century has been one of the erosion of religion as authority regarding the truth of the world. We see this especially with cosmology, where science took over as the authoritative voice. As science advanced, so religion retreated from empirical claims. Science and its attended technologies have stepped in to the gap left by the retreat of religion. At least this is true at the level of theory, although the Church did not give up its claim to empirical knowledge without a fight. The situation is complex in so far as there were a number of competing cosmologies that challenged the traditional, official Church view, namely the Copernicans, the Neo-Platonists, and the Biblicists. The Neo-Platonists held a geocentric, epicyclical model of the universe that was compatible with the biblical account and argued against Galileo and the Copernicans. But there were high stakes involved, and in 1610 the Church began a sustained attack on the ideas and person of the Italian philosopher-scientist Galileo Galilei (1564–1642) which was to last till the end of his life and beyond.[6] In that year, in *The Starry Messenger*, Galileo declared that he had discovered moons around Jupiter through the telescope he had constructed, but the Church condemned his discovery as going against Holy Scripture and therefore as being false. Further discoveries, that the moon reflected the light of the sun rather than being "a great light" in itself, and the discovery of sun spots (*The Sun Spot Letters* of 1613), were similarly condemned.

The Church was deeply threatened by Galileo's evidence for the Copernican theory of the heliocentric universe, that the earth was rotating daily around its own axis and yearly around the sun, and fought against the theory by condemnations of Galileo and his work, which culminated in his being summoned before the Inquisition in 1615. Under threat of imprisonment Galileo promised to obey the injunction that the earth does not move around the sun. In the following year Pope Paul V declared that the doctrine of the double revolution of the earth, around its own axis and around the sun, was false as it contradicted scripture. Further condemnations occurred but Galileo was allowed to publish the *Dialogo* in 1632 which, although it supported the Copernican view, contained a preface signed by Galileo condemning that view. The text was widely circulated throughout Europe and the pious preface taken with a pinch of salt by most people. This roused the ire of the Church again, particularly the Pope, and Urban VIII sent Galileo before the Inquisition once more where, under threat of torture, he was made to recant his view that the earth moved.

In hindsight it is easy for us in the twenty-first century to support Galileo's view against the Church, but we must remember that at the time, his was simply another view and not the truth that we understand today. Indeed, some of Galileo's ideas proved to be false, such as his denial of the eliptical shape of the planetary orbits. The condemnation of Galileo in 1633 also needs to be seen in the context of the threat to the Church by the Protestant reformation and establishing the authority of the Church in matters of biblical interpretation;[7] and his constantly critical attitude to the Church authorities did not help his case. Galileo spent the rest of his life in exile and even after his death his ideas were condemned. Only as late as 1822 did the Church officially allow the Copernican system to be taught, and the works of Galileo were removed from the Index only in 1835.[8]

The rise and gradual acceptance of the heliocentric view of the universe marks an end to the religious cosmology of the kind we had seen accepted by religious elites in the medieval period through Dante to the seventeenth century. By the end of the seventeenth century the Inquisition, although it lasted in Spain up to the nineteenth century, had lost its force. Religion in a sense retreated behind its own walls and focused on the moral universe as the realm of its operation rather than the physical universe. The shift to a heliocentric worldview is significant in that it marked a shift in the collective western perception of human reality from its central position in the Christian cosmological imagination. The world is now seen, as Taylor observes, to be but one small part of a much vaster universe, our sun just one star in a galaxy, and our time but a small fragment of the immense stretches of time behind us in which we were formed which "hides the process of our genesis, of our coming to be."[9] With John Locke after thirty years of religious war in Europe, religion was relegated to the private realm, although the Churches continued to make a claim upon the public sphere of discourse. The conflict with science exemplified in the argument with Galileo reflected badly on the Church, both Catholic and Protestant, and in time reinforced the secularist view that the Church was irrational and backward looking. The floodgates of science had been opened and the Church could do nothing to stop its inexorable march through to Isaac Newton and the theory of gravitation that explained the orbit of the planets in the solar system in 1687. As Taylor observes, there was a transformation in outlook between the seventeenth and nineteenth centuries from a view that we inhabit a fixed cosmos to the view of a vast, evolving universe.[10]

But the biggest threat to organized religion was to come in the nineteenth century, not from physics but from biology, with the publication of Charles Darwin's *Origin of Species* in 1859. Darwin desisted from publication of his eloquent book for some twenty years, a book which significantly threatened the Christian theory of creation and humanity as the summation of creation. Darwin showed that species change through time due to "the accumulation of innumerable slight variations" and that these variations are due to natural selection, "that there is a struggle for existence leading to the preservation of the profitable deviations of structure and instinct."[11] This natural selection "acts by competition, it adapts and improves the inhabitants of each country only in relation to their co-inhabitants."[12] This was as great a threat, if not greater, to traditional Christian theory than Galileo and its importance was clearly understood by the most astute theological minds of the time. If natural selection is true, then the traditional Christian narrative of the creation of Adam and Eve and human descent thereafter is not.[13] Even up to the present day, debate about this continues with serious theologians accepting evolution through natural selection but arguing for a "theistic evolution," that is, that evolution is God's action in the world – evolution is simply the way God creates.

Among the most prolific has been Arthur Peacocke, a professional scientist who argues for the compatibility of science and religion. While there are still biblical literalists, the general orientation of Christian theology has been to argue that God creates through the processes that science unveils. Rather than the eighteenth- and nineteenth-century idea of a mechanized universe with God, if there is one, as a detached instigator of natural laws, Peacocke argues for a continuous creation. God is continually active in creation and forms new species which develop out of old ones. Rather than God being detached, outside of the world, Peacocke's view is that the world is embedded within God and that the entire world is filled with God's presence; a doctrine of panentheism.[14]

He cites the analogy of the self and body: as we are to our bodies so God is to the universe, an image found not only in Christianity but particularly in the theology of the Hindu Vaishnava Ramanuja.[15] On this view the Christian doctrine of creation is quite compatible with science. What science shows us is the *how* of creation and to some extent the *why*, but what Christianity points to is the larger *why* of creation, the purposes of creation as far as we can discern them. The response to this larger question, as Peacocke observes, is not found in science. Rather the exploration of the *why* is the realm of religion; the response to the ultimate questions of life.

Other religions have responded to modern physics and biology but not to the degree that Christianity has. This is partly because there is a long and one might add antagonistic exposure of Christian theology to science which has by now developed a sophisticated understanding that integrates empirical findings with theological doctrines. There are Hindu claims that all modern scientific knowledge is found in the Vedas, but there has been little credible, serious Hindu theological response to developments in modern science although this is beginning to happen. In 1975 a famous book by Fritjof Capra *The Tao of Physics* claimed that "eastern mysticism," including Buddhism, views the world in a similar way to quantum physics. He argued that the truths of physics expressed in a complex mathematical language are also expressed in the technical languages of mysticism, particularly Buddhism. "Quantum theory," he writes, "forces us to see the universe not as a collection of physical objects, but rather as a complicated web of relations between the various parts of a unified whole."[16]

Eastern mysticism, claims Capra, has the same view as imaged by the interconnected cosmic web which in Buddhism represents interrelatedness and in Hinduism represents all things connected by the thread of the *brahman*. Buddhism has had a generally positive response to modern science in recent years particularly by the Dalai Lama who sees Buddhism as compatible with it.[17] In Buddhism there is no *theos*, no creator God that might be an obstacle to scientific understanding, and Buddhism has been taught as an open inquiry into the nature of reality, coming to the conclusion, in its Mahayana form, that the ultimate reality of the world is empty of essence. According to Buddhism the universe is a continuous, never ending process of cause and effect – described in Buddhism as the twelve links of dependent origination (*pratītyasamutpāda*) which keeps beings bound in the cycle of suffering and rebirth.[18] On this view the Buddha anticipated the developments of modern science, particularly quantum mechanics.[19] The difference between physics and Buddhism is that while physics describes the truth of reality as empty, Buddhism presents a way to directly experience that reality. More recently, Buddhism has been seen to be compatible with cognitive science. While empirical investigation of the brain states of meditators has been going on for some time,[20] this kind of work has received a new impetus with cognitive science and the willingness of mainly Western Buddhists to work with these developments.

Whereas the main focus of concern for Christianity has been evolutionary biology because this has seemed to directly challenge the centrality and uniqueness of human beings in creation, the main focus of concern for Buddhism has been physics and psychology because both make claims about the ultimate nature of reality as "empty" and Buddhism is deeply concerned with meditative states of consciousness. As with all religions and science, we find a selective process of concern and different aspects of science will engage with different aspects of the religions. But whatever science has to say about the nature of the world would not affect the teachings of the Buddha, whose main concern is freedom from entanglement in suffering and rebirth. No matter what the nature of the world, the ultimate human purpose is freedom from it through entry into *nirvana* (in one formulation of Buddhism) or awakening to the truth of Buddhahood, the truth of the emptiness of appearances, in the here and now.

One of the problems, particularly with books such as Capra's, is that while religions are generally resistant to change, and are in many ways conservative because they pass what they regard as vitally important cultural knowledge through the generations that needs to be preserved, modern science is not. Science progresses by the destruction of old theories. Indeed, as Popper reminds us, scientific claims are not provable but *falsifiable* and science develops by disproving old theories and testing new ones.[21] We should therefore be hesitant about leaping to conclusions that a particular religious tradition is saying virtually the same thing as a scientific proposition. Science is constantly changing and has undergone major paradigm shifts in the last centuries from Newtonian to quantum mechanics, which itself is undergoing rapid change as new particles are discovered. Buddhism and other religions for that matter, while they clearly change, do not undergo such rapid change and are not like scientific theories: religions are not falsifiable unless they make empirical claims and even then they are resistant to falsifiablity as we have seen in the case of Galileo and Darwin. It is highly questionable that because a religious tradition contains ideas that seem to resemble science at a certain stage in the history of science, that this points to a timeless truth. But although I am somewhat skeptical about claims of interconnection between science and religions, we do need to probe further in relation firstly to complexity and secondly in relation to the limits of language in religion and science.

Complexity and Constraint

The highest profile debate between science and religion since the nineteenth century has been over evolution. There have been massive advances in our understanding of the development of species, including the human species, in recent years with, to name one important development, the human genome project and the mapping of the all the genes of the human body.[22] Darwin would have been fascinated by the genetic evidence, the actual mechanism of how characteristics are transmitted, not available to him at that time, although Mendel had established the principle of genetic selection. Advances in paleontology have mapped more precisely the development of the human species from earlier forms and have even demonstrated that parallel species of human being have cohabited the planet up until fairly recent times.[23]

Kauffman summarizes the developments that have lead to contemporary biology. Before Darwin there were "rational morphologists" who were interested in the variety of types of organism and who sought, in Kantian fashion, for a relatively few underlying, universal principles to account for the diversity of living beings. This eventually developed into "branching phylogenies" and natural selection.[24] Kauffman outlines four strands that lead from rational morphology to contemporary biology, namely Darwin's theory of natural selection; Mendel's discovery of the basic laws of genetic transmission; Weissman's concept of germ plasm (a substance contained in a complex structure, the germ cell, due to which offspring resemble their parents); and population genetics.[25] All of these have formed the contemporary discipline, which is supported by recent developments in neuroscience and the mapping of the human brain in relation to evolution.

Theories of cognition show how the brain has developed and how specific parts of the brain are concerned with specific functions. This is complicated by the way our brains interact with culture: which is dominant, nature (brain chemistry) or nurture (culture)? Some years ago ethology, the science of animal behavior, transformed into sociobiology, itself a precursor of evolutionary psychology.[26] These disciplines attempted to understand animal behavior through reference to a deeper biological conditioning. With sociobiology we have the attempt to link behavior directly to the genes which in the seventies became highly contentious. When Edward Wilson wrote *The Insect Societies* and later *Sociobiology* there was little interest amongst the broader public. But when he applied the same principles, the same biological reductionism to the human case in *On Human Nature* there was much public debate and passion.[27]

What these developments have in common is that they maintain a link between cultural behavior and genes, that culture is "on the leash of the genes"[28] although, as Bowker describes at length, there are strong and weak theories about whether that leash is long or short. On the one hand, the strong thesis maintains that culture can always be "mapped back onto the genes: it cannot be an autonomous process,"[29] whereas weak theory implies a long leash, that culture functions autonomously to the genetic code. The purpose of culture in the strong theory is genetic adaptability to ensure the transmission of the genes through the generations, to ensure the maximal conditions for the reproductive survival of the genes. Culture, on this view, is a mechanism for the protection of the genes – a sophisticated way of saying, with Bishop Butler, that a hen is simply an egg's way of making another egg. Religions have been key institutions for ensuring the continued replication of the genes, of particular note being the family formed and reinforced by religious sanction.[30] Richard Dawkins has called cultural ideas that go through the generations and protect the gene pool, *memes*. Almost any cultural product can be a meme, including ideas, fashions, technology, and architecture, and even Darwinian theory itself.[31] The idea of God is a meme although its function is lost in the past and we can now regard it as a virus. The God meme is otiose and even dangerous.

In an important critique of Dawkins' idea, Bowker shows the inconsistency in his argument. For example, memes cannot be isolated as an essence in the sense that particular properties without which it could not exist cannot be identified. The analogy with the gene is therefore very remote because genes can be identified with a high degree of specificity; genes are "chain-like molecules of nucleic acids," such as DNA and RNA, found in the nucleus of cells which make up living beings.[32] Dawkins' meme does not even approach this level of specificity and, as Bowker argues, there are far better accounts of cultural transmission. The relationship between cultural productions, such as religions, and the genetic code simply cannot be established other than in a vague way. In Bowker's terms, following Susan Oyama, the phenotype is "a consequence of a developmental process in which the activity of gene transcription and the context of cultural constraint play their part but not in any standard or invariant or even exclusive way."[33] Human nature is a result of the combination of genes and culture, which, in Bowker's important way of expressing this, form "a network of constraint that controls all eventualities into their outcome, into their being what they are."[34]

A simple biological reductionism to explain human beings is inadequate to the task because the complexity is too great. Complexity shows that effects "can have an irreducible tangle of causes."[35] In technical terminology, the network of constraints gives rise to the particular phenotype; thus we might say that a seagull is the result of the network of constraints that have included a particular genetic code, the mating of its parents, the environment in which it was reared and now lives – a rocky coast in the Hebrides or a land-fill site in Brighton – the food it consumes and so on. There is a feedback loop entailed in so far as the organism that has emerged as a result of the network of constraints can affect particular elements in that network; thus the gull can breed, can eat a particular fish, can cause an accident through being sucked into a plane's engine, can give delight to a small child, can be the subject of a poem, and so on. But the point is that emergentist properties are still material: put simply by Drees "wetness is a property of drops of water, but it isn't a property of individual molecules of H2O."[36]

Kauffman in particular has been at the forefront of developing complexity theory. Natural selection alone cannot account for evolution; we also need the idea of self-regulation and holism. Organisms, and indeed all of nature, display great complexity as the result of lower-level factors (such as gene selection) but this complexity has an effect on the development of an organism and "we must understand how selection interacts with systems which have their own spontaneously ordered properties."[37] Kauffman goes into some of the detail of these emergent properties and argues that we can understand the origin of life itself in terms of emergent properties of "a modestly complex mixture of catalytic polymers, such as proteins or catalytic RNA, which catalyze one another's formation."[38] That is, the detailed interaction and building up of molecular compounds that affect each other produced life, which itself cannot be understood purely by reduction to these processes but supervenes on those processes. There is a spontaneous, higher-level organization that emerges from the lower-level genetic layer. In contrast to the view that evolution is an ad hoc process, Kauffman argues that it is purposive in the sense that the emergent properties are the reason, as it were, for the organism to evolve in precisely the way that it does. The organism is as it is because of the network of constraints operating upon it, to use Bowker's terms, but is not wholly reducible to that network. In a sense there is a teleology involved: an organism which results from natural selection which affects the particularity of genetic cell formation, is complemented by a higher-level, self-regulating system. Self-organization of organisms is so "profoundly immanent in complex regulatory networks," Kauffman writes, that "selection cannot avoid that order";[39] as complexity increases, as it does when protein molecules are distinguished from each other by only one amino acid position, selection "is less able to alter properties of system."[40] Far from being random and ad hoc, complexity theory tells us that natural selection is goal-orientated and the resulting systems are self-regulating.

This relationship between two sets of systems is not a kind of dualism – it is not that the organism exists independently of the network of constraints that comprise it – and we cannot, of course, leap to theistic conclusions from this failure of eliminative reductionism. The relationship between network of constraints (call it A) and resultant system (call it B) is not some kind of ontological independence. Indeed, the term "supervenience" might be used here, a technical term borrowed from the philosophy of mind. McLaughlin and Bennett define it as:

> A set of properties A supervenes upon another set B just in case no two things can differ with respect to A-properties without also differing with respect to their B-properties. In slogan form, "there cannot be an A-difference without a B-difference."[41]

Thus an exact copy of El Greco's *A View of Toledo* (to use McLaughlin and Bennett's example) or the Mona Lisa (to use Chalmers's example), is different from the original in so far as it is a forgery but it is also exactly like the original in shape, size, weight, color, and so on. The properties of the forgery can be said to supervene on the microphysical properties, for one cannot change these properties without also changing the properties of the forgery. A-properties affect B-properties but not necessarily the other way around, so shape supervenes on physical properties, "any two objects with the same physical properties will necessarily have the same shape,"[42] but value does not supervene in this way, thus "an exact physical replica of the Mona Lisa is not worth as much as the Mona Lisa."[43] Emergent properties supervene on that from which they emerge but are not identical to them in all respects. Some philosophers of mind, such as Chalmers, regard supervenience as the key to understanding consciousness, which remains a mystery in spite of developments in neuroscience and cognition.[44]

The self-regulating, supervenient system that is life is the product of natural selection but cannot be reduced to selection. But we might speak of selection itself as the creator of order, as Kauffman himself does,[45] an order which could allow humanity to find anew a place in the universe through this new science of complexity that shows that order is not accidental. In *Reinventing the Sacred* Kauffman goes beyond science in speaking of the reintegration of science with the ancient Greek idea of the good life and argues that complexity theory shows us that agency cannot be accounted for in reductionist terms. While resisting the language of theism, he nevertheless argues that humanity as self-regulating and morally driven needs to work towards a global ethic of toleration in a world civilization. Kauffman's vision may or may not appeal – it certainly underestimates the grip of traditions upon people – but the important point is that organizational systems, such as societies and religions, display emergent properties resistant to explanation in purely reductionist ways. The new science of complexity, thinks Kauffman, is "breaking the Galilean spell" that the natural world can be explained by physical laws.[46]

Like the economy and society, religions are self-regulating systems. The idea of a self-regulating system – homeostatic system[47] – means that the system cannot be explained only in terms of the lower-level factors or network of constraints that comprise it. An emergent property is a distinct entity that arises in a hierarchical system as the consequence of the lower levels but which itself cannot be accounted for only in terms of those lower levels. A hive of bees, for example, is a society of bees as a coherent, self-ordering group that is the result of a whole range of constraints including the genetic code of the bees and the environment. The network of constraints produces phenomena that cannot be explained simply by reference to any particular part of that network. Religions might be seen to be rather like this as extremely complex self-regulating systems. We might add that the specification of constraints cannot exclude the possibility of supernatural agency, which cannot be ruled out simply on a priori grounds.[48]

In the kind of language I have been using here, the human encounter with mystery is mediated by cultural forms in complex ways and the constraints that result in those complex forms are genetic, historical, and the mystery of life itself. Thus complexity produces emergent properties that cannot themselves be reduced to or accounted for in any direct way to specific material causes. Religion might be said to be emergent in being the consequence of complex processes which do not rule out the possibility of non-physical constraint.[49] A phenomenological perspective is necessarily open to the possibility that transcendence erupts in history. Furthermore, religions as emergent properties from immensely complex sets of constraint can arguably in turn affect those constraints. Thus Weber has convincingly argued at a macro-level that religion has been an important factor in the formation of modern capitalism. Religions also have an affect at a micro-level on human persons: they provide reasons for undertaking certain actions, and guide our judgments and behavior. At least for billions of human beings, self-understanding and the purposes and meaning of life are constrained by

religions and we already have seen the ways in which we internalize traditions and make them our own.

The Ontology of Process

The constraints that form an event into its outcome, to use Bowker's
terminology, are inexhaustibly complex in that the specification of all
constraints would probably be infinite. Recent thinking in physics speaks
of the "multiverse," the possibility that there are trillions of universes and
many possible histories of them with the complexity of constraint accounted
for by M-theory: a range of theories at the quantum level that brings together
the four laws of physics (gravity, electromagnetic force, and the strong and
weak nuclear forces).[50] Such complexity is certainly a challenge to human
explanatory powers, but it is also an opportunity to deepen our engagement
beyond the first-level of descriptive interpretation.

The idea of complexity controlled by constraints opens up the possibility of
a phenomenology as ontology and the exploration of those constraints which
are open to religion as an expression of the real. If religion speaks from within
the world or from within the real, then our inquiry into religion becomes an
inquiry into reality of which we are inseparably a part. Such inquiry is a kind
of entry in thought and in imagination into the sublime and an entry into
mystery. Indeed, the data of religions necessitates that we inquire further into
that immanence of which we are a part and into that transcendence,
although, by definition, it will always be out of reach. With regard to
aesthetic experience, Taylor makes the following claim:

> And there are certain works of art – by Dante, Bach, the makers of Chartres
> Cathedral: the list is endless – whose power seems inseparable from their
> epiphanic, transcendent reference. Here the challenge is to the unbeliever,
> to find a non-theistic register in which to respond to them without
> impoverishment.[51]

This epiphanic sentiment can be applied more broadly beyond art to religion
and its impact upon human subjectivity more generally. While Taylor's
theistic language might seem to restrict the impact of this idea, the overall
sentiment is surely apposite. If religions speak from within the real, if they are
central to human reality in showing us something about the nature of the
universe of which we are a part, as they claim, then not to understand them in
this deeper context is to misunderstand them. The data of religions necessitates our deeper exploration and the raising of ontological questions. It is not
that the answer to these questions will be the same, indeed there can be no
answer to these questions, but what we do have is endless possibility of

human enrichment through engaging with that which is behind appearance, which constrains those appearances into their particularity.

Such ontological language might be criticized for its theistic implications. But it is not a theological claim, because it does not stand within a theological tradition. Clearly a second-level ontological inquiry can and should be done from within the boundaries of traditions. This is traditional theology – reasoning about transcendence from within the boundaries of a semantically dense, textual practice, as in the case of Ghazali or Kshemaraja. But such an inquiry can also be done from within phenomenology in the academy, an inquiry that cuts across the particularities and languages of traditions. This is arguably a worthwhile enterprise because we live in the globalized, pluralistic world and many of us are hybrids, standing within a number of traditions, insiders and outsiders simultaneously, and yet for whom deeper philosophical engagement with the real is demanded. This kind of inquiry might be rejected out of hand from a perspective of methodological atheism, but to do so would be without justification other than the history of an a priori incredulity towards religious claims.

Phenomenological inquiry of this kind is ontology and therefore no different from other ontological inquiries. Heidegger understood this when he discussed the modes in which being shows itself, and in his early lectures on the phenomenology of the religious life.[52] A phenomenological inquiry of this kind is simply the articulation of the modes in which religion shows itself to us in experience, not in terms of content (that would be the task of a descriptive hermeneutical phenomenology, our first-level phenomenology) but in terms of process and the examining of the ways in which religion appears within human consciousness, enacted within communities.

But what could such an inquiry look like? I would submit that a second-level phenomenology would always be vague about substance but a phenomenology of religion of the kind attempted here could make a claim that different religions share in a structure of reality at the level of *process*, particularly the process of the intensification of subjective meaning along with bringing the subject into direct confrontation with the real through practices of prayer, asceticism, and moral action. There is an ethical dimension here that religions make claims that the structure of reality entails a certain kind of perception and that this perception is ethical as well as cosmological. Ethics is not simply law, although it does become that in many religions, but is also built-in to human perception. I see the suffering child and respond at a visceral, non-discursive level. Even traditions of transgression such as some Buddhist and Hindu tantric traditions, in order to break out of restriction imposed by mainstream tradition, assume an ethical structure to reality that can be disrupted. This is not a claim about content – the particular ontologies of religions are so diverse – but it is a claim about procedure and about the legitimacy of theological voices in making second-level ontological claims. If religions speak from within the real, from within the mystery and strangeness of the world, then human beings must inevitably listen; indeed the attraction of the voice from the real is so great that they can do no other, and yet it is a voice that, in the end, says nothing and reaches into silence.

The mystery and strangeness of the world resists human knowing and resists expression, and yet that mystery inevitably and inexorably draws us towards it. There is a deep unknowability about the world that religions recognize and that is also shared in scientific inquiry.[53] While some religions are suspicious of ineffability claims, many understand transcendence in those terms. Our argument has been that religions, while differing on metaphysical grounds and in terms of particular narratives and practices, all share an orientation to the world or process that can be described as a kind of mediation or mode of encountering mystery. While elaborate theological accounts of the world have been developed in the history of religions, all these theologies share a sense that this in the end is inexpressible. What then can be said about silence? Well, surprisingly traditions say quite a lot or perhaps skirt around the edges of a deep, cosmic silence of the unknowable universe and, in theistic language, a deep cosmic silence of an unknowable God. Such silence is articulated certainly in theological treatises, but also in poetry, in music, and in the plastic arts. This deep unknowability of the world is both a closed door, for nothing can be said, and an invitation, for unknowability is an endless deepening.

Conclusion

This chapter has examined the interface between religion and science by surveying the history of antagonism between Christianity and a scientific worldview in which we looked at Galileo's struggles and the ultimate triumph of scientific theory, particularly as regards cosmology, over theological accounts of the world. Perhaps the greatest threat to Christian theology was Darwin's theory of evolution through natural selection, although contemporary theologians see no conflict in natural selection being regarded as the way in which God creates. But natural selection is just one side of the evolutionary process and complexity theory has arisen in evolutionary biology in recent years which maintains that complex systems cannot be accounted for wholly in terms of the parts that make them up. That is, self-organization has an important role to play in the development of complex systems. Religions might be seen in terms of complex systems which emerge from other factors but cannot be reduced to those other factors. Religions show themselves in complex ways and the possibility of their opening out transcendence cannot be ignored. Indeed, the data of religions necessitate a second-level phenomenological inquiry, which is an ontological inquiry that cuts across traditions. Such a phenomenology is not so much about content – the religious traditions are so diverse – but is about process and the ways in which human communities engage with the world, with the real, through the practices of asceticism, prayer, and ethical action demanded by religious traditions. Such an inquiry is also open to the aesthetics of religions and shows the proximity of religion to the arts, a topic to which we will now turn.

Notes

1. Needham's volumes on the history of science in China bears witness to this. See also Staal, F., "The Indian Sciences," in Flood, G., *The Blackwell Companion to Hinduism* (Oxford: Blackwell, 2003), pp. 346–409. See also Fara, Patricia, *Science: A Four Thousand Year History* (Oxford: Oxford University Press, 2010), which does not, unfortunately, deal adequately with science in India; a massive lacuna in an otherwise very competent book.
2. Staal observes that this distinction is a feature of "a very particular, if not peculiar, cultural development," that particularly stems from Wilhelm Dilthey in the nineteenth century. Staal, "Introduction," in Flood (ed.), *The Blackwell Companion to Hinduism* (Oxford: Blackwell, 2003), pp. 346–7.
3. Needham, J., *Science and Civilization in China*, 18 vols. But for an abridgement, see Needham, J., *The Shorter Science and Civilisation in China: An Abridgement of Joseph Needham's Original Text* (Cambridge: Cambridge University Press, 1980).
4. Staal, "Introduction," p. 346.
5. Hayashi, Takao, "Indian Mathematics," p. 370, in Flood (ed.), *Blackwell Companion*, pp. 360–75.
6. The standard biography of Galileo is Drake, Stillman, *Galileo* (Oxford: Oxford University Press, 1980). See also Pitt, Joseph C., *Galileo: Human Knowledge, and the Book of Nature: Method Replaces Metaphysics* (Dordrecht: Kluwer, 1992); Levere, Trevor H. and William R. Shea (eds), *Nature, Experiment, and the Sciences: Essays on Galileo and the History of Science in Honour of Stillman Drake* (Dordrecht: Kluwer, 1990); and Machamer, Peter, *The Cambridge Companion to Galileo* (Cambridge: Cambridge University Press, 1998).
7. Drees, Willem B., *Religion and Science in Context: A Guide to the Debates* (London: Routledge, 2010), p. 25.
8. On his relationship with the Church, see Langford, Jerome J., *Galileo, Science and the Church* (Ann Arbor: University of Michigan Press, 1992).
9. Taylor, C., *A Secular Age* (Cambridge, Mass. and London: Belknap Press, 2007), p. 326.
10. Taylor, *A Secular Age*, p. 327.
11. Darwin, Charles, *The Origin of Species* (London: John Murray, 1901 (1859)), p. 380.
12. Darwin, *Origin*, p. 389.

13. For an account of the theological reception of Darwin, see Welch, Claude, *Protestant Thought in the Nineteenth Century*, vol. 2. (New Haven: Yale University Press, 1985); Gregory, F., "The Impact of Darwinist Evolution on Protestant Theology in the 19th century," in Lindberg, D.C. and R.I. Numbers (eds), *God and Nature: Historical Essays on the Encounter Between Christianity and Science* (Berkeley: University of California Press, 1986), pp. 369–89, and Ronald C. Numbers, "The Creationists," in the same volume, pp. 391–423.

14. See for example Peacocke, Arthur R., *Intimations of Reality: Critical Realism in Science and Religion* (Notre Dame, Ind.: University of Notre Dame Press, 1984), pp. 11–53; Peacocke, Arthur, "Articulating God's Presence in and to the World unveiled by the Scientist," pp. 143, 145–52, in Peacocke and P. Clayton (eds), *In Whom We Live and Move and Have Our Being: Panentheistic Reflections on God's Presence in a Scientific World* (Grand Rapids: Erdmans, 2004), pp. 137–54.

15. See Hunt Overzee, Ann, *The Body Divine, the Symbol of the Body in the Work of Teilhard de Chardin and Ramanuja* (Cambridge: Cambridge University Press, 1992).

16. Capra, Fritjof, *The Tao of Physics* (Bungay: Fontana, 1975), p. 142. For a more recent version of the thesis, see Jones, Richard H., *Science and Mysticism: A Comparative Study of Western Natural Science, Theravada Buddhism, and Advaita Vedanta* (Lewisburg, PA: Bucknell University Press, 1986), and *Piercing the Veil: Comparing Science and Mysticism as Ways of Knowing Reality* (New York: Jackson Square Books, 2010).

17. Tenzin Gyatso, The Dalai Lama XIV, *The Universe in a Single Atom: The Convergence of Science and Spirituality* (New York: Morgan Road Books, 2005). Buddhism must accept a hypothesis that turns out to be true (p. 25) and abandon aspects of Abhidharma cosmology (p. 85).

18. For an account of causation in Buddhism, see Kragh, Ulrich Timme, *Early Buddhist Theories of Action and its Result: a Study of Karmaphalasambandha, Candrakiriti's Prasannapada verses 17.1–20* (Wien: Vienna: Universität Wien, 2006). Kalupahana, David J., *A History of Buddhist Philosophy: Continuities and Discontinuities* (Honolulu: University of Hawaii Press, 1992).

19. There is burgeoning literature on science and Buddhism. See particularly Lopez, Donald S. Jr., *Buddhism and Science: A Guide for the Perplexed* (Chicago: University of Chicago Press, 2008); Dalai Lama, *The Universe in a Single Atom: The Convergence of Science and Spirituality*; McMahan, David, "Modernity and the Discourse of Scientific Buddhism," *Journal of the American Academy of Religion*, vol. 72 (4), 2004, 897–933; Wallace, B. Alan, *Hidden Dimensions: The Unification of Physics and Consciousness* (New York: Columbia University Press, 2007); Wallace, Alan B., (ed.), *Buddhism and Science: Breaking New Ground* (New York: Columbia University Press, 2003).

20. e.g. Naranjo, Claudio and Robert E. Ornstein, *On the Psychology of Meditation* (London: George Allen and Unwin, 1972).

21. Popper, Karl, *The Poverty of Historicism* (London: Routledge, 2002 (1957)), pp. 131–7. For an account of Popper's philosophy, see Corvi, Roberta, *An*

Introduction to the Thought of Karl Popper, trans. Patrick Camiller (London: Routledge, 1997).

22. Lee, Thomas F., *The Human Genome Project: Cracking the Genetic Code of Life* (New York, London: Pleunum Press, 1991).

23. e.g. Apart from Neanderthals we know of *Homo floriensis* or "flores man," who lived in Indonesia up to 12,000 years ago. Goldenberg, Linda, *Little People and a Lost World: An Anthropological Mystery* (Minneapolis, Minn.: Twenty-First Century Books, 2007).

24. Kauffman, S., *The Origins of Order: Self-Organization and Selection in Evolution* (New York: Oxford University Press, 1993), p. 3. See also *At Home in the Universe: The Search for the Laws of Self-Organization and Complexity* (New York: Oxford University Press, 1993).

25. Kauffman, *Origins*, p. 8.

26. For a comprehensive introduction, see Rossano, Matthew J., *Evolutionary Psychology: The Science of Human Behavior and Evolution* (Hoboken, NJ: John Wiley & Sons, 2003). Rossano argues that religion had a favorable adaptive function. Shamanism involved with healing through supernatural agency had a positive effect upon people involved in healing rituals (pp. 157–8).

27. Wilson, Edward O., *The Insect Societies* (Cambridge, Mass.: Belknap Press of Harvard University Press, 1971); *Sociobiology: The New Synthesis* (Cambridge, Mass.: Belknap Press of Harvard University Press, 1975); *On Human Nature* (Cambridge, Mass.: Belknap Press of Harvard University Press, 1978).

28. Wilson, E., *On Human Nature*, p. 32. For an excellent discussion, see Bowker, John, *Is God A Virus?* (London: SPCK, 1995), pp. 11–17, 35–46.

29. Bowker, *Is God a Virus?* p. 64.

30. Bowker, *The Sacred Neuron: Extraordinary New Discoveries Linking Science and Religion* (London: Tauris, 2005), p. 162.

31. Dawkins, R., *The Self Gene* (Oxford: Oxford University Press, 1976), pp. 192–5.

32. Bowker, *Is God a Virus?* p. 19.

33. Bowker, *Is God a Virus?* p. 87.

34. Bowker, *Is God a Virus?* p. 88.

35. Coveney, P. and R. Highfield, *Frontiers of Complexity: the Search for Order in a Chaotic World* (London: Faber and Faber, 1996), p. 328f. Quoted in Bowker, John, *The Sacred Neuron*, p. 4.

36. Drees, Willem, B., *Religion and Science in Context: A Guide to the Debates* (London: Routledge, 2010), p. 33.

37. Kauffman, *Origins*, p. xvi.

38. Kauffman, *Origins*, p. xvi.

39. Kauffman, *Origins*, p. xvii.

40. Kauffman, *Origins*, p. 38.

41. McLaughlin, Brian, and Bennett, Karen, "Supervenience," *The Stanford Encyclopedia of Philosophy* (Summer 2010 Edition), Edward N. Zalta (ed.) (http://plato.stanford.edu/archives/sum2010/entries/supervenience/; accessed August 25, 2010).

42. Chalmers, David J., *The Conscious Mind: In Search of a Fundamental Theory* (Oxford: Oxford University Press, 1996), p. 33.
43. Chalmers, *Conscious Mind*, p. 34.
44. Chalmers is eloquent on this matter: "Consciousness however is as perplexing as it ever was. It still seems utterly mysterious that the causation of behaviour should be accompanied by a subjective inner life." *Conscious Mind*, p. xi. Indian philosophies and religions have thematized consciousness to a degree not found in other religions and there is rich potential for comparative philosophy here.
45. Kauffman, *Origins*, p. 11.
46. Kauffman, S., *Reinventing the Sacred: A New View of Science, Reason and Religion* (New York: Basic Books, 2008), p. xi.
47. Bowker, John, *The Sense of God* (Oxford: Clarendon Press, 1973), pp. 50–1.
48. Bowker, *The Sacred Neuron*, p. 6.
49. See Peacocke, A. and P. Clayton (eds), *The Re-Emergence of Emergence: The Emergentist Hypothesis from Science to Religion* (Oxford: Oxford University Press, 2006).
50. M-theory originates with Edward Witten and is advocated by Steven Hawking and Leonard Mlodinow; see their *The Grand Design* (London: Bantam Press, 2010).
51. Taylor, *A Secular Age*, p. 607.
52. Heidegger, Martin, *The Phenomenology of the Religious Life*, trans. Mathias Fritsch and Jennifer Anna Gosetti-Ferencei (Bloomington and Indianapolis: Indiana University Press, 2004).
53. See John Bowker (ed.), *Knowing the Unknowable: Science and Religions on God and the Universe* (London: I.B. Tauris, 2009).

8

The Union of Nature and Imagination

Some seven months after the death of his wife, John Constable wrote to his friend John Fisher in July 1829 that "the whole object and difficulty of the art (and indeed of all the fine arts) is to *unite imagination with nature*."[1] This is precisely what the great early romantic landscape painters sought to achieve in the early nineteenth century. The understanding of art as the unity of imagination and nature points to an understanding of art as a creative force somewhat akin to that of the creator himself. In the present chapter we therefore need to examine this idea more closely, to argue that the distinctive characteristic of religious art has been its cosmological orientation and to show how some contemporary art seeks to re-establish the cosmological link broken with the development of secularism. There is a close proximity between religion and art; both show us something about the world, both unleash the imagination, and both give concrete expression to intellectual and emotional vision.

The idea of art as a general category that included literature and music as well as painting had only begun to emerge fifty years before Constable's letter, influenced by the concept of *Kunst* ("Art") in German romanticism. Goethe's friend Carl Philip Moritz wrote a book *On the Plastic Imitation of the Beautiful* (*Über die bildendeNachahmung des Schönen*) which was precisely about the representation of nature through the imagination and the artist's ability to recreate as being parallel to the creativity of "the great totality of nature" herself.[2] While Constable was far too down to earth to adopt such pantheistic views, the understanding of art as the imaginative

The Importance of Religion: Meaning and Action in Our Strange World,
First Edition. Gavin Flood.
© 2012 Gavin Flood. Published 2012 by Blackwell Publishing Ltd.

recreation of nature became pervasive and defining. The artist mediated the vastness of nature and yet contained that vastness within the canvass, mediated nature through culture. Indeed, art became a quasi-religious activity, something which has arguably continued to the present day, and the artist almost akin to a priest. Although this is not a language that Constable would have recognized, we might say that the artist shows us something that would otherwise remain hidden and that only comes into view indirectly through the imagination. While the nature and definition of art has changed, the insight that art unites imagination with nature is still pertinent if we replace "nature" with "our strange world." Art shows us something about the world that only comes into view indirectly and which could be said in no other way and is inseparable from the telling.

Art and the Real

There are many definitions of art, from aesthetic theorists of the nineteenth century such as John Ruskin's, who (echoing Constable) saw art as the articulation of the truth of nature, to postmodern theorists such as Clement Greenburg's, for whom modernist art is purely reflexive, concerned with critiquing art itself. Modernist art, particularly initiated by "the supreme smasher of icons,"[3] Marcel Duchamp, spurned a tradition of art as critique which challenged orthodox social and religious values through to the present. Andres Serrano's *Piss Christ* (1987), a large photograph of a crucifix immersed in the artist's urine, which, although hauntingly beautiful for some, caused much controversy,[4] and Chris Ofili's *VirginMary* (1999),[5] made partly of cow dung, come to mind as examples of contemporary iconoclasm.

The meaning and social function of art changes over the centuries and some philosophers of art, notably Jerrold Levinson, have argued for the irreducible historicality of the concept of art. He writes: "whether something is art now depends, and ineliminably, on what has been art in the past. I claim, in other words, that the concrete history of art is logically implicated in the way the concept of art operates."[6] On this view, art is an artifact that is intended to be art as some prior artifact was so intended. The intentionality of art is defined by its historical location and its implicit reference back to the past. Artists in modernity claimed through their art – such as Marcel Duchamp's "Fountain" or Tracy Emin's bed – that everyday objects could be conceived as art when "repositioned" and "reconceived."[7] It is surely correct that works of art must be understood within their historical timeframe; the rejection of tradition in art, which has been underway for almost a hundred years, can only be understood in relation to what went before. Duchamp would make no sense unless seen in the context of artistic formalism and romantic expressivism against which he was reacting, and it is surely not coincidental that Duchamp presented his urinal in 1917,[8] one of the bloodiest years of the First World War.

Works of art are communication to an audience of concerns that reflect their times and function both to reinforce cultural values and categories and to challenge those values and categories. At an earlier time of romantic aesthetics it would have been apposite to speak of art only in terms of the beautiful and of the sublime, as giving access to the sublime. While that language is still available to us, as a way of characterizing art *tout court* it no longer suffices and we need the idea of imagination that produces artifacts as mediations of the world. If art is intended to evoke aesthetic response, disgust might be one of those responses in late modernity or the cathartic release of tension and visceral energy as in the performance art of Hermann Nitsch.[9] One of the ironies is that the challenge to art has itself become mainstream and respectable, as the great British institution of the Turner Prize shows along with the absorption of potentially shocking art (Damian Hirst is the prime example) into mainstream culture, particularly through the patronage of wealthy collectors such as Charles Saatchi. Art is market-driven in the modern world (and perhaps always has been). This is not intended to be a necessarily critical remark, but an observation that makes us reflect on the meaning of art, its place in modern life, and its global applicability

But while accepting Levinson's historicist point, there are arguably patterns in the production of artwork that we can identify and that are pertinent to the connection between art and religion. We need some account of art to show this connection. In the following pages I shall, with some exceptions, restrict my examples and most of my discussion to Western art. I think, however, that this is partly justified in a book such as this because of the massive global impact of modernism. (The main disjunction is not between "East" and "West," but arguably between "modern" (including postmodern) and "pre-modern" or "traditional.")

Kant thought that art can give us a sense of the beautiful and the sublime and while that may not be an adequate or exhaustive characterization of what art is, it is nevertheless still part of what art can do. Indeed, much of postmodern art has been concerned with the sublime and the attempt to articulate what cannot be articulated. Thus Lyotard refers to the Russian artist Malevich as attempting to express the sublime in his white paintings (and we might add, in his black paintings too[10]). It all depends, of course, on what we mean by "artwork." By artwork *I* mean artifacts – both objects and music – intentionally produced (although not necessarily devoid of function) that communicate. Such forms of communication are a kind of cultural sign in imagination that points in two directions, one back to their author or authors, and the other to the audience who receive the work in the mode of address. Following Roman Jakobsen, communicative acts are characterized by a message initiated by an addresser to an addressee. Such a message entails contact between addresser and addressee, a code or form of expression such as a text or painting, and a context that addresser and addressee understand.[11]

This somewhat old-fashioned semiotics is still useful in highlighting the work of art as communication. The "message" of art is characterized firstly by addressivity: there is an author or authors of an artwork and an audience of reception. Secondly, the artwork is an expression, both of authorial intention and of something outside of authorial intention that we might refer to as the real or the world, part of which is the sublime. While an artwork is produced by an artist or group of artists, it not only expresses the artist's meaning but can express something outside or beyond the artist's intentionality, which partly accounts for art's enduring nature. This is especially true with regard to the beautiful and the sublime. In the pre-modern world there was the idea that art represented beauty (if not truth and goodness as well) and while that idea is eroded by a certain nihilism of postmodern art, it will never be wholly lost because of the very nature of human beings and, arguably, because of the structure of reality itself. Art speaks from within the real and expresses reality in a way that could not be done in any other form of communication: "If I knew what it meant I wouldn't have to dance it," remarked Isadora Duncan. Thirdly, the mode in which art speaks is mimetic; that is to say, mimesis or imitation is central to the artwork, be that imitation of the natural world in a Romantic canvass by Constable or representation of aesthetic emotion in the case of the simul-taneously full and spacious canvases of Jackson Pollock.

If art possesses these characteristics of address, expression, and imitation, it also possesses a quality that is hard to define, a quality that can evoke emotion but emotion which also involves thinking. This quality of being able to evoke frisson, particularly in music, is in one sense individual – what moves one person might not move another – but is also intersubjectively agreed to over long periods of time. Kant spoke of this aesthetic as apprehen-sion of the beautiful and the sublime, where the sublime exceeds the beautiful and refers to the capacity of the mind to apprehend the limitless, particularly the greatness of nature accompanied by a sense of reason's ability to transcend nature.[12]

This sense of the Romantic sublime is well expressed in the canvases of Casper David Friedrich, who painted stunning, mountainous landscapes with a figure, his back turned towards us, contemplating the scene. But not only does art convey a sense of the transcending sublime, it also conveys a more intimate sense of subjectivity. When we stand before Manet's barmaid at the Courtauld Gallery in London, we sense a collapse of time and the presence or subject of the painting engages with our own subjectivity; indeed the subjectivities of ourselves, the subject of the painting, and the artist meet to reveal something to us that would not otherwise come into view. A similar experience might happen with Zhang Xiaogang's blood-line portraits whose serious faces stare out at us with an almost haunting quality. This quality is arguably that of beauty, which certainly lies in the eye of the beholder, but more than this in the work itself; that an artwork is beautiful is not simply in the mind but is a judgment arrived at through the intersubjective agreement of the community of reception over a period of time.

John Bowker has argued that cognitive science shows us that there are conducive properties in certain objects – such as fine works of art – that elicit a "language of satisfaction" and there are innumerable instantiations of this throughout history. Conducive properties lead to particular emotions such as fear of snakes but also to emotions of awe and beauty which "depend on those parts of the neocortex dealing with the higher stages of sensory processing."[13] Be that as it may, there are arguably agreed standards of skill and execution in art that evoke aesthetic responses, the language of satisfaction, that hold for particular communities of reception; the language of satisfaction also evoked in religions. In the case of what is explicitly religious art, images and paintings of gods and angels are apprehended in particular, ritual circumstances. Thus people are ushered before the image of the goddess Kanyakumari in the temple at Cape Cormorin at the tip of India for a few moments to receive her vision (*darśana*) and the image evokes a particular response of awe. We find a parallel situation at the tomb of Christ in Jerusalem where pilgrims are ushered out after a few short moments before the tomb and an icon, but the evocation of aesthetic and devotional emotions is arguably not dissimilar. The conducive properties of the images and the context of sacred presence produce devotional emotion in the participants. Here art reflects something beyond the devotees; it participates in the reality to which it points and also imitates that reality, that power, thereby mediating the encounter with mystery for the community of reception, for the devotees who have waited for so long for their short encounter.

Cosmological Art

But this quality of mimesis is precisely why Plato rejected art, particularly painting. Art was an imitation of the world which itself is a reflection of the higher, pure form. In the *Republic*, Socrates reasons with Glaucon that there are three kinds of bed: one created by a god, one created by a carpenter, and one created by a painter. The god's bed represents the true nature or being of the carpenter's bed, whereas the painter's bed is an imitation of the carpenter's. The painter imitates what others have made and so is three times removed from the ideal form.[14] Thus art is an imitation of an imitation and takes us away from the real rather than bringing us into it; painting is essentially deceptive. But, luckily, Plato's dim view of art did not dominate even the classical world, although his idea of the form of truth, beauty, and goodness did come to have a central place in western metaphysics and, indeed, art and aesthetics. Rather than a moving away from the real, from truth, beauty, and goodness, art comes to be seen as a representation of the real; an attempt to achieve and participate in beauty, truth, and goodness. Art comes to be not a pale reflection of a reflection but a participation in the real and a manifestation of it. Thus in the early Church, particularly the Eastern Orthodox Church, we have the development of the idea of God as infinite beauty and the purpose of worship as participation in the beauty of God: *philosophia*, the love of wisdom, is accompanied by *philokalia*, the love of beauty. Human beings come to be seen by the Church Fathers as having a longing for beauty, which is a longing for God of whom humans are a reflection. Thus Gregory of Nyssa says that human being manifests divine beauty[15] and Gregory Nazianzus makes the point that we approach God, not by comprehension (given God's "infinite magnitude"), but by participation.[16]

We see the same thing in Hindu, Buddhist, and Jain art of the early medieval period. The wonderful temples of Tanjavore, Cidambaram, and Khajuraho, or the stupas at Sanchi, bear witness to a revelatory aesthetic in which the cosmos, peopled with divine beings, is represented in stone. The icon at the center of the temple, protected by the ferocious door guardians, embodies the deity in concrete form. The god has a body in the sound form of a mantra and in the spatial form of the stone icon.

Participation is a key to understanding pre-modern religious art. Through the icon the worshiper comes to participate in the divine and to share in the being of God; the intensity of meaning is linked to the intensity of the encounter. Many of the medieval theologians saw the world as a manifestation of God's ineffable beauty and conceptualized the universe in words of Umberto Eco, as "filled with light and optimism."[17] One of the first to understand the universe in this way was the fifth- or sixth-century mystical theologian Pseudo-Dionysius the Areopagite, who writes:

> But the super-essential Beautiful is called Beauty because of the beauty communicated by it to all beautiful things in accordance with their nature ... It calls all things to itself, whence it also names Beauty, and it gathers together all in all in itself ... From this Beautiful all things have their being ...[18]

Whether Dionysius directly influenced Gothic architecture is now open to doubt, but Dionysius articulates a general vision that influenced late medieval mysticism and was an indirect influence on late Gothic architecture.[19] This beauty comes to be represented in pictorial form, in the icon, which in spite of a period of iconoclasm, comes to be predominant in the Orthodox Church to the present day. Of course, it is the liturgy and the presence of

Christ in the "holy gifts" of bread and wine that is the central idea of Christian worship, but pictorial representation comes to be an integral aspect of it from icons in Orthodox Christianity to medieval wall paintings on the naves of parish churches, to façades of Gothic cathedrals such as Notre Dame, where Christian cosmology is graphically represented. At Notre Dame we see the last judgment and the fate of the blessed and the damned, a tradition that culminates in Michelangelo's frescoes on the ceiling of the Sistine Chapel in the Vatican. There is some debate about the degree to which theology influenced art in medieval Europe, from Hans Belting's standard history of the medieval image,[20] who claims a sometimes antagonistic relationship between theology and image (in which image is seen to threaten theology), to Freedberg's view of the importance of theology in understanding the image.[21] But whether image threatens theology or is formed by it, it functions to convey a sense of divine presence and to put people in touch with that power.

The idea of beauty in the world being a reflection of the form of the beautiful, and human life participating in it, is a cosmological understanding of beauty characteristic of the medieval world, which carries on into modernity in some theologians such as Pavel Florensky. A similar cosmological vision is found not only in the West but elsewhere too, particularly in India. By way of illustration let us take two brief examples, Pavel Florensky (1882–1937), a Russian theologian executed in the Gulag, and some nine hundred years earlier in Kashmir, the non-dual theologian Abhinavagupta, who articulates a vision of participation and aesthetic experience as religious experience.

Pavel Florensky

For Florensky there is an inseparable relationship between beauty, being, and truth existentially realized when a person transcends their limits and moves towards God in the process of deification. The sanctified human being is therefore the model of art, the true work of art, as it were. Florensky writes:

> A spirit-bearing person is beautiful, beautiful in two ways. This person is beautiful *objectively*, as an object of contemplation for those who are around. This person is also beautiful *subjectively*, as the focus of a new, purified contemplation of what is around. In the saint, the beautiful, original creature is revealed to us for contemplation.[22]

The saint is the embodiment of wisdom and one who has achieved the vision of the trinity and is in communion with it; he or she has achieved *theosis* or deification, a fundamental doctrine of the patristic tradition. As a human being can ascend to heaven and experience the heavenly light that shines from him or her, so art can reflect this process, particularly the art of the icon. Indeed, for Florensky this experience is the basis of art and the icon is proof of God's existence.[23] Echoing Plato, Florensky regards everyday art, secular art, as the art of ascent or naturalism that gives a false image of reality in contrast to the art of descent or symbolism which expresses the experience of the higher, heavenly world. Western art went down a wrong path at the Renaissance for Florenssky and is merely an outer shell, "the imitation of sensual reality ... which nobody needs."[24] Art on this view is revelatory and ontological. It reveals or opens out in the world a higher reality in which it participates and through the artwork the community of reception in turn can participate in the being it symbolizes. My being can become transformed through contact with the transcendent power expressed through the artwork, which itself parallels the human icon of the saint. My being is transformed not as a solitary, Cartesian monad but as part of the communion which is the church.

These two styles of art, that of descent – the sacred art of symbolism – and that of ascent – secular art of mere representation – reflect different kinds of culture. The culture reflected in the art of descent is "contemplative-creative," in contrast to the former, reflected in the art of ascent, which is "predatory-mechanical." Contemplative-creative culture is in turn associated with inwardness, and predatory-mechanical culture is associated with externality and a scientific attitude to life exemplified in the philosophy of Kant. External art for Florensky is characterized by a realism that is not actually realism at all, in contrast to the inner art of the icon that is true realism in the sense that it brings us into the real through the disruption of normal perspective and mere representation. The true purpose of life is to turn from the external towards the internal and to establish ourselves within God who is our true home. Thus Florensky's vision of art is wholly integrated into his ontology and highly Orthodox theology. While his denunciation of post-Renaissance, western art might seem somewhat sweeping and unwarranted, there is an uncompromising logic to Florensky's vision. His understanding art as symbolism is the way humanity enters into the real. Through the church we live a fuller, more complete existence, which moves away from a thin, deluded state of being outside the grace of God. Florensky's vision of art is something most people would probably reject but it is a lucidly clear articulation of a consistent position that stands at the end of a long tradition of the Orthodox theology of the icon.

Abhinavagupta

Turning to a different continent and nine hundred years before Florensky, we have a conception of art that in many ways parallels his. Abhinavagupta

(c. 975–1025 CE) was a Shaiva Brahmin in Kashmir who wrote on aesthetics, philosophy, and exegetical theological works commenting on a genre of text, believed to be revealed by the god Shiva, called Tantra. These texts regarded themselves as an alternative or new revelation for humanity, in contrast to the ancient Vedas. At the heart of Abhinavagupta's philosophy is the idea that in reality there is but one power of consciousness and all distinction between subject of knowledge, object, and method is illusory, caused by beginningless ignorance of our true nature as consciousness. This ignorance keeps us bound in the cycle of reincarnation. The goal of his system of philosophy and practice is freedom from the cycle of suffering which is at the same time the realization of the truth of one's true nature as the light of pure consciousness. This apparently simple doctrine becomes extremely complex in its exposition in different arenas of life and practice and in the different systems of revelation that he systematically interprets.

Abhinavagupta has a conception of art – there was painting at his time or perhaps frescoes on a wall, music, theatre, temple sculpture and wooden sculptures in Kashmir that have survived – although he focuses on the arts of speech. While the bulk of Abhinavagupta's work concerned scriptural exegesis of the tantric traditions, he is most well known for his work on aesthetics and his commentary (*locana*, "the eye") on a work of poetics by Anandavardhana (ninth century), the *Dhvanyaloka* or *Light on Suggestion* that concerns the transformation of basic human emotions or persistent moods (*sthāyi-bhāva*) into aesthetic flavors (*rasa*); thus bravery is transformed into heroism (*vīrya*), anger into fury (*raudra*), desire into the erotic (*śṛṅgara*), laughter into comedy (*hāsya*), grief (*śoka*) into compassion (*karuṇa*), and so on.[25] Abhinavagupta does not comment on the plastic arts but is concerned with the aesthetics and transformative power of drama and poetry. Specifically both Anandavardhana and Abhinavagupta maintain that poetic language has an evocative function that expresses meanings indirectly or implicitly. This suggested meaning is called *dhvani*, the power inherent in language itself to communicate indirectly and to suggest meaning in imagination which is inexplicit and cannot be directly expressed as long as the power of *dhvani* is maintained.[26] A number of (fairly complicated) examples are given in the text but one will suffice to illustrate this idea:

> Striking the nail with the tip of another,
> And revolving her joggling bracelet,
> With her foot, the anklet jingling,
> She was scrawling softly on the ground.[27]

This poetry indirectly expresses the emotion of bashfulness and also indicates how Sarasvati, the goddess of speech herself, reveals herself through suggestion. This realization, says Abhinavagupta, is accompanied by pleasure or relish (*camatkāra*) which is not merely entertainment but an epiphany, a manifestation of bliss (*ānanda*) which comes from the absolute reality (*brahman*).

Aesthetic flavor (*rasa*) evoked by *dhvani* is thus for Abhinavagupta much more than aesthetic but reveals or "flashes forth" the pure light of consciousness which vibrates in the heart. Indeed, the highest aesthetic emotion of tranquility (*śāntarasa*) is expressed here as identical with the shining forth of absolute consciousness and so the sensitive reader or "same-hearted one" (*sahṛdaya*) becomes filled with this power. The emotion that is aroused through a drama and extended to poetry by Anandavardhana,[28] becomes a vehicle for a religious experience, and aesthetic pleasure, as Isayeva observes, is regarded as an ontological category.[29]

The aesthetic that both Florensky and Abhinavaupta are conveying is premodern and cosmological. While, of course, they are speaking about different contents, the basic form of art being an epiphany or manifestation from a higher or more profound world is shared. Art here becomes an opening out of a reality that would otherwise be closed and evokes an experience of participation beyond the limited individual, even momentarily. That these two thinkers are separated by almost a thousand years and as many miles suggests to us firstly that religious meanings can be expressed through artistic media and secondly that religious meanings are cosmological and participatory. The cultural and historical gap between Orthodoxy and Shaivism seems to collapse when it comes to the structure of aesthetic experience and sensibility (although not its content). The meaning of art in these examples only makes sense in the context of a religious cosmology in which the meaning of a human life is related to the greater meaning of the cosmos in the traditions. For Florensky the purpose of life is deification, which has the specific connotation of participation in the holy trinity, for Abhinavagupta the purpose of life is recognition of one's true identity with absolute consciousness. In both cases, art – the icon and poetry – can become vehicles for those realizations because they are thought to be integral to the structure of the real.

Secular Art

That such a conception of art as Florensky's should still exist in the twentieth century says something about the persistence and resilience of tradition (especially in communist Russia). The point where art went wrong for Florensky was with the Renaissance, where there is a turning away from the theophanic and participatory model of art to a more human, less formalized conception in which the particularity of human emotion bound up in history comes to the fore.

No longer willing to simply participate in the unfolding of a cosmic drama, art turns to the human, even when dealing with religious themes, and humans come to be portrayed in their subjective truth and their fragility. We can almost smell the horse in Caravaggio's conversion of St Paul or taste the salty bread in the sudden recognition of the disciples in his Emmaus. Through the centuries since then we have witnessed a separation of art from religion with the further development of status art in portraiture of the rich and famous, and in the seventeenth-century realism of Rembrandt, Vermeer, and the still life of Louise Moillon, one of the few women to gain recognition at the time. In Britain alone we have Gainsborough, Stubbs, and Reynolds celebrating the country life of the elite and we also have the beginnings of romanticism, which was to flower in the nineteenth century. With the eighteenth century we have a turn towards the ancient past and the classical aesthetic.

This new Hellenism inspired the late eighteenth through to the nineteenth century, particularly instigated by Winckelmann (1717–68), whose vision of the beauty, the "tranquil grandeur" and "noble simplicity" of ancient Greece was to have a deep impact on the nineteenth century,[30] even on Nietzsche. Classicism gives way to romanticism, and Constable exquisitely expresses a nature that is contained within a frame and humanly controlled in a way that Hegel would have approved.

Towards the end of the nineteenth century, and once we move into the twentieth century, we have the development of modernism and while it is difficult to seriously maintain a teleological view of art history, there is a sense in which modernism is the outcome of an inexorable march that began with the development of art outside of the ecclesium. With modernism comes critique, the critique of the past and critique of art itself – thus with Gerhard Richter, painting comes to be wholly reflexive, about painting rather than about the world.[31] Yet while modernism is very diverse, with Richter painting about painting, Lucian Freud painting in realistic vein what he sees before him, and others rejecting painting altogether, there are shared features all the same. Peter Gay has characterized the diversity of modernists as being united by two themes, the lure of heresy "that impelled their actions as they confronted conventional sensibilities" and the turn to the self, "a commitment to principled self-scrutiny."[32]

It is not, of course, that the modernists began the search for the self and human nature – there is a world history of this from the Buddha, to Plato, to Augustine, the list in endless – but with the advent of modernity poets, artists, and novelists' self-scrutiny "became essential to their unorthodox enterprises."[33] This self-scrutiny took one direction in a materialistic and even atheistic conviction of modernist giants such as Samuel Beckett and Virginia Wolf in literature, Pollock and, in a different vein, Bacon in painting, but the route of introspection also took a spiritual direction for others, particularly Kandinsky and Mondrian in painting, and Eliot and Yeats in poetry, up to the contemporary video artist Bill Viola and environmentalists such as Andy Goldsworthy. Autobiographical art should be mentioned in this connection as part of the expressive movement whose representatives include Frida Kahlo, Tracey Emin, and, arguably, Louise Bourgeois.

Re-Spiritualizing Art

The turn to the spiritual in modernism is interesting in that the art of artists who describe themselves in this way is not religious in any traditional sense. Perhaps the most famous example here is the founder of abstraction, Vasili Kandinsky, a classic modernist rebelling against the old, yet who described his art in terms of spirituality. He presents an account of a moment of almost a mystical experience in 1909 or 1910 when he saw one of his paintings lit up with an inner glow and he realized that representation of the external world was actually an obstacle to his art. Gay questions whether this was an actual experience or "the dramatised condensation of a more protracted retreat from the ideal of mimesis," but either way, when Kandinsky set art against nature it "was an epochal event in the history of modernism."[34]

Kandinsky's turn to abstraction was not gradual and he thenceforth produced the abstract canvases he is famous for. He was deeply influenced by theosophy and in 1912 wrote a famous essay *On the Spiritual in Art*, the same year as the first exhibition of the *Blaue Reiter* (the "Blue Rider") group of which he was a part. This was accompanied by the publication of another essay, the *Blue Rider Almanach*, which again supported a turn to spirituality in the arts. *On the Spiritual in Art* is a sort of manifesto, according to which artists should work only from internal truths without regard to external form and without regard to material considerations driven by greed.[35] In the text he describes the search for abstract art and different routes towards it, including Rossetti and Burne-Jones; he describes the interrelation of color and form as the outer expression of inner meaning, and how form-harmony "must rest on a corresponding vibration in the human soul"[36] – a vibration driven by inner need. Much of the work is devoted to an account of the forms and colors of art – the eternal triangle and the combination of colors such as blue and yellow.

Art for Kandinsky is about the expression of inner meaning and the harmony of form that corresponds to something within human subjectivity. Every artist, Kandinsky writes, is a creator for something within that needs expression; he is "a child of his age" who expresses the spirit of his age and is a servant to art.[37] Kandinsky thought that there is a strong link between music and art and even saw his canvases as representations of music: simple forms he described as melodic while complex forms were symphonic and we can read the history of art through this lens. Thus Cezanne is melodic for

Kandinksy and Russian icons and Japanese art, along with the "old German masters," are symphonic, like the symphonies of Mozart and Beethoven.[38]

Although his treatise is clearly modernist, there are parallels in the religious art we have discussed. While not participatory in the cosmic sense we have seen, it is nevertheless expressive of an inner world that to Kandinsky's view is to be distinguished from the outer, materialism of his age. There are parallels with Florensky, and indeed he is schooled within the Russian tradition, but his work marks a new direction, a spirituality which is spontaneously inward and set against any standards of tradition and conformity. Kandinsky's spirituality is very modern and very non-traditional, seeing a new vision in a new world.

Contemporary art is marked by its variety but there is clearly a tradition of art in the spirit of Kandinsky that has severed the link with formal religion. Influenced both directly and indirectly by Freud, this new kind of art emphasizes catharsis, purification through the expression of emotion and instinct. Much performance art is like this and can involve blood letting and body sculpting. In Germany, Hermann Nitsch's *Das Orgien Mysterien Theater* ("Orgy Mystery Theatre") offers a six-day performance which is an "aesthetic ritual" with "no other pretext than the mystical glorifying of our being-here." This performance involves inordinate disinhibition and the expression of instinct and emotion, the celebration of emotional excess, blood, the expression "joyful lust," and the building up on emotional energy that erupts in a climax to foster "intensive sensory sensations and lead later to an orgiastic, sado-masochist acting out," including the killing and disemboweling of animals and the experiencing of "raw flesh, damp bowels still at body temperature, bloodied feces, blood warmed from the slaughter," all of which produces a "dionysic dismemberment situation" and an irruption of "mystic aggression and cruelty." Interestingly, Nitsch associates all of this with Holderlin's understanding of the tragic and the idea that "man's inner core" becomes one with the power of nature in rage. A catharsis or frenzied abreaction releases dammed up energy and achieves a tranquility and sense of union, being "spread across life."[39]

This heady mixture of psychoanalysis and German romanticism is spiritual art a long way from Kandinsky's canvases as the expression of inwardness. Nitsch's "dismemberment situation" seems particularly European, articulating a spirituality with its roots in German romanticism and European paganism. It is consciously anti-Christian in its embrace of sacrifice, its pantheism, its appeal to Dionysius, and in looking back to Greek tragedy. We can see a connection between Nitsch and Nietzsche, and the *Orgien Mysterien Theater* seems to derive much of its inspiration from Nietzsche. Here we have art not for its own sake, but as a tool for a cleansing purification and a liberation of the self from its own repression; perhaps a uniquely German form of contemporary art that sacrifices Apollonian rationality to Dionysian catharsis.

The forces at work on contemporary art are complex and diverse. On the one hand we have clearly secular pieces in a nihilistic spirit that are essentially critical, if humorous and sometimes sardonic, while on the other we have artworks that looks to a new optimism and revitalized spirituality. Gilbert and George are good representatives of the nihilistic or critical tendency, highly skeptical of religion, whose exhibition in London in February 2007[40] presented religion through a pastiche of images that showed religions to be essentially oppressive and, in contrast to their own art, without humor.[41] Damian Hirst arguably likewise gives voice to a nihilism where, in the end, death takes all. Although widely differing in their styles and skill, other conceptual artists can be placed in this tradition of skepticism and iconoclasm, particularly Rachel Whiteread, Tracey Emin, and Sarah Lucas.

On the other hand we have work that is not nihilistic but celebrates life; a new age spirituality closely linked to the environment. An example here is the Cuban artist Ana Mendieta who conjoined the events of birth and burial by being buried beneath a pile of stones at an old temple in Yagul, Mexico. The stones were gradually displaced by her inhalation and exhalation, slowly revealing her body. The whole event was filmed (*Untitled (Burial Pyramid)* 1974)[42] and repeated with mud the following year (*Untitled (Genesis Buried in Mud)* 1976). Perhaps Mendieta is most famous for the film of her standing naked, clutching a chicken whose throat had been cut, its body in death throes, its blood splattering her body (*Chicken Piece*, 1972).[43] She wrote that "I wanted my images to have power, to be magic. I decided that for the images to have magic qualities I had to work directly with nature. I had to go to the source of life, to mother earth."[44] Her work is an attempt to reconnect with the universe and to link her female body to the earth – a union of imagination with nature. This is a conscious, chthonic spirituality that reveres the environment and the earth as the source of life, almost diametrically opposed to forms of religion that seek to connect with a transcendence or power beyond the world.

Other examples in this genre could be cited. Andy Goldsworthy's work is perhaps on the edge of seeing nature in spiritual terms, along with Richard Long, famous for his walks. The connection with the earth links this group of artists to the pre-Christian religions of prehistoric people when art was inseparable from life, according to the art critic Lucy Lippard.[45] There are a number of artists who combine modern technology "with ancient wisdom" in creating interactive land art such as observatories and arrangements of stone.[46] Antony Gormley likewise arguably falls within the ambit of this autochthonous spirituality in his emphasis on the body, his own body, as his point of contact with the world,[47] thereby linking him to the mystical tradition of Boehme, Blake, and Brown (see p. 93).

In some ways the source of this environmental art is Joseph Beuys (1921–1986), whose influence on later artists is very great. Beuys exemplifies the artist as a shamanic figure. He worked sometimes with very large, stone installations and he has been complicit in the mythologizing of his life. As a young man in the Luftwaffe, his plane was forced to crash land in the steppes of Russia. He was pulled from the plane's wreckage by tribesmen who wrapped him in fat; he was ill for a long time but gradually came back to life, returned from the dead as it were, nursed back to life by the tribesmen. This experience governed his life and vision of the artist as akin to a shaman who goes into the next world and returns with a gift. Beuys' large pieces are environmental art that show us something of the world and he needs to be understood as being like a shaman revealing something about the world to us. Nature, as it were, speaks through the shaman.

What is interesting about land art and the work of artists such as Mendieta, Beuys, Goldsworthy, and Gormley is that they seem to be attempting to reconnect with a sacred cosmos. Although not in this tradition of sculpture, the video artist Bill Viola shares similar concerns. His hauntingly beautiful images reflect nature and offer a meditation on stillness, transience, and the inevitability of death.[48] Rather than accepting a mechanized, machine-like material universe which is now devoid of spirituality with secularization, and rather than accepting what they regard as dissatisfactory forms of traditional religion, these artists create new forms that while looking to the future draw from the ancient past with an emphasis on the land, on mother earth, on natural cycles, and on the body. We might even say that they reflect romanticism and express the union of nature with imagination that Constable commended.

Conclusion

In discussing so vast a topic as art and religion I am aware that so much more needs to be said and so many other examples could illustrate the points I have tried to make. Nor have I mentioned music, which is so central to the development of religion where, as in the plastic arts, we have the development of secular music but also the re-appropriation of religion in its mystical aspects from within the musical world (e.g. Olivier Messiaen, Sophia Gubaidulina, Meredith Monk, Jonathan Harvey[49]). We have seen the close parallels between art and religion and described how religious art shares a common structure in the idea of cosmological participation. Art is used in the service of religion and comes to express religious ideas. We have traced here the gradual separation of religion from secular art since the seventeenth century but with modernity we have the development of new forms of art that reject formal religion but embrace the idea of spiritual meaning, that art shows us something about the world that is more than simply material. If in some sense art is the voice of a society, then the contemporary situation speaks through a variety of voices, some of which are sympathetic to religious meanings, while others seek to go beyond religion in a secularist but plural world. It is to the political ideas and how they relate to religious ideas that underpin the contemporary global situation, upon which the broader artistic culture sits, to which we must, lastly turn.

Notes

1. Leslie, C.R., *Memoirs of John Constable Composed Chiefly of his Letters* (London: Phaidon Press, 1951 (1845)), p. 177. This had in fact been said to him by another painter John Jackson.
2. Boyle, N., *Goethe: The Poet and the Age*, vol. 1 (Oxford: Oxford University Press, 1991), p. 496–7.
3. Gay, Peter, *Modernism: The Lure of Heresy from Baudelaire to Beckett and Beyond* (London: Heinnemann, 2007), p. 167.
4. See Lucy Lippard, "The Spirit and the Letter," *Art in America*, vol. 80 (4), April 1990, pp. 238–45 (http://www.usc.edu/schools/annenberg/asc/projects/comm544/library/images/502.html; accessed September 2, 2010).
5. http://arts.guardian.co.uk/pictures/image/0,8543,-11504640117,00.html.
6. Levinson, Jerrold, *Contemplating Art: Essays on Aesthetics* (Oxford: Oxford University Press, 2006), p. 13.
7. Levinson, *Contemplating Art*, p. 28.
8. http://sdrc.lib.uiowa.edu/dada/blindman/2/04.htm (accessed September 2, 2010).
9. www.nitsch.org (accessed August 3, 2010).
10. Lyotard, Jean-François, *The Postmodern Condition*, trans. G. Bennington and Brian Massumi (Manchester University Press, 1986), pp. 77–8. See also Stephanie Rosenthal, *Black Paintings* (Munich: Hausterkunst, n.d.).
11. Summarized by Terence Hawkes, *Structuralism and Semiotics* (London: Routledge, 1977), pp. 82–3.
12. See Jean-François Courtine (ed.), *Of the Sublime*, trans. J.S. Librett (Albany: SUNY Press, 1993).
13. Bowker, John, *Sacred Neuron: Extraordinary New Discoveries Linking Science and Religion* (London: Tauris, 2005), p. 49.
14. Plato, *Republic* X 597a–598d, ed. John M. Cooper (Indianapolis and Cambridge: Hackett, 1997).
15. Evdokimov, Paul, *The Art of the Icon: A Theology of Beauty*, trans. Steven Bigham (Redondo Beach: Oakwood Publications, 1990 (1972)), pp. 10–11.
16. Beeley, Christopher A., *Gregory of Nazianzus on the Trinity and the Knowledge of God* (Oxford: Oxford University Press, 2008), pp. 228–9.
17. Eco, Umberto, *Art and Beauty in the Middle Ages*, trans. H. Bedin (New Haven: Yale University Press, 1986), p. 17.

18. Dionysius the Aereopagate, trans. Board of Scholars, *The Divine Names* (Fintry: The Shrine of Wisdom 1957), pp. 34–5.
19. Panofsky, E., *Gothic Architecture and Scholasticism* (La Trobe, PA: Archabbey Press, 1951), pp. 16–17; P. Frank, *Gothic Architecture* (New Haven: Yale University Press, 2000).
20. Belting, Hans, *Likeness and Presence: A History of the Image before the Era of Art*, trans. E. Jephcott (Chicago: Chicago University Press, 1994). For an excellent survey of the field, see Jeffrey F. Hamburger, "The Place of Theology in Medieval Art History: Problems, Positions, Possibilities," in Hamburger and A.-M. Bouche (eds), *The Mind's Eye: Art and Theological Argument in the Middle Ages* (Princeton: Princeton University Press, 2006).
21. Freedberg, D., *The Power of Images: Studies in the History and Theory of Response* (Chicago: Chicago University Press, 1989), e.g. pp. 11–12, 94–8. Also see George Pattison, *Art, Modernity, and Faith: Towards a Theology of Art* (London: Macmillan, 1991).
22. Florensky, Pavel, *The Pillar and the Ground of Truth*, trans. Boris Jakim (Princeton: Princeton University Press, 1997) p. 324.
23. Bychkov, Victor, *The Aesthetic Face of Being: Art in the Theology of Pavel Florensky*, trans. R. Pevear and L. Volokhonsky (New York: St Vladimir's Seminary Press, 1993), p. 42.
24. Floresnky, quoted in Bychkov, *Aesthetic Face*, p. 43.
25. Abhinavagupta *Locana*, 1.5. K. Krishnamoorthy (ed. and trans.), *Abhinava-gupta's Dhvanyāloka-Locana with Anonymous Sanskrit Commentary* (New Delhi: MeharchandLachhmandas, 1988).
26. For a good account, see Natalia Isayeva, *From Early Vedanta to Kashmir Shaivism* (Delhi: Sri Satguru Publications, 1995), pp. 163–80.
27. *Locana* 1.5.
28. Raja, Kunjunni, *Indian Theories of Meaning* (Madras: Adyar Library, 1963), p. 285. Also P.V. Kane *The History of Sanskrit Poetics* (Delhi: Motilal, 1961), p. 350.
29. Isayeva, *From Early Vedanta*, p. 175.
30. See Davies, Oliver, *The Creativity of God* (Cambridge: Cambridge University Press, 2004), pp. 58–63.
31. Buchloh, Benjamin H.D., *Neo-Avantgarde and Culture Industry* (Cambridge, Mass. and London: MIT Press, 2003), p. 365.
32. Gay, Peter, *Modernism: the Lure of Heresy from Baudelaire to Beckett and Beyond* (London: Heinemann, 2007), pp. 3–4.
33. Gay, *Modernism*, p. 5.
34. Gay, *Modernism*, p. 130.
35. Kandinsky, V., *On the Spiritual in Art*, trans. Michael T.H. Sadler (London: Tate, 2006 (1912)), pp. 10–11.
36. Kandinsky, *On the Spiritual in Art*, p. 57.
37. Kandinsky, *On the Spiritual in Art*, p. 66.
38. Kandinsky, *On the Spiritual in Art*, p. 111.
39. www.nitsch.org (accessed August 3, 2010).
40. http://www.tate.org.uk/modern/exhibitions/gilbertandgeorge/rooms/exit.shtm (accessed September 3, 2010).

41. Gilbert and George, *Major Exhibition, Tate Modern* (London: Tate, 2007), e.g. pp. 18–81, "Mass" and "Was Jesus a Hetrosexual?"
42. http://www.sfmoma.org/multimedia/videos/193.
43. http://wn.com/Ana_Mendieta (accessed September 3, 2010).
44. Cited in Ben Tufnell, *Land Art* (London: Tate, 2006), p. 70.
45. Lippard, Lucy, *Overlays: Contemporary Art and the Art of Prehistory* (New York: The New Press, 1995), p. 4.
46. Tufnell gives a list in *Land Art*, p. 110.
47. Tufnell, *Land Art*, p.132.
48. e.g. Viola, Bill, *The Passing* (Paris: Editions à voir, 2007 (1991), DVD).
49. For an engaging account of the "spiritual" dimensions of composition, see Jonathan Harvey, *Music and Inspiration* (London: Faber and Faber, 1999).

9

Religion and Politics

Religion has always been deeply implicated with politics and lies behind many political ideals. In his inaugural address in January 2009, Barak Obama underlined this connection when he proclaimed:

> The time has come to reaffirm our enduring spirit; to choose our better history; to carry forward that precious gift, that noble idea passed on from generation to generation: the God-given promise that all are equal, all are free, and all deserve a chance to pursue their full measure of happiness.[1]

The American ideals of equality and freedom are deeply rooted in a Christian ethic and textual tradition. While one of the claims of this book is that the religious imperative cannot simply be reduced to power, the formation of religions as institutions has always been closely implicated in the formation of states and the legitimizing of particular social and political structures.

Many contemporary thinkers have claimed that religion can be understood in terms of power relationships and that the discourse of religion hides a (generally oppressive) will to power. By contrast many religious communities claim that religion is the wellspring of their life's energy and that tradition cannot be explained only in terms of politics and the will to power. While the secularization paradigm continues to develop in some western countries where the churches continue to empty,[2] elsewhere in the world there is a resurgence of religion, and religions now play an important part in global politics.[3] The secular, liberal idea that religions are dying out is simply wrong in the global context. As a senior figure in the World Bank said in 2009, the vast reach of religions and interfaith work of organizations such as the World

The Importance of Religion: Meaning and Action in Our Strange World,
First Edition. Gavin Flood.
© 2012 Gavin Flood. Published 2012 by Blackwell Publishing Ltd.

Faiths Development Dialogue and the Tony Blair Faith Foundation are important for social cohesion and inter-communal relationships.[4] The place of religion in politics and the public sphere should not be assessed purely negatively in the wake of the terrible events of 9/11 where religion and politics were intertwined in a devastating way, but it also needs to be assessed in terms of the realistic contribution religions can make to reconciliation in our future world.

The theory of religious action and the tradition-specific understanding of the self that I have presented in earlier chapters can be seen as orientations in moral space. These orientations are controlled by a religion's goals. The orientations of tradition and modernity are generally opposed; the former towards goals which are soteriological and/or eschatological, the latter to goals of self-fulfillment and authenticity. I will broadly argue that religious orientation can be tradition-specific yet function in a pluralistic, democratic context. Problems come when political representations of the self conflict in the public arena (as we have in the issue of girls wearing the hijab in secular schools in France). In this final chapter we need to situate the discussion about the place of religion in public space; the secular model of neutral public space, the inclusivist model of democratic public space, and the exclusivist model of public space contested by different religious traditions. The place of religion is contentious. Some argue for an extreme secularism that there should be no place for religious voices in serious public debate that informs the legislature, while others argue for the importance of religion in public debate and the need for religious perspectives on legal and moral issues facing a society.

Religion in the Public Sphere

As the world's population approaches seven billion in 2011 and the world faces attendant problems of resource management and distribution, the question of ideology and the place of belief system in public discourse becomes highly relevant. For the human future these environmental and economic problems, which are also political problems, will have to be solved and to do that issues of identity, conflict resolution, and what people understand to be the purpose and meaning of life have to be addressed. Shared solutions to shared problems entail mutual understanding and the ability to negotiate conflict and disagreement. If, as I have argued, religions are central to human subjectivity, to the meaning of our lives and the stories we tell about ourselves, then religions will need to have a stronger voice in the public sphere through reasoned debate, even though some contemporary religious expressions would see the destruction of that very sphere (some Islamicist and some Christian fundamentalisms for example).

But first we need a brief reminder of the history of the problem. Sitting in his rooms in Christ Church College Oxford, John Locke (1632–1704) was weary of the English Civil War that had ended not too long earlier and the thirty years of war that had torn Europe apart and which had finally (mostly) ended with the Peace of Westphalia in 1648. He saw that an end to such conflicts lay in the idea of toleration, the toleration of religions by the state which could be fostered by a strict division between the state and the church. The corollary to this would be that religion would be relegated to the private realm leaving the public sphere for governance. The state should ensure the commonwealth or "society of men" for the pursuit of life, liberty, health, and private property but should not interfere in matters of religious conscience. For the interests of the state, it matters not to which religion one belongs as the role of the citizen is to obey the legislature and carry out his or her obligations and self-interested actions within the framework of law. If, however, a religion interferes with the state, then we reach the limits of tolerance; religious dissent which becomes political cannot be tolerated for Locke.[5] Locke laid the foundations for the theory of the state in the following centuries and the development of the secular age. It was not that Locke dismissed the relevance of religion – he was not a French Encyclopedist of the following century – but he wanted to restrict its power to matters of conscience and morality established through reason that supported God's revelation.

The roots of the public/private distinction with regard to religion go back before Locke to the medieval period with the idea of the *saeculum*, century or age, which is used in opposition to religion, where religion designates being within a monastic order. Thus people in the saeculum are living a regular life in ordinary time as opposed to those outside the saeculum in the monastery living a religious life in higher time "closer to eternity."[6] Locke, implicitly drawing on this distinction, advocated the de-politicization of religion in the sense that a non-political institution should have no quarrel with the state and the state should have no problem with the private practices and beliefs of its citizens. Along with other deists, Locke was responsible for the emphasis on reason and the idea of rational religion, a religion of ethics arrived at through thoughtful effort. As we have already seen, this development led to the Enlightenment and contributed to the scientific critique of religion. But what are the political implications of this development? And how does this affect us today?

Locke is one of the founders of the modern discourse about society and the idea of a social contract (of which Hume was so disparaging). The public sphere is the shared arena where subjectivities can be displayed and where the institutions that an individual invests in can find articulation. The control of the public sphere means power for the one who controls it and we have seen examples of this already. The Church, in its battle with Galileo, was not only fighting over contested notions of truth but also over power, over who controlled the public space of discourse, over whose truth wins out in the end. In our own day, religious groups vie for media attention and highly voluble public debate can be heard throughout the world over political and moral matters, from stem cell research and abortion, to debate about the links between religion and terrorism, to whether one can wear a cross or the hijab in a French school. The public realm is occupied by contesting voices, which is as it should be, but problems come when contestation has to result in decision, and finally legislation, which is linked to the idea of who defines the public sphere. Religion is a hot topic in this area, particularly in Europe.

While there was public debate in all civilizations prior to the rise of the West, the very idea of the public sphere as we understand it today has developed in the western democracies since the seventeenth and eighteenth centuries. John Locke was an important voice but also Kant's understanding of Enlightenment as autonomy rather than heteronomy. Charles Taylor defines it in a useful way as:

> a common space in which the members of society are deemed to meet through a variety of media: print, electronic, and also face-to-face encounters; to discuss matters of common interest; and thus to be able to form a common mind about these.[7]

We might complement this with Habermas' contention that the public sphere is "a space of reasoned communicative exchanges."[8] Salvatore claims that the public realm constitutes a "third sphere" along with economics and political system.[9] The public sphere is thus closely associated with the media and the forms of communication, particularly since the information revolution that has occurred in the post-1945 period, although its formation can be found, according to Habermas, in the coffee houses and salons of Europe with the rise of bourgeois class.[10] Indeed, it is central to modern, global society where communication across thousands of miles is instant. But this public space is not simply a neutral forum for conveying information; it is rather a place of discourse and is integral to the governments we have and the laws we abide by. It is essential to democracy and implicitly against fundamentalism, whether religious or secular, if by that term we mean groups who intend disruptive violence to others.[11] The discourse in the public sphere influences legislation and governance and is in turn influenced by them. It is the realm wherein debate can take place not only about legislation and governance but about the deeper values that inform them, about what it is to lead a good life and what justice is. While almost every conflict in the world has a religious component, it is also at the level of discourse in the public sphere where conflicts of value occur. Indeed, one of the most important debates concerns which values the public sphere should be guided by: the values of religions or the values of secularism? What is the place of religions in the public sphere (and more broadly in the global community)?

In a popular book entitled *The Cube and the Cathedral* George Weigel offered two alternative visions of Europe.[12] The book raises the question as to why, in spite of the vital role that Christianity has played in the formation of Europe, it was not mentioned in the European Union constitution. This is the inevitable development of what Locke had articulated, if not actually started: the complete expulsion of religion from discourse about the state. The Cube is a colossal cube-shaped piece of art entitled "La Grande Arche de la Défense," erected by president Mitterrand in the business quarter of Paris; it symbolizes a secularized Europe in which religion is completely expunged from the public sphere. The Cube was intended by its Danish and French architects and engineer to be a monument to humanity and humanitarian ideals. By contrast, the cathedral of Notre Dame built in the twelfth century is a still living monument to the power of Christianity. Which, asks Weigel, represents the best future for Europe, the purely secular vision devoid of any religious orientation or a future in which religion, specifically Christianity, is at the heart of moral renewal? The responses to this question are complex and made more complex by the demographic make-up of Europe with large Moslem populations and other religions and ethnicities. While the situation may be different in the Americas and in Asia, the case of Europe serves to highlight some important issues about the place of religion in the public sphere and political and social life.[13]

While the public sphere of the West, if we might call it that, is clearly important in terms of world power and universality, conducted primarily through the medium of English, it is not the only public sphere: China is particularly important and will be in the future as the centre of civilization shifts once again from West to East and Islam has conducted discussion in a parallel public sphere.[14] In a sense there was a public sphere in south Asia conducted through the medium of Sanskrit; the Sanskrit cosmopolis spread from Kashmir to Cambodia in the medieval period, although the concerns of discourse were primarily epistemological and ontological and social criticism at the level of discourse was largely absent.[15] But at present it is the public sphere as formed in relation to western nation states that has become a global integrated network of discourse.

Religions are global systems that have proven to be very resilient to secularization and have adapted and transformed to modernity. In spite of the dominance of science in terms of the truth of empirical claims and the development of sophisticated technology, religions have been remarkably adaptable, especially to computer technology and the internet. Literalist or fundamentalist forms of religion have adopted modernity; the internet has been used to spread messages of Islamic groups, of Falun Gong, of

Catholicism, and all significant religious groups. But while virtual communities are important, religions cannot function only in virtual terms. As we have seen, religions address fundamental human needs and entail bodily exploration and being in community. Religions bring their communities into presence and into the present, using technology in the service of their generally ancient purposes.

In theory, a purely technological religion is conceivable – one thinks of the novels by William Gibson such as *Neuromancer* where the hero exists is a virtual world or the feminist cyborg vision of Donna Harraway that Richard Roberts has highlighted[16] – but in practice this would probably never occur as long as we are the bodily creatures that we are. The public discourse of religion is predicated upon the bodily life of religion; religion in the public sphere is secondary to the practices of prayer, asceticism, worship, and the ritual reception of text along with modes of fellowship and social organization that religions foster. Alongside traditional practices, religions have tended to welcome new technology and globalization, especially traditions which have a missionary imperative as new technology functions in the service of disseminating their truth.

In spite of religious differences, religions which exist in close connection with each other, particularly in the western democracies, participate in the global economy, global communication, and local political institutions. All are stakeholders in contemporary political life and all have some vision of what the ideal society would be, or more specifically, what kind of political discourse would foster the development of a good life. It is over this question, what would constitute the good life and what would be the shape of a politics that promotes it, that differences and conflict occur between religions and between religions and the secular state.

On the one hand we have extreme fundamentalist positions that interpret scriptures very literally and tend to be highly conservative in their social mores, especially with respect to the rights of women, while on the other we have a libertine, secular ideology that is fundamentally amoral and claims that the highest good is simply a successful life in the world seen in terms of worldly prosperity or even the maximization of pleasurable experience. There are more nihilistic versions of this latter position and there is a spectrum of views between these extremes. Thus we have a variety of new religious movements and what have become known as "quasi-religions" and humanist and atheistic systems that cross the "boundary" between the religious and the secular, as Kim Knott has lucidly pointed out.[17] Most religions that engage with modernity are critical of the secular state, particularly what are perceived to be its moral shortcomings, but want to engage with it and want to participate as citizens in the countries to which they belong. Most religious people today negotiate multiple identities as religious persons, as holders of jobs, as parents, as children, as politicians, and as citizens.

The Secular Public Sphere

The issue of the compatibility of the citizen with competing religious claims came out in France where the policy of *laïcité* has brought the authorities into conflict with religious minorities. As Roger Trigg observes, the term *laïcité* is hard to translate although it denotes the neutrality of the state towards all religions and specifically refers to three values, freedom of conscience, equality of religions in law, and political neutrality.[18] In 2003 President Chirac remarked that the French Republic is composed of citizens and "cannot be segmented into communities."[19] Part of the policy has been the banning of all religious accoutrements from public places such as schools in 2004. This ban has included a prohibition on the display of crucifixes, turbans, and most controversially of the Moslem woman's head covering as an expression of modesty (*hijab*), which is a highly sensitive issue in a country with five million Moslems. In the case of the hijab, this aggressive secularism claims that such legislation is being true to the emancipatory spirit of the Enlightenment and is in fact liberating women (even if they claim they do not wish to be liberated!). While the aim of *laïcité* is integration, this is a model that goes against much of the spirit of liberalism in marking a boundary of toleration beyond which a society will not go and having a view of citizenship which is highly conformist to state policy. On this view, to be a good citizen is to conform to the dictates of the secular state; there is a conflict between the citizen and the member of a religious community.[20]

Arguably there are other models of secularism which are more tolerant and less centralized that the French version. Part of this can be understood as a defensive response to threat and indeed attack from the extreme Islamicist groups which is perceived more broadly as an attack by Islam on the West. To defend the West's way of life, so the argument goes, we need legislation which ensures and safeguards the citizen. But this is arguably an impoverished view of citizenship which extols sameness and vapid conformity to state authority. Another model of secularism would be one in which difference is celebrated, in which religions have a legitimate place (in the role of education for example).[21] The problems here arise when there is a perception that a group of people are sharing in the benefits of the secular state, such as freedom of expression, while at the same time offering a rhetoric and pattern of action which undermines that state and openly declares hostility toward it.

The philosopher who has most clearly developed a notion of a tolerant public sphere is Jürgen Habermas. For Habermas the public sphere is a realm in which different traditions can converse and his task has been, in Adam's words, "to identify *rules* for argumentation that transcend tradition."[22] Habermas acknowledges that all discourse is situated within a particular location and accepts the view that to assess whether an argument is in accordance with reality one would need to stand in a position outside both the argument and reality, which is impossible. But what we can do is communicate effectively and the task of the public sphere is the clarification of the communicative act. Speech communities come to consensus about events but it is only possible to distinguish between genuine and false consensus on the grounds of the possibility of an unconstrained arena for dialogue that speakers have access to.[23] This is the "ideal speech situation," which presupposes a mode of discourse that transcends the particularity of culturally bound communication. Through discourse we can remove distortions to our self-understanding, which is the task of the social sciences. Human communication is universal and different traditions can transcend their limitations and participate in this universal human quality. But this in a sense begs the question. There are particular languages and particular lifeworlds that we all inhabit, but the ideal speech situation would seem to entail a "language" of moral action that exceeds the boundaries of particular tradition. It is clearly possible for us to think and speak beyond the limits of our cultures, but the space in which this speech takes place is itself predicated upon a particular cultural life. This is not necessarily problematic, but there is need to argue for the validity and universal applicability of that particular form of life. For many, this optimum ideal speech community comes close to liberal democracy.

While the values of the Cube seem to end up with a monolithic, intolerant state in which any public display of religious affiliation is suppressed, on the other hand the values of the Cathedral are from a bygone age. We no longer live within the sacred canopy of a Christian cosmos and of necessity have had to adapt to a new situation. At worst, the sacred canopy of faith creates intolerant and crushing regimes, particularly for women, as we see in the various kinds of fundamentalism that have cut themselves off from liberal political and legal structures (such as Mormon polygamous sects). Surely there is way of living and acting between the Cube and the Cathedral? Surely as contemporary human beings we can display tolerance or, more strongly, "affection" or "friendship" towards others who live in very different forms of culture? Even when this is difficult, friendship towards others becomes a kind of asceticism which, in the end, can be transforming of the social matrix.

But first we need to ask the question as to whether there is a convincing reason why people from different cultures and religions should share public discourse other than the practical contingencies that not to do so leads to misunderstanding and conflict. There is clearly an element of self-interest in the dialogue of religions with each other and with the secular state. As Milbank observed some time ago, tolerance is a value that has developed within a particular liberal milieu and is only held by those who share in that view.[24] Thus dialogue is only undertaken by those who share the values of tolerance. A traditional Hindu Brahmin, for example, who was not schooled through a liberal, English education, would not be particularly interested in dialogue or learning about the other. There is a history of insularity in the

Brahmanical case – not so much a hostility to the other but simply an indifference to modes of discourse outside those of the Brahmanical, Sanskrit tradition. The Brahmanical tradition engaged in rigorous internal debate between rival traditions but shows no interest in intellectual engagement with other, external systems of the "foreigners" or *mlecchas*, especially the Moslems.[25]

For Christianity and Islam there was some internal impulsion towards intellectual engagement with other traditions, namely conversion, but clearly the idea of tolerance of plurality is a modern phenomenon, although we must not forget periods in history where the cross fertilization of ideas has flourished, as in thirteenth-century Spain where Jewish, Moslem, and Christian intellectuals engaged in discussion. The imperative to coexist and engage in conversation is even more necessary in the contemporary context. Of course, the traditional Brahmin intellectual has no particular interest in shared debate in the public sphere, but the shrinking world and the development of global economies and global politics necessitates that intellectual traditions engage with each other: it is a demand of modernity that traditions so engage. While it is important that intellectual traditions exist within the boundaries of their own coherence – Islamic philosophers still debate in Qumm in Iran, Hindu philosophers still debate in Varanasi, Jewish philosophers still debate in Jerusalem – there also needs to be intellectual engagement in the public sphere because it is desirable, according to most people, to avoid violent conflict and resolve issues of shared interest through dialogue rather than aggression. It might well be possible to have Alasdair MacIntyre's educational institutions based wholly on internal, traditional concerns (thus we might have Catholic universities, Hindu universities, and so on) as developed in his Gifford Lectures,[26] but there is some compulsion with globalization for these traditions to mutually engage with each other.

For modern liberalism the idea of tolerance that we should all get along, seems to be a fairly uncontentious claim. However, liberal tolerance is not as politically and culturally neutral as it might at first appear. To bring the problems into sharper relief let us look at the counter-view which extols the virtues of tradition and makes a strong claim for the religious voice in the public sphere. Let us call this the traditionalist view. We can then look at a version of the secularist view concerning the neutrality of the public sphere and finally outline the beginnings of a modified traditionalist view focused on the citizen.

The Traditionalist View

If Habermas is the theorist of universal communication in the European context, one of the most influential political and moral philosophers to espouse the values of liberalism in recent years has been John Rawls (1921–2002), whose *A Theory of Justice* (1971) attempted to establish a rationality for justice based on principles that we could all agree to given an original situation in which we all subscribe to a basic social structure. If people were placed behind a "veil of ignorance"[27] without prejudicial knowledge of their own and others situations, they would practice "justice as fairness." Given such equality it would be rational to choose a kind of society that has a framework of individual liberties as well as concern for the least well off. This depended on a view of the self as neutral and unencumbered by prejudice and tradition. In a way not dissimilar to Habermas' ideal speech situation, Rawls argues that social and political institutions that favor individual rights are conducive to human flourishing. In contrast to this position, communitarian criticism of the idea of the "unencumbered self" and liberal neutrality developed a view that we are beings located in history, traditions, and communities and our choices are inevitably informed by our situations and locations. These thinkers, particularly MacIntyre and Sandel, developed what became known as communitarianism, that the self is embedded within communities and the individual is shaped by the ambient society and culture. Although he does not directly engage with Rawls, Milbank can be understood in this context, as can Gavin D'Costa and Stanley Hauerwas.[28]

For MacIntyre, liberal individualism that develops from the Enlightenment is unable to provide a moral basis for society because of its tendency to moral relativism and its lack of the idea of a shared human *telos* other than individual desires and purposes. This critique of liberalism is echoed by Sandel, who claims that liberal ethics is wrong because the idea of neutrality is impossible as we "can never wholly escape the effects of our conditioning."[29] It is simply an illusion that we can stand, as it were, outside of ourselves and our histories. For MacIntyre justice and virtue are ideas with histories and specific to traditions of thinking, of particular importance being the classical and Christian tradition. In *After Virtue* he articulates a deep skepticism about the state of moral discourse in modernity; we live in a morally impoverished and fragmented environment in which the language of morality has been forgotten. The Enlightenment project which has sought to develop a neutral moral space and an objective perspective on human life independent of tradition and historical context, has failed. What is needed is a revisioning of the moral landscape and a return to the Aristotelian paradigm of teleology. In the face of modernity's failure to produce a flourishing human community we need to base an account of practical reason on the idea that human beings have a goal and that goal should be development towards the good, which in effect means the development of virtue. This is essentially a recollection of the ideal of virtue which has been lost. The modern self is emotive in the sense that moral judgments are seen to be merely the expression of preference and this is true not simply in moral philosophy but culturally.[30]

It is not possible to correct this loss of moral discourse from within the paradigm of modernity. We need to retrace our steps, as it were, and revert to the Aristotelian view of teleology, that as human beings we have moral purpose beyond ourselves, beyond our own will, beyond our autonomy, and the satisfaction of our own desires. Through developing virtue (*arête*) we can live a good life and this also entails recognizing that we are kinds of beings who make sense of our life in terms of narrative. Human actions are characterized by narrative.[31] Indeed, in contrast to the fragmented nature of the self of modernity, a coherence to the self is needed with the development of a virtue ethics, that there is a narrative coherence to my life. If a life is to be understood as "more than a sequence of individual actions and episodes," then we need to see our actions as part of a larger whole and what emerges is the truth that "man is in his actions and practices, as well as in his fictions, essentially a story telling animal."[32] The story of my life is not simply isolated but is part of a broader matrix of stories "always embedded in the story of those communities from which I derive my identity."[33] On this view, religion is integral to the kinds of being we are and we are deeply formed by the historical tradition in which we find ourselves.

This is a persuasive argument in many ways. As human beings we inhabit communities with histories and our identity is deeply related to the story of our life. Who we are is how we have acted and what has formed us, what the events or narratives are that have formed us into the particularity of ourselves. Who I was in the past has continuities with who I am now and who I will be in the future. Narrative for MacIntyre, as for Ricoeur, is essential to the unity of a person's life and the emphasis on narrative is an antidote to the fragmentation of modernity. As human beings we have a purpose or goal and that goal only makes sense in the context of the story of who we are; the story of who we are, in turn, is very much tied up with the story of our community and traditions. In late modernity these stories can be very complex, as we live in an increasingly hybrid world, we marry across racial and cultural boundaries, we are born to diverse traditions and ideologies. Even so our narrative identities are made coherent by living life the best we can and assimilating the disruption of our narratives through the overwhelming nature of the encounter with mystery.

A modified traditionalist view that acknowledges the communitarian critique of liberalism while at the same time recognizes the necessity of pluralism and acceptance in the public sphere would seem to be a good way forward. Genuine interest in what other traditions have to say is of fairly recent origin and comes out of a liberal tradition of tolerance, which itself arguably develops from a Christian understanding of love and a desire for the ontology of peace. Religions have on the whole sought to defend their boundaries and their truth against the claims of other, rival, traditions. Even Hinduism which is often lauded for its tolerance of different perspectives on the world was traditionally less generous towards other views than is sometimes supposed. Different Hindu traditions such as the Shaivas argued equally against their dualist cousins as against the Buddhists, and although they acknowledged that other traditions had access to truth, their truths were of a lower order in a hierarchy of views. While there are passages from scripture that justify equality before God (such as the *Bhagavad Gita*), it is also true that most Hindu temples in the South will not let lower castes or outsiders into the central shrine (although technically illegal) for fear of pollution.

Comparative theology, in which different religions intellectually engage with each other in the public sphere on an even footing, is of recent origin. Frank Clooney describes the enterprise as a response to twenty-first century religious diversity in which the meaning of the contemporary religious situation must be decided with reference to the other.[34] Scriptural reasoning likewise wishes to intellectually engage with diverse traditions through the reading of scripture (see p. 145). This has political implication in providing a model of religious engagement in the public sphere that is true to the roots of tradition yet open to the truths of the other. Both comparative theology and scriptural reasoning are attempts to intellectually discuss religion in the public sphere which both recognize the problematic nature of liberal neutrality and individualism and also recognize the problematic idea that we are locked into particular cultural worlds and particular narratives from which we cannot escape.

Fundamentalism

I have so far avoided speaking about "fundamentalism," partly because the term is somewhat pejorative of millions of people in the "majority world,"[35] and partly because it signifies a highly diverse and complex phenomenon not necessarily linked to violence. Pentecostal and charismatic churches throughout the world form a significant section of world Christianity – there were an estimated 523 million Pentecostals in 2001[36] – and have already and will continue to play a role in national and global politics. Similarly, Islamicist groups, while linked to an ideology of violent overthrow of the West, play an important and complex part in world politics. Indeed, the word "complex" is appropriate as the modern "fundamentalism" is often a different kind of modernism in the guise of tradition. Ali Shariati, Casanova reminds us, was the intellectual father of the Islamic revolution; he translated Fanon's *Les Damnés de la Terre* ("The Dammed of the Earth") using the Qur'anic term "the disinherited" (*mostaz'afin*) which had a wide impact and illustrates the cross-fertilization of ideas.[37] We cannot tar all these groups with the same brush and there are instances in which local communities have been greatly aided by Islamicist groups in times of national crisis such as natural disasters (flooding, earthquakes, tidal waves). The moral judgment about fundamentalism depends very much upon where one stands and many of these groups have strong local support.

Fundamentalism is a response to modernity and reflects human insecurity at losing the certainties of an old cosmology and social structure. Clearly the rise of science and the development of technology have threatened traditional religious worldviews along with changing social attitudes (as Taylor has described). Some religious groups react to these rapid changes by simply rejecting them in favor of an inward-looking worldview and closing themselves off from evidential refutation. An example here is the Fundamentalist Church of Jesus Christ of Latter Day Saints (FLDS Church) which is an offshoot of the mainstream Mormon Church over the issue of polygamy. The FLDS continued to practice polygamy and the president of the Church, Warren Jeffs, regarded as the "prophet, seer, and revelator," was convicted in 2007 of rape as an accomplice through arranging three marriages of minors (including a fourteen-year-old girl) to older men, although the conviction of ten years imprisonment has since been overturned (2010).[38]

Such groups are examples of the desire to cling to a tradition (even a recent tradition) because of the sense of purpose and meaning it brings to people's lives but at the cost of rationalization and abiding by the norms of the broader society. Here we have a good example of where religious law (polygamy) conflicts with actual, secular law (the prohibition of polygamy, the prohibition on child marriage) and the reification of the religious word from the mouth of a man regarded as a prophet. What is important for world politics is the degree to which such groups can be brought into the public sphere and their practices moderated in the context of broader consensus. Within the public sphere such groups could be encouraged to voice their legitimate concerns. As Terry Eagleton said long ago, an ideology is effective because it gives voice to genuine needs and desires.[39] The structures of religion that I have been speaking about here – the internalization of the text, the development of the ritual habitus, the way the need for meaning is met – are all present in fundamentalism. The issue facing the world is the way in which these kinds of religion, which are really forms of encounter between tradition and modernity, can be given voice that is not disruptive of the public sphere. The fundamentalist can also be a citizen.

The Religious Citizen

There are many problems facing the world's democracies, apart from environmental problems such as global dimming or global warming (whatever is the latest idea), namely the survival of liberal democracy, the integration of multiple worldviews into political coherence, the maintaining of social stability in the light of social fragmentation, the problems of global capitalism such as poverty, the support of corrupt governments, and so on. Having raised some of the problems of the religions in relation to the contemporary democratic state, in this last section I wish to outline an argument for the compatibility of the citizen of the state and global economy with religions.

We have seen the critique of liberalism which stresses the culturally and religiously embodied nature of the self: we are born into narrative, religious traditions which can claim primacy over us, more than the claims of the state. One of the important questions is the degree to which the claims of the state take precedence over the claims of tradition. Where should our loyalties lie? To tackle this question we need to look at the primary claim on us of the modern, democratic state as that of citizenship. Regardless of ethnicity, religion, or sexual orientation, the state demands that we be its citizens to enjoy its benefits and meet its obligations.

The concept of citizenship is an invention of the West derived from the Greek idea of the *polis*; the citizen (*politos*) is a member of a political community who has certain obligations to that community and who, in turn, is awarded certain rights or privileges.[40] By implication, and in historical reality, the citizen on this view was distinguished from "the other," the non-citizen, particularly slaves and women.[41] Democracy entails citizenship and the legitimacy of democracy arises from the presupposition that it is a form of governance that promotes the equal interests of all its members.[42] The idea of the citizen therefore entails certain liberal values that have developed in the history of the West and are now universalized. But the idea of the citizen is not a natural category, and while all societies throughout the world have had political participation, the idea of the citizen with its particular nuances has developed since the Renaissance (for example, there is no direct Sanskrit equivalent for the term "citizen"). In modern democracies, this concept is one in which, as T.H. Marshall reminds us, the citizen is a member of the political community who has "civil rights," civil, political, and social, such as the right of assembly, freedom of speech, freedom of movement, freedom of conscience, the right to own property, and the right of equality before the law.[43] This conception is linked to the idea of recognition by others (in interpersonal relationships and in the public sphere) and dignity.[44]

The citizen also has obligations, to the state (such as paying tax), to fellow citizens, and the obligation to abide by the law. In cases where there is a conflict between the obligation to the state and the obligation to religious law, there can be problem: the values of a particular religious community may be antithetical to citizenship, as in the case of certain fundamentalist religious groups. War would be a good example here. The state wishes a citizen to go to war on its behalf but the religious community to which he belongs might not acknowledge its legitimacy, as did happen in the First World War for example. Here the conscientious objector's values are in conflict with his legal obligation.

One solution to the potential conflict between religious obligation and the legal obligations of the citizen would be the selective endorsement of rights. In *Multicultural Citizenship* Will Kymlicka argues for the rights of minorities but within the broad framework of liberal democracy. There are, he says, good group rights that should be legally protected such as the rights of ethnic minorities to education and health care and there are bad group rights which should not be legally protected and discouraged, particularly the restriction of individuals in a community in the name of group solidarity. Thus the argument by a particular religious or cultural minority that women's rights should be restricted because this is in accordance with their traditions should not hold up because this conflicts with the values of liberalism and upholding the individual. Liberal democracies should not support the demand by minority cultures to restrict the basic rights of its own members.[45] But the problem here is on what grounds does the liberal tradition claim the importance of individual rights over the rights of communities to behave in certain ways? If, for example, an African ethnic community practices female circumcision – a highly controversial practice – on what *moral* grounds does the liberal society prohibit this? Of course, there are legal grounds, but the only appeal is to the liberal ideal of individual human rights and appeal to the notion of equality; that is, the values of liberalism. Which model dominates, the values of liberalism or the values of a particular tradition could, in the end, simply be a question about power: liberalism has the power to impose its view on the ethnic minority. On this view, the discourse of liberalism, when it comes down to it, is a discourse about power and an extension into modernity of the colonialist enterprise.

But this argument for moral relativism does not stand up. While of course there is no neutral ground from which to assess moral claims, there is a strong argument that the rights of minority traditions and ethnicities in the liberal state can be ensured so long as they do not infringe upon the rights of the individual to lead a successful life (as they did in the case of the FLDS Church). Success might mean the degree of human flourishing, a vague term that we can take to mean something like enabling the maximum conditions in which a person can fulfill their goals. These goals are individual but also communal in that an individual's identity is closely bound up with the narratives of tradition and justice, and these cannot be separated from aims which are constrained by the values and stories of tradition. As MacIntyre observes, "the story of my life is always embedded in the story of those communities from which I derive my identity."[46] While a general principle might be that cultural identities need to be respected by the liberal state (that is, the law), when traditional values and practices clash with the law in a way that is detrimental to the flourishing of the individual (as arguably in the case of female circumcision and polygamous marriage of children), then the state has the right to intervene. Where one draws the line is a delicate issue and one open to debate. Thus the argument wears rather thin when applied to a cultural practice such as wearing a full veil, but there is a strong argument for legal intervention in cases where individual flourishing can be judged to be compromised, especially where the health of a person is at stake.

On the one hand, there is a case for multiculturalism in the contemporary world and recognition of minority rights and the right of respecting different cultural practices. On the other hand, there is the right of the liberal state to ensure practices of equality and promotion of what it regards as human flourishing. What should take precedence, culture or the individual? Judgments in these matters could never be absolute and need to be negotiated in the cut and thrust of history. But it is precisely in the public sphere where these issues can and should be debated. Stout as well as Trigg have advocated a view of the compatibility of religious voices with democratic ideals in the public sphere. Stout, along with MacIntyre, is critical of the exclusion of religion from the public sphere and while he owes his liberal allegiance to Rawls, disagrees with Rawls about the need to silence religion. Stout makes the point that religions that participate in conversation must adhere to the values of the public sphere and, indeed, implicitly do so in the very act of conversing.[47]

I would agree with those who claim there is legitimacy to religious voices in the public sphere, although there must be limits to this if those religious voices are calling for the killing of doctors who perform abortions or calling for suicide bombers to disrupt the liberal state as much as possible. Then the state has the obligation to the majority of its citizens to protect the values and institutions that are so threatened. But we must be cautious. There is a danger in the liberal state supported by law, not allowing dissonant voices – and the history of the state developing out from Judeo-Christian roots can be read as a history that oppresses women, for example, through the association of death and violence with the symbolic realm of discourse.[48] There are limits to the religious voice constrained by law. But the public sphere is not the main arena of religious activity. Religions, as I have argued in earlier chapters, are concerned with the development of subjectivities which are kinds of narrative identity wherein we encounter the mystery and strangeness of the world. Religions do address issues of public concern and have a legitimate voice in the democratic public sphere, but the life of religion is not in conversation but in bodily practices and forms of community that generally entail submission to the narrative of tradition and inner transformation. Religions are still fundamentally cosmological in their claim that human meaning is found in being located within a cosmos and having a life trajectory within that which, for some religions, takes one outside of that cosmos. Rather than public conversation limited to ethics and law,[49] the lifeblood of religions is in practice, communion, and calling to action in response to the overwhelming mystery of the world.

This is not so much an appeal to the old Lockean distinction between the private world in which religion can operate and the public world of governance from which religious voices are banished, but it clearly draws on that kind of distinction. We live in a secular and religious world, as David Ford says, that has the right to have a voice in the public sphere. At the end of the day, the state is oblivious to the mystery of life. This is left to religions and to other cultural forms of mediation including art.

The strength of religions lies in their ability to mediate the encounter with mystery, particularly at the interstices of life such as birth and the great transition called death. While the language of rights and the clamor for rights is important in the public sphere, at the end of the day the subjective internalization of tradition and the exploration of its meaning in my subjectivity is what religion is fundamentally about, where subjectivity is not the isolated, individual monad but is part of the dynamic cultural narratives that make up who we are. The subject in her bodily being inhabits a world which is simultaneously political, social, and above all mysterious once we shift perception through religious technologies of liturgy, prayer, and asceticism. Certainly our being is defined to some extent by the state and our moral being is our political being, but more than this, our moral being is our religious being, which is linked to the deep structures of the universe. As citizens we abide by the law but pursue our enlightenment or salvation in the communities to which we belong and from which we draw the sap of our life.

Conclusion

In this chapter we have surveyed the idea of religion in the public sphere and argued for the compatibility of the expression of religious and non-religious views. The idea of the public sphere has arisen out of the distinction between church and state and between private and public that has developed since the seventeenth century. John Locke was especially important in making clear the distinction between the private realm of religion and the public realm of governance. This separation led in due course to the relegation of all religious affairs outside of governance. In France this somewhat aggressive secular-ization called *laïcité* has served promote the French state to its citizens and exclude religious voices from the public sphere – and also religious behavior such as the wearing of the hijab. Traditionalists by contrast would wish to see a more prominent public voice of religions. The issues are complex because human beings have allegiances to the nation state as citizens and to other communities such as religions, ethnic groups, and sexual identities. Problems come when secular law conflicts with religious and cultural injunction (as in the case of wearing the hijab).

Arguably being a citizen is not incompatible with allegiance to religious traditions and in some countries, particularly the United States, is almost a precondition for what is regarded as good citizenship. This chapter has argued that a religious humanism is possible that draws on the cosmological resources of traditions while yet acknowledging the need for religious subjectivity to interface with a secular, public world of governance.[50] In some ways this is to defend a liberal position deriving from Locke that relegates governance to the public realm and religion to the private realm in an attempt to avoid the violence of religious conflict. Yet such a religious humanism remains at the level of discourse and cannot substitute for the power of religious action and speech. Such a position does advocate the legitimacy of religious traditions' responses to the world as mystery and unfathomable strangeness, to their claim to lay hold of the world of life, and the rights of traditions to operate within different moral orientations but necessarily within secular law (itself suffused with a Christian, moral orientation). While, in my view, we must uphold the values of democratic cultures against theocracies, these values embrace pluralism and the multiple voices that express the religious imperative. The religious imperative and the kinds of subjectivity that it expresses are legitimate ways in which human beings respond to strangeness and mystery.

Notes

1.   Obama, Barack *The Inaugural Address 2009* (London: Penguin, 2009), p. 5.
2.   In 1900, 27% of the population belonged to a Church; in 2000 it was 10%. Bruce, Steve, *God is Dead: Secularization and the West* (Oxford: Blackwell, 2002), pp. 66–8. On the secularization thesis, see Ingleharrt Ronald and Pippa Norris, *Sacred and Secular: Religion and Politics Worldwide* (Cambridge: Cambridge University Press, 2004), who argue for a link between this distinction and economic development; poorer countries being in thrall to "sacred" ideas. For a response to Charles Taylor's *A Secular Age* (Cambridge, Mass.: Belknap Press for Harvard University Press, 2007), see Warner, Michael, Jonathan Vanantwerpen, and Craig Calhoun (eds), *Varieties of Secularism in a Secular Age* (Cambridge, Mass.: Harvard University Press, 2010).
3.   Beyer, P., *Religion in Global Society* (London: Routledge, 2006), pp. 81–6.
4.   Marshall, K., "Concluding Remarks," *Faith and Development*, Accra, Ghana, July 3, 2009 (http://siteresources.worldbank.org/DEVDIALOGUE/Resources/ KatherineMarshall.pdf; accessed August 6, 2010). Also see Katherine Bell,

World Bank: from Reconstruction to Development to Equity (London: Routledge, 2008).

5. John Locke *Essay Concerning Toleration*, in David Wooton (ed.), *Political Writings of John Locke* (New York: Mentor, 1993). I have been guided by the useful presentation and discussion of Locke in Paul Griffiths, *Problems of Religious Diversity* (Oxford: Blackwell, 2001), 103–11.

6. Taylor, Charles, *A Secular Age*, p. 55. See also J. Casonova, *Public Religions in the Modern World* (Chicago: Chicago University Press, 1994).

7. Taylor, *A Secular Age*, p. 185.

8. Habermas, J., *Between Naturalism and Religion*, trans. Ciaran Cronin (Malden and Cambridge: Polity, 2008), p. 12.

9. Salvatore, A., *The Public Sphere: Liberal Modernity, Catholicism, Islam* (New York: Palgrave Macmillan, 2007), p. 3.

10. Habermas, J., *The Structural Transformation of the Public Sphere*, trans. T. Burger (Cambridge: Polity, 1989).

11. I have not dealt with the issue of religious violence. There is a large body of literature here but see, for example, Hent de Vries, *Religion and Violence: Philosophical Perspectives from Kant to Derrida* (Baltimore: Johns Hopkins University Press, 2002); John Hinnelss and Richard King (eds), *Religion and Violence in South Asia: Theory and Practice* (London: Routledge, 2007).

12. Weigel, George, *The Cube and the Cathedral* (New York: Basic Books, 2005).

13. For an illuminating consideration of the European identity and religion, see Richard Roberts "The Souls of Europe: Identity, Religion and Theology," in *Religion, Theology and the Social Sciences* (Cambridge: Cambridge University Press, 2002), pp. 217–47. Also see Seyla Benhabib, *The Claims of Culture: Equality and Diversity in the Global Era* (Princeton: Princeton University Press, 2002), pp. 147–77; Ramadan, Tariq, *The Quest for Meaning: Developing a Philosophy of Pluralism* (London: Allen Lane, 2010).

14. See Salvatore, Armando, *The Public Sphere: Liberal Modernity, Catholicism, Islam* (New York: Palgrave Macmillan, 2007); Salvatore, Armando and Dale F. Eickelman (eds), *Public Islam and the Common Good* (Leiden: Brill, 2006).

15. Although there was a Buddhist critique of the Vedic order. Pollock, Sheldon, *The Language of the Gods in the World of Men* (Chicago: Chicago University Press, 2006), pp. 51–9. There was social critique of caste but more at the level of action and religious movements in the medieval period (particularly *bhakti*) rather than discourse.

16. See Roberts, Richard H., *Religion, Theology and the Human Sciences* (Cambridge: Cambridge University Press, 2002), pp. 282–8.

17. Knott, Kim, "Inside, Outside, and the Space Between: Territories and Boundaries in the Study of Religion," p. 53. *Temenos*, vol. 44 (1), 2008, pp. 41–66.

18. Trigg, Roger, *Religion in Public Life: Must Faith Be Privatised?* (Oxford: Oxford University Press, 2007), p. 116.

19. Quoted by Trigg, *Religion in Public Life*, p. 118.

20. The concept of community itself is complex. For a discussion of the term, see Michael Freeden, *Liberal Languages: Ideological Imaginations and Twentieth-*

Century Progressive Thought (Princeton: Princeton University Press, 2005), pp. 41–50.

21. D'Costa, Gavin, *Theology in the Public Square: Church, Academy and Nation* (Oxford: Blackwell, 2005), pp. 1–37.

22. Adams, N., *Habermas and Theology* (Cambridge: Cambridge University Press, 2006), p. 8.

23. See Adams, *Habermas and Theology*, pp. 23–48.

24. Milbank, cited in D'Costa, Gavin, *Christianity and World Religions: Disputed Questions in the Theology of Religions* (Oxford: Wiley-Blackwell, 2009), p. 49. For a critique of liberal tolerance, see Wendy Brown, *Regulating Aversion: Tolerance in the Age of Identity and Empire* (Princeton: Princeton University Press, 2008). Brown argues that tolerance "functions as a supplement to liberal tolerance that cannot sustain itself" (p. 174) because liberalism itself favors male dominance rooted in autonomy and self-interest (p. 154).

25. See Halbfass, Wilhelm, "Traditional Indian Xenology," in his *India and Europe: An Essay in Understanding* (New York: SUNY Press, 1988), pp. 172–96.

26. MacIntyre, A., *Three Rival Versions of Moral Inquiry* (Notre Dame, Ind.: Notre Dame Press, 1990).

27. Rawls, John, *A Theory of Justice* (Cambridge, Mass.: Harvard University Press, 1971), p. 136.

28. D'Costa, *Theology in the Public Square*; Hauerwas, Stanley, *The Hauerwas Reader*, ed. John Berkman and William Cavanaugh (Durham, NC: Duke University Press, 2001).

29. Sandel, Michael J., *Liberalism and the Limits of Justice* (Cambridge: Cambridge University Press, 1982), p. 11.

30. MacIntyre, Alasdair, *After Virtue: A Study in Moral Theory* (London: Duckworth, 1981), p. 22.

31. MacIntyre, *After Virtue*, p. 208.

32. MacIntyre, *After Virtue*, pp. 204, 216.

33. MacIntyre, *After Virtue*, p. 221.

34. Clooney, Francis X., *Comparative Theology: Deep Learning Across Religious Borders* (Oxford: Wiley-Blackwell, 2010), pp. 8–9.

35. This term is used by Alan Anderson, *Introduction to Pentecostalism* (Cambridge: Cambridge University Press, 2004), p. 15. This was brought to my attention by David Westurlund in his review of Steve Bruce's *Fundamentalism*, in *Temenos*, vol. 44 (1), 2008, pp. 176–80. On fundamentalism, see Steve Bruce, *Fundamentalism*, second edition (Cambridge: Polity, 2008).

36. Anderson, *Pentecostalism*, p. 11.

37. Casanova, José, *Public Religions in the Modern World* (Chicago: Chicago University Press, 1994), p. 4.

38. http://en.wikipedia.org/wiki/Warren_Jeffs (accessed August 6, 2010).

39. Eagelton, Terry, *Ideology: An Introduction* (London and New York: Verso, 1991), p. 45.

40. Benhabib, Seyla, *Situating the Self: Gender, Community and Postmodernism in Contemporary Ethics* (Cambridge: Polity, 1992), p. 162.

41. On the *polis* and its sacred nature, see Vernant, Jean-Pierre, *The Origins of Greek Thought* (Ithaca: Cornell University Press, 1982), pp. 49–69.
42. See Benhabib, *The Claims of Culture*, pp. 105–6.
43. Marshall, T.H., "Citizenship and Social Class," p. 10, in *Citizenship and Social Class and Other Essays* (London: Cambridge University Press, 1950), pp. 1–84.
44. See Taylor, Charles, "The Politics of Recognition," in Amy Gutman (ed.), *Multiculturalism* (Princeton: Princeton University Press, 1994), pp. 25–73. See also Malory Nye, *Multiculturalism and Minority Religions in Britain* (London: Routledge, 2001).
45. Kymlicka, Will, *Multicultural Citizenship: A Liberal Theory of Minority Rights* (Oxford: Clarendon Press, 1995), p. 152.
46. MacIntyre, *After Virtue*, p. 205.
47. Stout, J., *Democracy and Tradition* (Princeton: Princeton University Press, 2004), pp. 65–77.
48. This is a vast area that is beyond the scope of this book to address. Reading the history of religions through a feminist lens is clearly an important project both for a "science of religion" and as a corrective practice for religions themselves. For a genealogical and feminist critique of religion that links religion to liberal democracy, see, for example, Grace Jantzen, *Foundations of Violence: Death and the Displacement of Beauty*, vol. 1 (London: Routledge, 2004); Pamela Anderson, *A Feminist Philosophy of Religion: The Rationality and Myths of Religious Belief* (Oxford: Blackwell, 1998).
49. On this, see Warnock, Mary, *Dishonest to God: On Keeping Religion Out of Politics* (London: Continuum, 2010), pp. 69–91.
50. On theological humanism, see David E. Klemm and William Schweiker, *Religion and the Human Future: An Essay on Theological Humanism* (Oxford: Wiley-Blackwell, 2008). They develop a model of human integrity and responsibility compatible with the view presented here. On the idea of an ethic of humanity, see Paul Heelas, "On things not being worse and the ethic of humanity," in P. Heelas, Scott Lash, and Paul Morris (eds), *Detraditionalization: Critical reflections on Authority and Identity* (Oxford: Blackwell, 1996).

Summary

We have come close to the end of a long journey along highways and byways that, while interesting paths in themselves, take us onward toward a destination. That destination is a general thesis about religion in relation to the world and how religion must be understood, primarily in terms of meaning and ways through life, rather than as propositions or theories about life. In these last pages I will restate the thesis and assess what has been established.

The general thesis I have presented is that religions are important as ways of living that create meaningful frameworks within which people build and live their lives. Far from being escapist fantasies, religions bring people into the world through their insistence on action that articulates both a cosmological and an ethical vision. This bringing of people into the world takes place through a cultural imagination that posits transcendent goals and develops cultural forms that articulate a desire for transcendence and a will to meaning. Religions (and I use the plural here) are always set within particular cultures, embodied in particular communities, and engender particular social practices that connect people to a goal that transcends or stretches the horizon of their own particularity of place and time. In the language I have developed, religions mediate the human encounter with mystery.

After surveying some of the vexed questions about whether we can speak of religion in the singular and whether there is an essence of religion, we have gone on to argue that religions mediate the encounter with mystery through the three categories of action, speech, and world. Firstly, religions need to be understood in terms of meaning that finds expression in action. Secondly, religions are articulated through speech; the speech of text repeated through

The Importance of Religion: Meaning and Action in Our Strange World,
First Edition. Gavin Flood.
© 2012 Gavin Flood. Published 2012 by Blackwell Publishing Ltd.

the generations, the speech of promise, and the speech of doctrine. Thirdly, religions need to be understood in terms of world; religions are fundamentally concerned with the world and how we negotiate its strangeness. We see this through religion's proximity to art, in how religion relates to science, and also to politics.

Through action we encounter the strange world, through action we push the boundaries of our horizon, and through action we impact upon or generate history. Our actions are unrepeatable, generally unpredictable, and the consequences always exceed us. In Chapter 1 I set this irreducible human truth in relation to the grand sweep of history, on the one hand, and subjective human action, on the other. Religion mediates the encounter with mystery through action that we can see in two ways: action as the product of historical process and action as impacting on historical process. Which has priority? Is it the structures that are beyond us within which we all live, or our ability to act upon those structures and that history? The general position of the book is both that religion can be understood as the consequence of long historical process but also that religious subjectivity can impact upon history through human action.

The first chapter examined this issue in relation to the processes of reification highlighted by the Marxist philosopher Lukács and rationalization developed by the sociologist Weber. On the one hand, we have the view that religion is the consequence of the social economy characterized by reification, taking relationships and processes to be things. On the other hand, we have the idea that religious subjects directly affect the social economy and that religion changes from magical practices to developed ethical structures and bureaucracies instituted by human agents. On the one hand, the subject of history for Lukács is the self-conscious proletariat, while on the other the subject of history for Weber is the self-conscious social actor. Clearly both processes of reification and rationalization are important for showing us how religion has developed in modernity, but these accounts do not exhaust the ways in which religions need to be understood. While the claims of religions vary greatly, particularly their sources of authority, be it the Bible or *Qur'an* or Veda, a pattern can be highlighted that we might call the mediation of mystery. This process involved the identification of knowledge and action, temporal mediation, and subjective meaning.

Religious actions, which embrace moral and ritual acts, are forms of cultural knowledge through which religious agents become aware of the world. Human will combines with knowledge in the religious act, which is always in time. Through time religions facilitate the human encounter with mystery, an encounter that can be described as a mediation of the world within a religious framework. This mediation of the world involves action as the performance of subjective meaning. An action embodies a way of thinking and always involves understanding and a purpose. The religious person acts in a particular way, taking Holy Communion, meditating on the breath, fasting at Ramadan, and thereby expresses the meaning of that act. Through religious action the person or community or persons recapitulates the memory of tradition and looks to the future within the present. We see, particularly in the ritual act, a kind of temporal collapse in which the text is enlivened in the present while simultaneously looking to the future.

To place emphasis on ritual is therefore to emphasize the body and to emphasize the place of culture in the formation of religious expression. The ritual act is characterized by the habitus, an idea originating in Marcel Mauss and developed by Bourdieu, or the bodily orientation set within the broader framework of the tradition. We illustrated this in Chapter 2 with Victor and Edith Turner's work among the Ndembu. Edith Turner in particular presents a remarkable account of experiencing ritual in which she saw a "tooth" being extracted from the body of a person possessed by a particular kind of witchcraft. There is a social scientific account of this rite that sets in the context of socio-economic conditions that allowed for its development, but Turner observes that there is another frame of reference, outside of the social scientific one, that has its own validity and sets human action within a cosmological framework. The phenomenology of sacrifice likewise shows us how religion locates human reality within a meaningful cosmos.

The focus on experience within the context of tradition is taken up in Chapter 3 with the idea of life as an inner journey, a view shared by the mysticism of many religions. In the spiritualities of religious traditions we can see the human encounter with mystery expressed particularly in a language of negation – the reality of transcendence cannot be expressed in words. The goal of understanding this mystery is through developing a spiritual habitus in which the practitioner conforms her life to tradition conceived as a journey to the tradition's goal, which is a way of locating human reality within a broader cosmos.

Crucial to locating human reality within a cosmos is text (explored in Chapter 4). Most religions claim to be revelations of something previously concealed. We see this with the Bible, regarded by many Christians as the word of God; we see this with the *Qur'an*; and we see this with the Hindu scriptures such as the *Bhagavad Gita*. These revelations are displays or attempts to show human communities some truth about the world. Sacred texts are therefore living entities that come alive for their communities of reception, above all in the ritual act. Indeed, we might understand religious action as forms of textual reception. This reception is not merely cognitive but a bodily act; the text is constantly reinvested with meaning through our shared gestures, postures, and expressions. This realization of the text in the liturgical present enlivens or in some sense brings back the past into the present field of meaning. This is simultaneously the collapse of the future into the present in the sense that the goals anticipated within the tradition are enacted and made real. Even though most followers of most religions have probably been illiterate in the histories of religions, nevertheless the text remains central in being enlivened and made relevant through ritual and also through the extra-ritual ethical act. This realization of the text in the ritual moment also entails the internalization of the text in the subjectivities of practitioners. The text is made one's own and experienced within subjectivity. It also entails the externalization of the text in moral acts outside of the restricted, ritual arena. The text is brought to life or realized in ritual but also brought to bear on everyday life and the moral choices that are constantly before us.

This account of text next led us to an account of language (Chapter 5) in recognition of the centrality of language for religions and the enigmatic place language holds in human reality in both belonging to me in a most intimate way (my language is filled with my voice for me) and in being beyond me, shared by everyone.

Our reflection on language led us to a consideration of universalism versus relativism. Some linguists, such as Anna Wierzbicka, argue that there are linguistic universals such as "I," "you," and "something" although this is at a level of abstraction that is inevitably vague. In contrast, linguistic relativists, earlier Sapir and Whorf and latterly Gumpertz and Lucy, have argued that languages or language groups are restricted to particular societies and that we are heavily constrained, if not determined, by our linguistic categories. On this view religious experience, intimately connected with language, is relative to different cultures.

From our study of language and these debates we can conclude that the evidence of linguistic anthropology shows us how grammatical structures inform and mould our experience in significant ways. But we might also argue that processes and patterns are shared across languages and we can see this especially in metaphor. Lakoff and Johnson in particular have shown how metaphor is closely linked to the body, with spatial orientation metaphors (up and down, etc.) and the container metaphor (inside, outside) being found in all languages. This is particularly important in religions where the cosmos is understood as a vertical axis with higher worlds located above our world and hells below. But even though language and the structures of language might be necessary conditions for the production of certain kinds of religious metaphor, we are still left with questions of truth and the justification of religious language in terms of rationality. Given that there are some universals of language structure, if not semantic units, then are there criteria of rationality through which such language can be judged? That is, are religions rational?

Again, the answer to this question is complex. If we understand rationality not simply in terms of logic but more broadly in terms of human practices that have developed over millennia for making judgments in order to achieve a particular end, then religions are generally rational. We explored this idea in Chapter 6 with particular reference to the rationality debate in the first few decades after the Second World War. On the one hand the philosopher of social science, Peter Winch, put forward a relativist view that different cultures have different standards of rationality and we cannot judge one through the standards of rationality developed in another. On this view, we cannot judge Azande belief in witchcraft as erroneous as this is to assume that western science, which is another language game, corresponds to reality, which is an unwarranted assumption.

The debate came into sharp focus in the exchange between the anthropologists Obeyesekere and Marshall Sahlins. Sahlins argued for the apotheosis in 1779 of Captain Cook, who was killed after being mistaken for a god. Obeyesekere, by contrast, argues that this is a European myth that places the rational European above the irrational native. While the debate lingers on, the data of religions suggest that they are indeed rational in the sense that they develop reasons for practices and speculative reasoning based on scriptural sources. Charles Taylor has furthermore suggested that we can make a distinction between theoretical and non-theoretical cultures, that rationality entails not merely cultural coherence, but that some cultures can theorize their practices and communicate them. We might argue therefore that rationality entails coherence and articulation. Religions contain coherence within the frameworks of their worldviews and practices. They also articulate good reasons for particular practices and transmit these through the generations. Indeed, it is vital for religions' survival to speak through the generations as well as spatially between communities. On this account, a culture is rational to the degree that it is coherent and the degree to which it can articulate reasons for particular practices. Clearly the major, textual religions are rational in this sense as can be seen, for example, in three contemporaries in the medieval period writing in different religious traditions in different continents: Al Ghazali in Tus explaining the Qur'anic verse on the "niche of the lights" in Arabic, Kshemaraja in Kashmir expounding a philosophy of pure consciousness in Sanskrit, and Anselm of Canterbury developing the ontological argument for the existence of God in Latin. All three figures are reasoning, yet they perform kinds of reasoning very different from the Enlightenment model of universal objectivity that we have inherited and that proclaims standards of truth independently of traditions of discourse. Rationality on this view is linked into science and is a kind of secondary commentary on a scientific understanding of the world.

Developing this angle in Chapter 7 we saw the ways in which religion and science overlap. In the West there has been a history of antagonism between religion and science since the seventeenth century and science along with its attendant technology have triumphed over religions where they make empirical claims (such as that the universe is not heliocentric). Science has taken over cosmology from which religion has generally retreated. But there are conceptions of science (such as that of Kauffman) that are not reductionist in any crude sense and some religious thinkers (such as Arthur Peacocke) have developed the possibility of overlap between science and religion.

One of the key ideas here is that of emergence; that given certain physical properties other properties emerge (such as wetness in relation to H_2O). Emergent properties cannot themselves be accounted for in a direct way in terms of material causation. We might see religions in this kind of way as emergent properties of immensely complex sets of constraints that can in turn affect those constraints. The constraints that form an event into its outcome, to use John Bowker's terminology, are immensely complex. This complexity – of which religions are an example – is an opportunity to deepen our understanding. Following Bowker's model, I have suggested that a first-level descriptive phenomenology might be followed by a deeper, ontological inquiry necessitated by that first-level description.

While I do not think that it is possible to assess or judge the metaphysical propositions of religions from a detached, scientific perspective, we can begin to raise questions about what is behind appearances and even the theological realities that make those appearances meaningful. This is a legitimate inquiry necessitated by the data of religions. I have argued here that religions share in the structures of reality at the level of process, such as the intensification of subjective meaning through the practices of prayer, asceticism, and moral action. It is in this second-level, ontological referent that supplies religious meanings, that we see from whence religious appearances derive their power. But this is not a theological claim as such; it is rather another way of saying that religions bring practitioners into the world and speak from the real. It is speaking from the real that guides actions in the real and gives life meaning and purpose for those who inhabit that world. The mystery and strangeness of the world resists explanation and yet draws us toward it in ways articulated through religions. Religious actions are ways in which the real is mediated and subjective meanings (which are also intersubjective) draw their source of power. This second-level ontological inquiry cuts across traditions and is not about content but rather about process and the ways in which human communities engage with our strange world.

But religions are not the only cultural forms that mediate our encounter with the real. Other cultural forms can do this too, notably art (as we saw in Chapter 8), although not in the sustained and communal way entailed by religion. Nevertheless there are close parallels and art has been used in the service of religion to express religious ideas. With the gradual separation of religion from the secular sphere in the West we have the development of purely secular art. In the twentieth century with modernism we have new forms of art that reject formal religion yet which nevertheless wish to articulate a sense of spirituality. We have seen this with the abstract painters such as Kandinsky. We also have a reinvigoration of art in a spiritual mode in some contemporary conceptual art, such as the video work of Bill Viola or the body sculpting of Ana Mendieta who tries to articulate a chthonic spirituality that gives expression to the voice of nature.

There is a political dimension here and many, although not all, contemporary artists seem to be aware of this. The mediation of mystery through art, and indeed through religion, has political implications. The last chapter of the book, Chapter 9, has tried to draw this out by focusing briefly on the history of the distinction between the public realm of governance and the private realm of religion and conscience articulated by John Locke in the seventeenth century. This distinction has governed to a large extent our modern understanding of religion and has lead to problems in exporting the western idea of religion to other cultures (as we saw in the Introduction). Some of the issues coalesce around the idea of the place of religion in the modern secular state. On the one hand there are secularists who argue that the public sphere is best served through being a neutral space in which, for Habermas following in the Enlightenment mode, there is clarity of communication. More traditionalist voices, such as MacIntyre, would wish to see traditions being given voice and a return to the values of virtue being demonstrated in public life. I have adopted a modified traditionalist view that acknowledges the communitarian critique of liberalism (Sandel versus Rawls) while recognizing the need for pluralism and acceptance in the public sphere.

At the end of this long journey it is for the reader to judge the success or otherwise of this project, but its significance arguably lies in taking seriously religious claims and offering a way in which we can understand religious behavior. There is also a methodological significance in showing how we can have a repristination of phenomenology as a theoretical discourse, chastened by postmodern theory and social science, which does not fall into a problematic essentialism but is cultural, linguistic, yet open to deeper ontological inquiry. There are further ramifications to the position I adopt, that it is certainly possible to be a good adherent of a religion alongside being a good citizen in the secular state. The state is not concerned with the mediation of mystery and so cannot fulfill most human needs and desires. But among the many cultural forms within which we live, the importance of religions lies in the ways they can and do mediate the encounter with our strange world and endow human lives with meaning in the overwhelming presence of death's darkness and the infinity of space surrounding us.

Epilogue

As we look to the future there are great challenges for religions ahead: adaptation to the conditions of modernity, particularly technology and economic growth, adaptation to environmental change, and adaptation of religious communities to each other. Technology, claimed Heidegger, is a way of revealing, of bringing something into presence that was hidden.[1] Although writing well before the advent of computers and the internet, Heidegger makes the astute observation that the future is technological and that the challenge to humanity is to grasp the essence of technology which is both a danger and an opportunity. Technology is an "enframing," the setting up of a structure that reveals (as physics applies apparatus "to the questioning of nature").[2] Religions have been remarkably adept at adapting to new technology, and computer-mediated communication has flourished. Islam, for example, has used the internet to great effect: Moslems can hear sermons preached thousands of miles away, the *Qur'an* is searchable in digital format, and Moslem organizations can easily display what they are about.[3] Other religions are similarly using the internet to spread their message or simply as a resource. Through the internet and through the dispersal of communities throughout the world, religions become global phenomena. But this kind of internet activity is always secondary to the living communities of traditions that enact and practice their prayers, dietary laws, marriage rules, death rites, and ethical codes. The essence of religions lies in their being ways of life, stories told and lived, which are pliable to the conditions of the age.

In an era of globalization and the internet, religions encounter each other in new ways and in new contexts. This is an opportunity for interfaith

The Importance of Religion: Meaning and Action in Our Strange World,
First Edition. Gavin Flood.
© 2012 Gavin Flood. Published 2012 by Blackwell Publishing Ltd.

dialogue and many religious people feel the need to pursue such dialogue. On the one hand, we have religious people being mutually suspicious of simply ignoring each other and pursuing their own goals and traditions; on the other hand, we have a desire among some for a grand ecumenism in which not only the Christian Churches but all religions can be united. This view, a kind of latter day deism, maintains that all religions are in essence the same or point to the same reality and is in contrast to claims to truth of a singular tradition (not only Christianity makes such claims but also Islam, Buddhism, and, indeed, all missionary religions). There are of course positions between these two where intelligent and responsible interfaith dialogue takes place. Within Christianity the ecumenical movement is strong with voices representing a range of Christian traditions from Rowan Williams, the Archbishop of Canterbury, to Raniero Cantalamessa, the Preacher to the Papal Household, to Nicky Gamble, the founder of the Alpha course at Brompton's Holy Trinity Church. Yet conversely the Anglican communion itself is under threat of splitting over the issue of homosexuality and its acceptance or otherwise in the priesthood. In such cases it is not so much interfaith dialogue that needs to take place but intra-faith dialogue.

One example of the high-level interfaith dialogue, already mentioned, is scriptural reasoning where Jews, Muslims, and Christians read their sacred texts together and apply these scriptures to repairing fissures between traditions and trying to improve the world. This usually takes place in the context of the secular university. It is pointless for interfaith dialogue to try to negotiate non-negotiable metaphysical claims, such as the doctrine of the trinity or the *Qur'an* being the word of God: Christians will not change their minds about the Creed through argument with non-Christians, nor would Moslems change their minds about the *Qur'an* through argument with Christians (although it is another matter for the philological study of the text to influence Islam as the philological study of the Bible has influenced Christianity over the years). But there are many other areas where dialogue can take place, particularly on ethical, political, and social issues. Whether wearing the hijab is oppressive of women would be a question open to interfaith dialogue or the question of animal welfare, stem cell research, euthanasia, abortion, and so on. These are often ethical issues that have arisen due to technology and to which religions have to respond or make a decision. Dialogue between religions on this kind of front is clearly important.

The issue of faith schools is another area important for inter-religious interaction and the relationship between religion and government. Faith schools of Jewish, Catholic, Protestant, Hindu, and Islamic communities have increased in the United Kingdom to about one in four at the time of writing, with government financial and intellectual support. The argument is that faith schools perform well and it is legitimate for communities to reinforce cultural difference and identity. The counter-argument is that faith schools are divisive and that pupils only meet people from the same world. There are also issues about the curriculum, the teaching of evolution for example in traditions that reject this. Far better, the argument goes, would be the abolishing of faith schools in the interests of wider citizenship so that pupils from a variety of ethnicities and religions interact – otherwise we have a situation like Northern Ireland where cultural and religious difference between Catholic and Protestant is reinforced by faith schools. This is a complex question and there are arguments on both sides. But arguably the demands of citizenship are not incompatible with the demands of religion nurtured through faith schools so long as they do not compromise on standards of truth and inquiry. One of the important issues is religious literacy. Knowledge of world religions is arguably essential for any educated citizen. As schools teach different languages, so they should teach about different religions, regardless of whether or not they espouse a particular one.

Lastly, religions are beginning to face the challenge of a changing climate. If George Monbiot is right and the future is bleak unless human beings adapt quickly by cutting carbon emissions,[4] then the resources that religions can muster to tackle this problem are considerable and religions will need to be part of this global movement. There are signs that religions are rising to the challenge, for example with Hindus in the United Kingdom developing the Bhumi project intended to stimulate Hindus to engage with environmental action at local level and supporting conservation projects in India such as cleaning the highly polluted river Yamuna. There is also a revival of "nature religions" in neo-Paganism and neo-Shamanism and more broadly the ecological movement for a sustainable human future on the planet is often understood in religious terms. Bron Taylor in an illuminating book has spoken of "dark green religion" as a loose affiliation of social groups that understand nature as sacred and, Taylor thinks, might replace traditional religions with a "terrapolitical earth religion."[5] And further transformation of religion awaits as humans move into space.

The danger of religions is great but then again so is their transformative potential. Predictions are usually wrong, but I would speculate that religions will survive as an important force so long as there is a human future. All species will die out in "the light of the eternity of the end," but in the meantime the human experiment has much potential as we strive for transcendence both in ourselves through spiritual technologies and collectively through material technology; yet in our hearts we remain bereft. Whether we call them "religions" or not, cultural forms that mediate the human encounter with mystery will continue as long as we wonder about our strange world and as long as our restlessness perpetuates our wandering: in the words of Thom Gunn "one is always nearer by not keeping still."[6]

Notes

1. Heidegger, Martin, "The Question Concerning Technology," trans. William Lovitt, p. 285, in *Philosophical and Political Writings*, ed. Manfred Stassen (New York: Continuum, 2003), pp. 279–303.
2. Heidegger, "The Question Concerning Technology," pp. 290–2.
3. See Bunt, Gary, *Virtually Islamic: Computer-Mediated Communication and Cyber Islamic Environments* (Cardiff: University of Wales Press, 2000).
4. Monbiot, George, *Heat* (London: Penguin, 2007).
5. Taylor, Bron, *Dark Green Religion: Nature, Spirituality and the Planetary Future* (Berkeley: University of California Press, 2010), especially ch. 8.
6. Gunn, Thom, "On the Move," *Selected Poems* (London: Faber and Faber, 1994), p. 7.

References

Adams, N. (2006) *Habermas and Theology*. Cambridge: Cambridge University Press.
Adams, N. (2006) Making deep reasonings public, in D.F. Ford and C.C. Pecknold (eds), *The Promise of Scriptural Reasoning*. Oxford: Blackwell, pp. 41–57.
Agamben, G. (1998) *Homo Sacer: Sovereign Power and Bare Life*, trans. D. Heller-Roazen. Stanford, CA: Stanford University Press.
Anderson, A. (2004) *Introduction to Pentecostalism*. Cambridge: Cambridge University Press.
Anderson, P. (1998) *A Feminist Philosophy of Religion: The Rationality and Myths of Religious Belief*. Oxford: Blackwell.
Anscombe, G.E.M. (1958) On brute facts. *Analysis*, 18, 69–72.
Armando, S. (2007) *The Public Sphere: Liberal Modernity, Catholicism, Islam*. New York: Palgrave Macmillan.
Armando, S. and Eickelman, D.F. (eds) (2006) *Public Islam and the Common Good*. Leiden: Brill.
Arnason, J., Eisenstadt, S.N., and Wittrock, B. (2005) *Axial Civilizations and World History*. Leiden: Brill.
Asad, T. (1993) *Genealogies of Religion: Discipline and Reasons of Power in Christianity and Islam*. Baltimore: Johns Hopkins University Press.
Bakhtin, M. (1993) *Towards a Philosophy of the Act*, trans. V. Liapunov. Austin: University of Texas Press.
Baquedano-Lopez, P. (2009) Creating social identities through doctrina narratives, in A. Duranti (ed.), *Linguistic Anthropology: A Reader*, 2nd edn. Oxford: Wiley-Blackwell, pp. 364–377.
Bataille, G. (1990) *The Accured Share*, trans. Robert Hurley. New York: Zone.
Batnitsky, L. (2006) *Leo Strauss and Emmanual Levinas: Philosophy and the Politics of Revelation*. Cambridge: Cambridge University Press.

The Importance of Religion: Meaning and Action in Our Strange World,
First Edition. Gavin Flood.
© 2012 Gavin Flood. Published 2012 by Blackwell Publishing Ltd.

Beattie, J. (1964) *Other Cultures: Aims, Methods, Achievements in Social Anthropology*. London: Routledge.

Beckett, S. (1976) *Endgame*. London: Faber and Faber.

Beeley, C.A. (2008) *Gregory of Nazianzus on the Trinity and the Knowledge of God* Oxford: Oxford University Press.

Bell, K. (2008) *World Bank: From Reconstruction to Development to Equity*. London: Routledge.

Belting, H. (1994) *Likeness and Presence: A History of the Image before the Era of Art*, trans. E. Jephcott. Chicago: Chicago University Press.

Benveniste, E. (1969/1973) *Indo-European Language and Society*. London: Faber and Faber.

Benhabib, S. (1992) *Situating the Self: Gender, Community and Postmodernism in Contemporary Ethics*. Cambridge: Polity.

Benhabib, S. (2002) *The Claims of Culture: Equality and Diversity in the Global Era*. Princeton: Princeton University Press.

Berger, P. (1967/1990) *The Sacred Canopy*. New York: Anchor.

Berlin, B. and Kay, P. (1969) *Basic Colour Terms: Their Universality and Evolution*. Berkeley: University of California Press.

Betz, R. (1994) Christianity as religion: Paul's attempt at definition in Romans, in U. Bianchi (ed.), *The Notion of "Religion."* Rome: Bretschneider, pp. 3–9.

Beyer, P. (2006) *Religion in Global Society*. London: Routledge.

Bianchi, U. (ed.) (1994) *The Notion of "Religion" in Comparative Research: Selected Proceedings of the XVI AHR Congress*. Rome: Bretshneider.

Bourdieu, P. (1990) *The Logic of Practice*, trans. R. Nice. Cambridge: Polity.

Bowie, A. (2004) *Introduction to German Philosophy: From Kant to Habermas*. Cambridge: Polity.

Bowie, F. (2000) *The Anthropology of Religion*. Oxford: Blackwell.

Bowie, F. (2004) Comment. *Current Anthropology*, 45(2), 176–177.

Bowker, J. (1973) *The Sense of God*. Oxford: Clarendon Press.

Bowker, J. (1991) *The Meanings of Death*. Cambridge: Cambridge University Press.

Bowker, J. (1995) *Is God A Virus?* London: SPCK.

Bowker, J. (ed.) (1997) *Oxford Dictionary of World Religions*. Oxford: Oxford University Press.

Bowker, J. (2005) *The Sacred Neuron: Extraordinary New Discoveries Linking Science and Religion*. London: Tauris.

Bowker, J. (ed.) (2008) *Conflict and Reconciliation: The Contribution of Religions*. London: Key Publishing House.

Bowker, J. (ed.) (2009) *Knowing the Unknowable: Science and Religions on God and the Universe*. London: Tauris.

Boyer, P. (2001) *Religion Explained: The Evolutionary Origins of Religious Thought*. London: Basic Books.

Boyle, N. (1991) *Goethe: The Poet and the Age*, vol. 1. Oxford: Oxford University Press.

Brague, R. (2007) *The Law of God: The Philosophical History of an Idea*, trans. L.G. Codrae. Chicago: Chicago University Press.

Brandom, R. (1994) *Making It Explicit: Reasoning, Representing, and Discursive Commitment*. Cambridge, MA: Harvard University Press.

Brown, N. (1959) *Life Against Death*. London: Routledge & Kegan Paul.

Brown, W. (2008) *Regulating Aversion: Tolerance in the Age of Identity and Empire*. Princeton: Princeton University Press.

Bruce, S. (2002) *God is Dead: Secularization in the West*. Oxford: Blackwell.

Bruce, S. (2008) *Fundamentalism*, 2nd edn. Cambridge: Polity.

Buchloh, B.H.D. (2003) *Neo-Avantgarde and Culture Industry*. Cambridge, MA: MIT Press.

Bujard, M. (2000) *Le Sacrifice au ciel dans la Chine ancienne: théorie et pratique sous les Han occidentaux*. Paris: École Française d'Extrême-Orient.

Bunt, G. (2000) *Virtually Islamic: Computer-Mediated Communication and Cyber Islamic Environments*. Cardiff: University of Wales Press.

Burguière, A. (2009) *The Annales School: An Intellectual History*, trans. J.M. Todd. Ithaca, NY: Cornell University Press.

Burkert, W. (1996) *Creation of the Sacred: Tracks of Biology in Early Religions*. Cambridge, MA: Harvard University Press.

Bychkov, V. (1993) *The Aesthetic Face of Being: Art in the Theology of Pavel Florensky*, trans. R. Pevear and L. Volokhonsky. New York: St Vladimir's Seminary Press.

Cantwell-Smith, W. (1991) *The Meaning and End of Religion*. Minneapolis: Fortress Press.

Capra, F. (1975) *The Tao of Physics*. Bungay, Suffolk: Fontana.

Carrette, J. (2007) *Religions and Critical Psychology*. London and New York: Routledge.

Casanova, J. (1994) *Public Religions in the Modern World*. Chicago: Chicago University Press.

Certeau, M. de (1988) *The Writing of History*, trans. T. Conley. New York: Columbia University Press.

Certeau, M. de (1992) *The Mystic Fable*, vol. 1: *The Sixteenth and Seventeenth Centuries*, trans. M.B. Smith. Chicago: Chicago University Press.

Chalmers, D.J. (1996) *The Conscious Mind: In Search of a Fundamental Theory*. Oxford: Oxford University Press.

Chomsky, N. (1965) *Aspects of the Theory of Syntax*. Cambridge, MA: MIT Press.

Cioran, E.M. (1992) *The Heights of Despair*, trans. I. Zarifopol-Johnston. Chicago: Chicago University Press.

Clarke, P. and Byrne, P. (1993) *Religion Defined and Explained*. London: Macmillan.

Clooney, F.X. (2010) *Comparative Theology: Deep Learning Across Religious Borders*. Oxford: Wiley-Blackwell.

Coakley, Sarah (ed.) (1997) *Religion and the Body*. Cambridge: Cambridge University Press.

Conze, E. (1961) *The Large Sutra on Perfection of Wisdom*. London: Luzak.

Cooey, P.M. (1994) *Religious Imagination and the Body: A Feminist Analysis*. Oxford: Oxford University Press.

Corbin, H. (1986) *Spiritual Body and Celestial Earth: From Mazdean Iran to Sh'ite Iran* trans. N. Pearson. London: Tauris.

Corvi, R. (1997) *An Introduction to the Thought of Karl Popper*, trans. P. Camiller. London: Routledge.

Cottingham, J. (2005) *The Spiritual Dimension: Religion, Philosophy and Human Value*. Cambridge: Cambridge University Press.

Courtine, J.-F. (1993) *Of the Sublime*, trans. J.S. Librett. Albany: SUNY Press.

Coveney, P. and Highfield, R. (1996) *Frontiers of Complexity: The Search for Order in a Chaotic World*. London: Faber and Faber.

Critchely, S. (1997) *Very Little, Almost Nothing; Death, Philosophy, Literature*. London and New York: Routledge.

Csordas, T.J. (ed.) (1994) *Embodiment and Experience: The Existential Ground of Culture and Self*. Cambridge: Cambridge University Press.

Csordas, T.J. (2004) Asymptote of the ineffable: embodiment, alterity, and the theory of teligion. *Current Anthropology*, 45(2), 163–185.

Darwin, C. (1859/1901) *The Origin of Species*. London: John Murray.

Davidson, D. (1984) *Inquiries into Truth and Interpretation*. Oxford: Clarendon Press.

Davies, O. (2002) Celtic Christianity, in M. Atherton (ed.), *Celts and Christians: New Approaches to the Religious Traditions of Britain and Ireland*. Cardiff: University of Wales Press, pp. 23–38.

Davies, O. (2004) *The Creativity of God*. Cambridge: Cambridge University Press.

Davies, O. (2010) Introducing transformation theology. www.oliverdavies.com (accessed June 10, 2010).

Davies, O. and Turner, D. (eds) (2002) *Silence and the Word*. Cambridge: Cambridge University Press.

Dawkins, R. (1976) *The Selfish Gene*. Oxford: Oxford University Press.

D'Costa, G. (2005) *Theology in the Public Square: Church, Academy and Nation*. Oxford: Blackwell.

D'Costa, G. (2009) *Christianity and World Religions: Disputed Questions in the Theology of Religions*. Oxford: Wiley-Blackwell.

Derrida, J. (1974) *Of Grammatology*, trans. G. Spivak. Baltimore: Johns Hopkins University Press.

Derrida, J. and Vattimo, G. (eds) (1998) *Religion*. California: Stanford University Press.

Dionysius the Aereopagate (1957) *The Divine Names*, trans. Board of Scholars. Fintry: The Shrine of Wisdom.

Doniger, W. (1998) *The Implied Spider: Politics and Theology in Myth*. New York: Columbia University Press.

Drake, S. (1980) *Galileo*. Oxford: Oxford University Press.

Drees, W.B. (2010) *Religion and Science in Context: A Guide to the Debates*. London: Routledge.

Dubuisson, D. (1998) *L'Occident et la religion: mythes, science et idéologie*. Bruxelles: Éditions Complexe.

Dupuy, M. (1990) Spiritualité, in M. Viller *et al.* (eds), *Dictionaire de spiritualité*. Paris: Beauchene, vol. 14, pp. 1142–1143.

Duranti, A. (ed.) (2009) *Linguistic Anthropology: A Reader*, 2nd edn. Oxford: Wiley-Blackwell.

Eagleton, T. (1991) *Ideology: An Introduction*. London and New York: Verso.

Eagleton, T. (2009) *Reason, Faith, and Revolution: Reflections on the God Debate*. New Haven: Yale University Press.

Eco, U. (1986) *Art and Beauty in the Middle Ages*, trans. H. Bedin. New Haven: Yale University Press.

Eisenstadt, S.N. (ed.) (1986) *The Origins and Diversity of the Axial Age*. Albany: SUNY Press.

Eliot, T.S. (1932) Thoughts after Lambeth, in *Selected Essays*. London: Faber and Faber, pp. 353–377.

Eliot, T.S. (1932) *Selected Essays*. London: Faber and Faber.

Eliot, T.S. (1944) *Four Quartets*. London: Faber and Faber.

Evans Pritchard, E.E. (1976) *Witchcraft, Oracles and Magic Among the Azande*. Oxford: Clarendon Press.

Evdokimov, P. (1972/1990) *The Art of the Icon: A Theology of Beauty*, trans. S. Bigham. Redondo Beach: Oakwood Publications.

Fara, P. (2010) *Science: A Four Thousand Year History*. Oxford: Oxford University Press.

Fitzgerald, T. (2000) *The Ideology of Religious Studies*. Oxford: Oxford University Press.

Fitzgerald, T. (2007) *Discourse on Civility and Barbarity: A Critical History of Religion and Related Categories*. Oxford: Oxford University Press.

Foley, W.A. (1997) *Anthropological Linguistics: An Introduction*. Oxford: Blackwell.

Ford, D. (2007) *Shaping Theology: Engagements in a Religious and Secular World*. Oxford: Wiley-Blackwell.

Ford, D. (2007) *Christian Wisdom: Desiring God and Learning in Love*. Cambridge: Cambridge University Press.

Ford, D. and Pecknold, C.C. (eds) (2006) *The Promise of Scriptural Reasoning*. Oxford: Blackwell.

Forman, R. (1999) *Mysticism, Mind, Consciousness*. Albany: SUNY Press.

Flood, G. (1992) Techniques of body and desire in Kashmir Śaivism. *Religion*, 22, 47–62.

Flood, G. (1999) *Beyond Phenomenology: Rethinking the Study of Religion*. London: Cassell.

Flood, G. (ed.) (2003) *The Blackwell Companion to Hinduism*. Oxford: Blackwell.

Flood, G. (2004) *The Ascetic Self: Subjectivity, Memory, and Tradition*. Cambridge: Cambridge University Press.

Flood, G. (2006) *The Tantric Body*. London: Tauris.

Flood, G. (2008) Dwelling on the borders: self, text, and world. *Temenos*, 44(1), 13–34.

Flood, G. (2008) Text reception and ritual in Tantric scriptural traditions, in J. Schaper (ed.), *Der Textualisierung der Religion*. Tubingen: Mohr Siebeck, pp. 241–249.

Florensky, P. (1997) *The Pillar and the Ground of Truth*, trans. B. Jakim. Princeton: Princeton University Press.

Frank, P. (2000) *Gothic Architecture*. New Haven: Yale University Press.

Frankenberry, N.K. (ed.) (2002) *Radical Interpretation in Religion*. Cambridge: Cambridge University Press.

Frankl, V.E. (1959/2004) *Man's Search for Meaning*, trans. I. Lasch. London: Rider.

Freedberg, D. (1989) *The Power of Images: Studies in the History and Theory of Response*. Chicago: Chicago University Press.

Freeden, M. (2005) *Liberal Languages: Ideological Imaginations and Twentieth-Century Progressive Thought*. Princeton: Princeton University Press.

Freeman, R. (1991) Purity and violence: sacred power in the Teyyam worship of Malabar. PhD thesis. University of Pennsylvania.

Freeman, R. (2003) The Teyyam tradition of Kerala, in G. Flood (ed.), *The Blackwell Companion to Hinduism*. Oxford: Blackwell, 2003, pp. 307–326.

Freud, S. (1925) The uncanny, in *Collected Papers*, vol. IV, trans J. Riviere. London: Hogarth Press, pp. 368 407.

Freud, S. (1928/1985) *The Future of an Illusion*, in *Civilization, Society and Religion, Group Psychology, Civilization and Its Discontents and Other Works*, trans. W.D. Robson-Scott. London: Penguin.

Frye, N. (1947) *Fearful Symmetry: A Study of William Blake*. Boston: Beacon Press.

Gadamer, H.-G. (1975/1993) *Truth and Method*, 2nd edn, trans. J. Weinsheimer and D.G. Marshall. London: Sheed and Ward.

Gay, P. (2007) *Modernism: The Lure of Heresy from Baudelaire to Beckett and Beyond*. London: Heinemann.

Geertz, C. (1973) *The Interpretation of Culture*. New York: Fontana.

Genette, G. (1980) *Narrative Discourse*. Oxford: Blackwell.

Gilbert and George, (2007) *Major Exhibition, Tate Modern*. London: Tate.

Gilson, E. (1938) *Héloise and Abélard: Études sur le moyen âge et l'humanisme*. Paris: J. Vrin.

Giovannelli, A. Goodman's aesthetics, in E.N. Zalta (ed.), *The Stanford Encyclopedia of Philosophy*, Summer 2010 edn. http://plato.stanford.edu/archives/sum2010/entries/goodman-aesthetics/ (accessed August 22, 2010).

Girard, R. (1976/1987) *Things Hidden Since the Foundation of the World*, trans. S. Bann and M. Meteer. London: The Athlone Press.

GodloveJr., T.F. (2002) Saving belief, in N.K. Frankenberry (ed.), *Radical Interpretation in Religion*. Cambridge: Cambridge University Press, pp. 10–24.

Goldenberg, L. (2007) *Little People and a Lost World: An Anthropological Mystery*. Minneapolis, Minnesota: Twenty-First Century Books.

Gombrich, R. (1997) Religious experience in early Buddhism. BASR Occasional Papers.

Goodman, N. (1976) *Languages of Art: An Approach to a Theory of Symbols*. Indianapolis: Hackett Publishing Company.

Gracia, J.J.E. (1995) *A Theory of Textuality: The Logic and Epistemology*. Albany: SUNY Press.

Greetham, D.C. (1999) *Theories of the Text*. Oxford: Oxford University Press.

Gregory, F. (1986) The impact of Darwinist evolution on Protestant theology in the 19th century, in D.C. Lindberg and R.I. Numbers (eds), *God and Nature: Historical Essays on the Encounter Between Christianity and Science*. Berkeley: University of California Press.

Griffiths, P. (1999) *Religious Reading: The Place of Reading in the Practice of Religion*. Oxford: Oxford University Press.

Griffiths, P.J. (2001) *Problems of Religious Diversity*. Oxford: Blackwell.

Grof, S. (1996) *Realms of the Human Unconscious*. New York: Souvenir Press.

Grondin, J. (1994) *Introduction to Philosophical Hermeneutics*, trans. J. Weinsheimer. New Haven: Yale University Press.

Gumpertz, J.J. and Levinson, S.C. (eds) (1996) *Rethinking Linguistic Relativity*. Cambridge: Cambridge University Press.

Gunn, T. (1994) *Collected Poems*. London: Faber and Faber.

Guthrie, S. (2005) *Faces in the Clouds: A New Theory of Religion*. Oxford: Oxford University Press.

Gutman, A. (ed.) (1994) *Multiculturalism*. Princeton: Princeton University Press.

Gyatso, T.(The Dalai Lama XIV) (2006) *The Universe in a Single Atom: The Convergence of Science and Spirituality*. London: Abacus.

Habermas, J. (1989) *The Structural Transformation of the Public Sphere*, trans. T. Burger. Cambridge: Polity.

Habermas, J. (2008) *Between Naturalism and Religion*, trans. C. Cronin. Cambridge: Polity.

Hadot, P. (1993) *Exercices spirituels et philosophie antique*. Paris: Albin Michel.

Halbfass, W. (1988) *India and Europe*. Albany: SUNY Press.

Hamburger, J.F. and Bouche, A.-M. (eds) (2006) *The Mind's Eye: Art and Theological Argument in the Middle Ages*. Princeton: Princeton University Press.

Harrison, P. (1990) *"Religion" and the Religions in the English Enlightenment*. Cambridge: Cambridge University Press.

Harvey, J. (1999) *Music and Inspiration*. London: Faber and Faber.

Hauerwas, S. (2001) *The Hauerwas Reader*, ed. J. Berkman and W. Cavanaugh. Durham, NC: Duke University Press.

Hawkes, T. (1977) *Structuralism and Semiotics*. London: Routledge.

Hawking, S. and Mlodinow, L. (2010) *The Grand Design*. London: Bantam Press.

Hayashi, T. (2003) Indian mathematics, in G. Flood (ed.), *Blackwell Companion to Hinduism*, pp. 360–375.

Hedley, D. (2005) The "future" of religion, in J. Lipner (ed.), *Truth, Religious Dialogue and Dynamic Orthodoxy Reflections on the Works of Brian Hebblethwaite*. London: SCM Press, pp. 96–111.

Heelas, P. (1996) On things not being worse and the ethic of humanity, in P. Heelas, S. Lash, and P. Morris (eds), *Detraditionalization: Critical reflections on Authority and Identity*. Oxford: Blackwell.

Heelas, P. and Lock, A. (1981) *Indigenous Psychologies: The Anthropology of the Self*. London: Academic Press.

Heelas, P. and Woodhead, L. (2000) *Religion in Modern Times: An Interpretative Anthology*. Oxford: Blackwell.

Heelas, P. and Woodhead, L. (2005) *The Spiritual Revolution: Why Religion is Giving Way to Spirituality*. Oxford: Blackwell.

Heesterman, J. (1993) *The Broken World of Sacrifice*. Chicago: Chicago University Press.

Heidegger, M. (1962) *Being and Time*, trans. J. McQuarry and E. Robinson. Oxford: Blackwell.

Heidegger, M. (2003) The question concerning technology, trans. William Lovitt, in M. Stassen (ed.), *Philosophical and Political Writings*. New York: Continuum, pp. 279–303.

Heidegger, M. (2004) *The Phenomenology of the Religious Life*, trans. M. Fritsch and J.A. Gosetti-Ferencei. Bloomington: Indiana University Press.

Hervieu-Léger, D. (2000) *Religion as a Chain of Memory*, trans. S. Lee. Cambridge: Polity.

Hilesum, E. (1981/1996) *Etty Hillesum: An Interrupted Life the Diaries, 1941–1943 and Letters from Westerbork*, trans. A.J. Pomerans. New York: Henry Holt and Co.

Hinnelss, J. and King, R. (eds) (2007) *Religion and Violence in South Asia: Theory and Practice*. London: Routledge.

Hirst, D. (1964) *Hidden Riches: Traditional Symbolism from the Renaissance to Blake*. London: Eyre and Spottiswood.

Hodgson, P. (ed.) (1944) *The Cloud of Unknowing and the Book of Privy Council*. Early English Text Society. Oxford: Oxford University Press.

Hoijer, H. (ed.) (1954) *Language in Culture*. Chicago: Chicago University Press.

Hollis, M. (1977) *Models of Man: Philosophical Thoughts on Social Action*. Cambridge: Cambridge University Press.

Honneth, A. (2006) *Reification: A Recognition-Theoretical View: The Tanner Lectures of Human Value*. www.tannerlectures.utah.edu/lectures/documents/Honneth_2006.pdf (accessed June 8, 2010).

Honneth, A., Butler, J., Geuss, R., and Jay, M. (2008) *Reification: a New Look at an Old Idea*. Oxford: Oxford University Press.

Horton, R. (1993) *Patterns of Thought in Africa and the West*. Cambridge: Cambridge University Press.

Hughes, G. (2003) *Worship as Meaning: A Liturgical Theology for Late Modernity*. Cambridge: Cambridge University Press.

Hunt Overzee, A. (1992) *The Body Divine, the Symbol of the Body in the Work of Teilhard de Chardin and Ramanuja*. Cambridge: Cambridge University Press.

Husserl, E. (1950) *Cartesian Meditations*, trans. D. Cairns. Dordrecht, Boston, London: Kluwer.

Ingalls, D.H.H., Masson, J.M., and Patwardhan, M.V. (trans.) (1990) *The Dhvanyāloka of Ānandavardhana with the Locana of Abhinavagupta*. Cambridge, MA: Harvard University Press.

Isayeva, N. (1995) *From Early Vedanta to Kashmir Shaivism*. Delhi: Sri Satguru Publications.

Jackson, M. (ed.) (1996) *Things as they are. New Directions in Phenomenological Anthropology*. Bloomington: Indiana University Press.

Jantzen, G. (1995) *Power, Gender and Christian Mysticism*. Cambridge: Cambridge University Press.

Jantzen, G. (2004) *Foundations of Violence: Death and the Displacement of Beauty*, vol. 1. London: Routledge.

Johnson, M. (1987) *The Mind in the Body: The Bodily Basis of Meaning, Imagination, and Reason*. Chicago: Chicago University Press.

Jones, R.H. (1986) *Science and Mysticism: A Comparative Study of Western Natural Science, Theravada Buddhism, and Advaita Vedanta*. Lewisburg, PA: Bucknell University Press.

Jones, R.H. (2010) *Piercing the Veil: Comparing Science and Mysticism as Ways of Knowing Reality*. New York: Jackson Square Books.

Kalupahana, D.J. (1992) *A History of Buddhist Philosophy: Continuities and Discontinuities*. Honolulu: University of Hawaii Press.

Kandinsky, V. (1912/2006) *On the Spiritual in Art*, trans. M.T.H. Sadler. London: Tate, 2006.

Kane, P.V. (1961) *The History of Sanskrit Poetics*. Delhi: Motilal.

Katz, S. (ed.) (1973) *Mysticism and Religious Traditions*. Oxford: Oxford University Press.

Katz, S. (ed.) (1978) *Mysticism and Philosophical Analysis*. Oxford: Oxford University Press.

Katz, S. (ed.) (1992) *Mysticism and Language*. Oxford: Oxford University Press.

Kauffman, S. (1993) *At Home in the Universe: The Search for the Laws of Self-Organization and Complexity*. New York: Oxford University Press.

Kauffman, S. (1993) *The Origins of Order: Self-Organisation and Selection in Evolution*. New York: Oxford University Press.

Kauffman, S. (2008) *Reinventing the Sacred: A New View of Science, Reason and Religion*. New York: Basic Books.

Kennedy, P. (forthcoming) *God's Career: The Evolution of a Deity*. London: Tauris.

Kierkegaard, S. (1983) *Fear and Trembling; Repetition*, ed. and trans. H.V. Hong and E.H. Hong. Princeton: Princeton University Press.

King, R. (1999) *Orientalism and Religion: Postcolonial Theory, India and "The Mystic East."* New York: Routledge.

Klemm, D.E. and Schweiker, W. (2008) *Religion and the Human Future: An Essay on Theological Humanism*. Oxford: Wiley-Blackwell.

Knott, K. (2005) *The Location of Religion: A Spatial Analysis*. London and Oakville: Equinox.

Knott, K. (2008) Inside, Outside, and the Space Between: Territories and Boundaries in the Study of Religion. Temenos, 44(1), 41–66.

Kolakowski, L. (1982) *Religion*. Glasgow: Fontana.

Kragh, U.T. (2006) *Early Buddhist Theories of Action and its Result: A Study of Karmaphalasambandha, Candrakiriti's Prasannapada verses 17.1–20*. Wien: Universität Wien.

Krishnamoorthy, K. (1988) *Abhinavagupta's Dhvanyālokalocana*. Delhi: Meharchand Lachhmandas.

Kristeva, J. (1984) *Revolution in Poetic Language*, trans. M. Waller. New York: Columbia University Press.

Kristeva, J. (2010) *Hatred and Forgiveness*, trans. J. Herman. New York: Columbia University Press.

Kymlicka, W. (1995) *Multicultural Citizenship: A Liberal Theory of Minority Rights*. Oxford: Clarendon Press.

Laerman, R. and Vershraegen, G. (2001) The late Niklas Luhmann on religion: an overview. *Social Compass*, 48(1), 7–20.

Lakoff, G. and Johnson, M. (1980) *Metaphors We Live By*. Chicago: Chicago University Press.

Langford, J.J. (1992) *Galileo, Science and the Church*. Arbor: University of Michigan Press.

Lash, N. (1996) *The Beginning and End of "Religion."* Cambridge: Cambridge University Press.

Lee, T.F. (1991) *The Human Genome Project: Cracking the Genetic Code of Life.* New York: Plenum Press.

Lemmon, E.J. (1965) *Beginning Logic.* London: Nelson.

Leslie, C.R. (1845/1951) *Memoirs of John Constable Composed Chiefly of his Letters.* London: Phaidon.

Levere, T.H. and Shea, W.R. (eds) (1990) *Nature, Experiment, and the Sciences: Essays on Galileo and the History of Science in Honour of Stillman Drake.* Dordrecht: Kluwer.

Levinson, S.C. (1997) Language and cognition. The cognitive consequences of spatial description in Guugu Yinithirr. *Journal of Linguistic Anthropology*, 7(1), 98–131.

Levinson, J. (2006) *Contemplating Art: Essays on Aesthetics.* Oxford: Oxford University Press.

Lewis, C.S. (1964) *The Discarded Image.* Cambridge: Cambridge University Press.

Lewis-Williams, D. (2010) *Conceiving God: The Cognitive Origin and Evolution of Religion.* London: Thames and Hudson.

Lienhart, G. (1987) *Divinity and Experience: Religion Among the Dinka.* Oxford: The Clarendon Press.

Lindberg, D.C. and Numbers, R.I. (eds) (1986) *God and Nature: Historical Essays on the Encounter Between Christianity and Science.* Berkeley: University of California Press.

Lippard, L. (1990) The spirit and the letter. *Art in America*, 80(4), 238–245.

Lippard, L. (1995) *Overlays: Contemporary Art and the Art of Prehistory.* New York: The New Press.

Lloyd, G. (1996) *Adversaries and Authorities. Investigations into Ancient Greek and Chinese Science.* Cambridge: Cambridge University Press.

Locke, J. (1993) *Essay Concerning Toleration*, in D. Wooton (ed.), *Political Writings of John Locke.* New York: Mentor.

Lopez, D.S. Jr., (2008) *Buddhism and Science: A Guide for the Perplexed.* Chicago: Chicago University Press.

Lovejoy, A.O. (1936/1964) *The Great Chain of Being.* Cambridge, MA: Harvard University Press.

Luckmann, T. (1990) Shrinking transcendence, expanding religion? Sociological Analysis, 51(2), 127–138.

Lucy, J. (1992) *Language Diversity and Thought: A Reformulation of the Linguistic Relativity Hypothesis.* Cambridge: Cambridge University Press.

Lucy, J. (1992) *Grammatical Categories and Cognition: A Case Study of the Linguistic Relativity Hypothesis.* Cambridge: Cambridge University Press.

Luhmann, N. (1982) *Funktion der Religion.* Frankfurt-am-Main: Suhrkamp.

Luhmann, N. (1984) *Religious Dogmatics and the Evolution of Societies*, trans. P. Beyer. New York and Toronto: Edwin Mellen.

Luhmann, N. (1995) *Social System*, trans. J. Bednary with D. Baelber. California: Stanford University Press.

Lukács, G. (1971) *Theory of the Novel*, trans. A. Bostock. London: Merlin Press.

Lukács, G. (1971) *History and Class Consciousness*, trans. R. Livingstone. Cambridge, MA: MIT Press.

Lyas, C. (1999) *Peter Winch*. London: Acumen.

Lyotard, J.-F. (1986) *The Postmodern Condition*, trans. G. Bennington and B. Massumi. Manchester: Manchester University Press.

McCarthy Brown, K. (1991) *Mama Lola: A Vodou Priestess in Brooklyn*. Berkeley: California University Press.

McCutcheon, R.T. (1997) *Manufacturing Religion: The Discourse on Sui Generis Religion and the Politics of Nostalgia*. Oxford: Oxford University Press.

McGinn, B. (1997) *The Foundations of Mysticism, Origins to the Fifth Century*. New York: Crossroad.

Machamer, P. (1998) *The Cambridge Companion to Galileo*. Cambridge: Cambridge University Press.

McIntosh, M.A. (1998) *Mystical Theology*. Oxford: Blackwell.

MacIntyre, A. (1981) *After Virtue: A Study in Moral Theory*. London: Duckworth.

MacIntyre, A. (1988) *Whose Justice? Which Rationality?* Notre Dame, Ind.: University of Notre Dame Press.

MacIntyre, A. (1990) *Three Rival Versions of Moral Enquiry*. Notre Dame, Ind.: University of Notre Dame Press.

McLaughlin, B. and Bennett, K., Supervenience, in E.N. Zalta (ed.), *The Stanford Encyclopedia of Philosophy*, Summer 2010 edn. http://plato.stanford.edu/archives/sum2010/entries/supervenience/ (accessed August 23, 2010).

McLellan, D. (1980) *The Thought of Karl Marx*, 2nd edn. London: Macmillan.

McMahan, D. (2004) Modernity and the discourse of scientific Buddhism. *Journal of the American Academy of Religion*, 72(4), 897–933.

McMahon, R. (2006) *Understanding the Medieval Meditative Ascent: Augustine, Anselm, Boethius, Dante*. Washington: Catholic University of America Press.

Malotki, E. (1983) *Hopi Time: A Linguistic Analysis of the Temporal Categories in the Hopi Language*. Berlin: Mouton.

Mandair, A.-P.D. (2009) *Religion and the Specter of the West: Sikhism, Indian, Postcoloniality, and the Politics of Translation*. New York: Columbia University Press.

Marianne 2 (2010) Les nouvelles guerres des religions: comment les clericalismes menacent la planète (March 26).

Marshall, K. (2009) Concluding remarks. *Faith and Development*. Accra, Ghana, July 3. http://siteresources.worldbank.org/DEVDIALOGUE/Resources/KatherineMarshall.pdf (accessed August 6, 2010).

Marshall, T.H. (1950) *Citizenship and Social Class and Other Essays*. London: Cambridge University Press.

Martin, D. (2005) *On Secularisation: Towards a Revised General Theory*. Aldershot: Ashgate.

Marx, K. (1844/1978) *Contribution to the Critique of Hegel's Philosophy of Right*, trans. S.K. Padover, in *The Essential Marx: The Non-Economic Writings*. New York: New American Library.

Masuzawa, T. (2005) *The Invention of World Religions Or, How European Universalism was Preserved in the Language of Pluralism*. Chicago: Chicago University Press.

Mauss, M. (1935/2006) Techniques of the body, trans. B. Brewster, in N. Schlanger (ed.), *Techniques, Technology and Civilization*. London: Routledge, pp. 77–96.

Merleau-Ponty, M. (1945) *Phénoménologie de la perception*. Paris: Gallimard.

Merleau-Ponty, M. (1962) *Phenomenology of Perception*, trans. C. Smith. London: Routledge.

Merleau-Ponty, M. (1968) *The Visible and the Invisible*, trans. Alphonso Lingis. Evanston, IL: Northwestern University Press.

Merleau-Ponty, M. (1993) *In Praise of Philosophy*, trans. J. Wild and J. Edie. Evanston, IL: Northwestern University Press.

Michael, T. (ed. and trans.) (1975) *Le Joyau du Śiva-yoga Śivayogaratna de Jñānaprakāśa*. Pondichery: Institut Français d'Indologie.

Milbank, J. (1990) *Theology and Social Theory: Beyond Secular Reason*. Oxford: Blackwell.

Minnis, A. (2983) Affection and imagination in *The Cloud of Unknowing* and Hilton's *Scale of Perfection. Traditio*, 39, 323–366.

Monbiot, G. (2007) *Heat*. London: Penguin.

Moosa, E. (2008) *Ghazali and the Poetics of Imagination*. Oxford: Oxford University Press.

Naranjo, C. and Ornstein, R.E. (1972) *On the Psychology of Meditation*. London: George Allen and Unwin.

Needham, J. (1980) *The Shorter Science and Civilisation in China: An Abridgement of Joseph Needham's Original Text*. Cambridge: Cambridge University Press.

Neville, R. Cummings (1996) *The Truth of Broken Symbols*. Albany: SUNY Press.

Nitsch, H., www.nitsch.org (accessed 8/3/2010).

Nye, M. (2001) *Multiculturalism and Minority Religions in Britain*. London: Routledge.

Obama, B. (2009) *The Inaugural Address 2009*. London: Penguin.

Obeyesekere, G. (1992) *The Apotheosis of Captain Cook; European Mythmaking in the Pacific*. Princeton: Princeton University Press.

O'Brian, J. and Palmer, M. (eds) (2007) *Atlas of Religion*. Berkeley: University of California Press.

Ochs, P. (2006) Philosophical warrants for scriptural reasoning, in D.F. Ford and C.C. Pecknold (eds), *The Promise of Scriptural Reasoning*. Oxford: Blackwell, pp. 121–138.

Otto, R. (1923) *The Idea of the Holy: An inquiry into the Non-Rational Factor in the Idea of the Divine and its Relation to the Rational*, trans. J.W. Harvey. Oxford: Oxford University Press.

Panofsky, E. (1951) *Gothic Architecture and Scholasticism*. La Trobe, PA: Archabbey Press.

Parry, C. (1994) *Death in Benares*. Cambridge: Cambridge University Press.

Partridge, C. (2006) *The Re-Enchantment of the West: Alternative Spiritualities, Sacralization, Popular Culture and Occulture*. London: T&T Clark.

Pattison, G. (1991) *Art, Modernity, and Faith: Towards a Theology of Art*. London: Macmillan.

Pattison, G. (1996) *Agnosis: Theology in the Void*. London and New York: Macmillan and St Martins.

Peacocke, A.R. (1984) *Intimations of Reality: Critical Realism in Science and Religion*. Notre Dame, IN: University of Notre Dame Press.

Peacocke, A. and Clayton, P. (eds) (2004) *In Whom We Live and Move and Have Our Being: Panentheistic Reflections on God's Presence in a Scientific World*. Grand Rapids, MI: Eerdmans.

Peacocke, A. and Clayton, P. (eds) (2006) *The Re-Emergence of Emergence: The Emergentist Hypothesis from Science to Religion*. Oxford: Oxford University Press.

Pike, K.L. (1967) *Language in Relation to a Unified Theory of Structure of Human Behavior*, 2nd edn. The Hague: Mouton.

Pitt, J.C. (1992) *Galileo: Human Knowledge, and the Book of Nature: Method Replaces Metaphysics*. Dordrecht: Kluwer.

Plato, *Republic*, in J.M. Cooper (ed.) (1997) *Plato: Complete Works*. Indianapolis and Cambridge: Hackett Publishing Company.

Polhemus, T. (ed.) (1983) *Social Aspects of the Human Body*. London: Penguin.

Pollock, S. (2006) *The Language of the Gods in the World of Men*. Chicago: Chicago University Press.

Popper, K. (1957/2002) *The Poverty of Historicism*. London: Routledge.

Raja, K. (1963) *Indian Theories of Meaning*. Madras: Adyar Library.

Ramadan, T. (2009) *Radical Reform: Islamic Ethics and Liberation*. Oxford: Oxford University Press.

Ramadan, T. (2010) *The Quest for Meaning: Developing a Philosophy of Pluralism*. London: Allen Lane.

Rappaport, R. (1999) *Ritual and Religion in the Making of Humanity*. Cambridge: Cambridge University Press.

Ricoeur, P. (1981) *Hermeneutics and the Human Sciences*, trans. J.B. Thompson. Cambridge: Cambridge University Press.

Ricoeur, P. (1984) *Time and Narrative*, vol. 1, trans. K. McLaughlin and D. Pellauer. Chicago: Chicago University Press.

Ricoeur, P. (1992) *Oneself as Another*, trans. K. Blamey. Chicago: Chicago University Press.

Roberts, R. (2000) Religion and the body in comparative perspective. *Religion*, 30, 55–64.

Roberts, R. (2011) *Religion and Social Theory*. Oxford: Wiley-Blackwell.

Roberts, R.H. (ed.) (1995) *Religion and the Transformations of Capitalism*. London and New York: Routledge.

Roberts, R.H. (2003) *Theology and the Social Sciences*. Cambridge: Cambridge University Press.

Ronald, I. and Norris, P. (2004) *Sacred and Secular: Religion and Politics Worldwide*. Cambridge: Cambridge University Press.

Rosenthal, S.(n.d.) *Black Paintings*. Munich: Hausterkunst.

Rossano, M. (2003) *Evolutionary Psychology: The Science of Human Behaviour and Evolution*. Hoboken: John Wiley & Sons, Inc.

Sahlins, M. (1995) *How Natives Think, About Captain Cook for Example*. Chicago: Chicago University Press.

Salvatore, A. (2007) *The Public Sphere: Liberal Modernity, Catholicism, Islam*. New York: Palgrave Macmillan.

Sandel, M.J. (1982) *Liberalism and the Limits of Justice*. Cambridge: Cambridge University Press.

Sartre, J.-P. (1996) *L'Existentialisme est un humanisme*. Paris: Gallimard.

Scarry, E. (1985) *The Body in Pain: The Making and Unmaking of the World*. Oxford: Oxford University Press.

Scheckner, R. (1993) *The Future of Ritual*. London and New York: Routledge.

Schimmel, A. (1964) *Mystical Dimensions of Islam*. Chapel Hill: The University of North Carolina Press.

Schipper, K. (1985) Vernacular and classical ritual in Taoism. *Journal of Asian Studies*, 45(1), 21–57.

Schipper, K. (1993) *The Taoist Body*, trans. K.C. Duval. Berkeley: California University Press.

Scholem, G. (1941) *Major Trends in Jewish Mysticism*. New York: Schocken Books.

Schutz, A. (1970) *On Phenomenology and Social Life*. Chicago: Chicago University Press.

Segal, R. (1992) *Explaining and Interpreting Religion: Essays on the Issue*. New York: Peter Lang.

Shaw, S. (2009) *Buddhist Meditation*. London: Routledge.

Shepherd, J. (ed.) (2009) *Ninian Smart on World Religions*, 2 vols. London: Ashgate.

Siebert, R.J. (1985) *Critical Theory of Religion: The Frankfurt School – From Universal Pragmatic to Political Theology*. Berlin, New York: Walter Gruyter.

Siebert, R.J. (2006) *The Critical Theory of Religion: From Religious Orthodoxy through Mysticism to Secular Enlightenment and Beyond: The Totally Other and the Rescue of the Hopeless*. Leiden: Brill.

Smart, N. (1996) *Dimensions of the Sacred: An Anatomy of the Worlds' Religious Beliefs*. London: Macmillan.

Smith, M. (2000) *The Origins of Biblical Monotheism: Israel's Polytheistic Background and the Ugaritic Texts*. New York and Oxford: Oxford University Press.

Solecki, R.S. (1972) *Shandar: The Humanity of Neanderthal Man*. London: Allen Lane.

Southwood, T.R.E. (2003) *The Story of Life*. Oxford: Oxford University Press.

Staal, F. (1988) *Rules Without Meaning*. New York: Peter Lang.

Staal, F. (1989) The independence of rationality from literacy. *European Journal of Sociology*, 30, 301–310.

Stout, J. (2004) *Democracy and Tradition*. Princeton: Princeton University Press.

Stroumsa, G.G. (2009) *The End of Sacrifice: Religious Transformations in Late Antiquity*. Chicago: Chicago University Press.

Stroumsa, G.G. (2010) *A New Science: the Discovery of Religion in the Age of Reason* Cambridge, MA: Harvard University Press.

Suzuki, D.T. (1953) *Essays in Zen Buddhism*, third series. London: Rider.

Tajfel, H. and Turner, J.C. (1986) The social identity theory of inter-group behavior, in S. Worchel and L.W. Austin (eds), *Psychology of Intergroup Relations*. Chicago: Nelson-Hall, pp. 276–293.

Tart, C.T. (ed.) (1990) *Altered States of Consciousness*, 3rd edn. San Francisco: Harper.

Taylor, B. (2010) *Dark Green Religion: Nature, Spirituality and the Planetary Future*. Berkeley: University of California Press.

Taylor, C. (1985) Interpretation and the human sciences, in *Philosophy and the Human Sciences: Philosophical Papers*, vol. 2. Cambridge: Cambridge University Press, pp. 15–57.

Taylor, C. (1985) Rationality, in *Philosophy and the Human Sciences: Philosophical Papers*, vol. 2. Cambridge: Cambridge University Press, pp. 134–151.

Taylor, C. (2007) *A Secular Age*. Cambridge, MA: Harvard University Press.

Tillich, P. (1957) *Dynamics of Faith*. New York: Harper & Row.

Torella, R. (1994/2002) *The Īśvarapratyabhijñākārikā of Utpaladeva with the Author's Vrtti*. Delhi: MLBD.

Trigg, R. (2007) *Religion in Public Life: Must Faith Be Privatised?* Oxford: Oxford University Press.

Tufnell, B. (2006) *Land Art*. London: Tate.

Turner, B. (1984) *The Body and Society*. Oxford: Blackwell.

Turner, D. (1983) *Marxism and Christianity*. Oxford: Blackwell.

Turner, D. (1995) *The Darkness of God: Negativity in Christian Mysticism*. Cambridge: Cambridge University Press.

Turner, E. (1992) *Experiencing Ritual: A New Interpretation of African Healing*. Philadelphia: University of Pennsylvania Press.

Turner, V. (1967) *The Forest of Symbols: Aspects of Ndembu Ritual*. Ithaca, NY: Cornell University Press.

Tweed, T.A. (2006) *Crossing and Dwelling: A Theory of Religion*. Cambridge, MA: Harvard University Press.

Urban, G. (1989) The "I" of Discourse, in B. Lee and G. Urban (eds), *Semiotics, Self and Society*. Berlin and New York: Mouton de Gruyter, pp. 27–51.

Urban, G. (2001) *Metaculture: How Culture Moves through the World*. Minneapolis and London: University of Minnesota Press.

Vernant, J.-P. (1982) *The Origins of Greek Thought*. Ithaca, NY: Cornell University Press.

Viola, B. (1991/2007) *The Passing*. Paris: Editions à Voir (DVD).

Visser, S. and Williams, T. (2009) *Anselm*. Oxford: Oxford University Press.

Vries, H. de (2002) *Religion and Violence: Philosophical Perspectives from Kant to Derrida*. Baltimore: Johns Hopkins University Press.

Vries, H. de (ed.) (2008) *Religion: Beyond a Concept*. New York: Fordham University Press.

Wallace, B.A. (ed.) (2003) *Buddhism and Science: Breaking New Ground*. New York: Columbia University Press.

Wallace, B.A. (2007) *Hidden Dimensions: The Unification of Physics and Consciousness*. New York: Columbia University Press.

Walters, C. (1961) *The Cloud of Unknowing and Other Works*. London: Penguin.

Ward, K. (2004) *The Case for Religion*. Oxford: Oneworld.

Ware, K. (1997) The body in Greek Christianity, in S. Coakley (ed.), *Religion and the Body*. Cambridge: Cambridge University Press, pp. 90–110.

Warner, M., Vanantwerpen, J., and Calhoun, C. (eds) (2010) *Varieties of Secularism in a Secular Age*. Cambridge, MA: Harvard University Press.

Warnock, M. (2010) *Dishonest to God: On Keeping Religion Out of Politics*. London: Continuum.

Waterfield, R. (1989) *Jacob Boehme: Essential Readings*. Wellingborough: Crucible.

Weigel, G. (2005) *The Cube and the Cathedral*. New York: Basic Books.

Welch, C. (1985) *Protestant Thought in the Nineteenth Century*, vol. 2. New Haven: Yale University Press.

Welton, D. (ed.) (1999) *The Body*. Oxford: Blackwell.

Westurlund, D. (2008) Review of Steve Bruce's *Fundamentalism*. Temenos, 44(1), 176–180.

Whitehouse, H. (2004) *Cognitive Theory of Religious Transmission*. Walnut Creek, CA: Alta Mira Press.

Whorf, B.L. (1956) *Language, Thought and Reality*, ed. John Carroll. Cambridge MA: MIT Press.

Wierzbicka, A. (1996) *Semantics: Primes and Universals*. Oxford: Oxford University Press.

Williams, R. (2002) *Lost Icons*. Edinburgh: T&T Clark.

Wilson, A.N. (1999) *God's Funeral*. New York, London: W.W. Norton and Co.

Wilson, E.O. (1971) *The Insect Societies*. Cambridge, MA: Belknap Press of Harvard University Press.

Wilson, E.O. (1975) *Sociobiology: The New Synthesis*. Cambridge, MA: Belknap Press of Harvard University Press.

Wilson, E.O. (1978) *On Human Nature*. Cambridge, MA: Belknap Press of Harvard University Press.

Winch, P. (1958) *The Idea of a Social Science and Its Relation to Philosophy*. London: Routledge & Kegan Paul.

Yao, X. (2000) *Introduction to Confucianism*. Cambridge: Cambridge University Press.

Index

The Importance of Religion: Meaning and Action in Our Strange World,
First Edition. Gavin Flood.
© 2012 Gavin Flood. Published 2012 by Blackwell Publishing Ltd.

244   *Index*